Developing a New Curriculum for Adult Learners

MICHAEL CARROLL, EDITOR

TESOL Language Curriculum Development Series

Kathleen Graves, Series Editor

TESOL Teachers of English to Speakers of Other Languages, Inc.

Typeset in Adobe Garamond with Frutiger Display
by Capitol Communication Systems, Inc., Crofton, Maryland USA
Printed by United Graphics, Inc., Mattoon, Illinois USA
Indexed by Pueblo Indexing and Publishing Services, Pueblo West, Colorado USA

Teachers of English to Speakers of Other Languages, Inc.
700 South Washington Street, Suite 200
Alexandria, Virginia 22314 USA
Tel 703-836-0774 • Fax 703-836-6447 • E-mail tesol@tesol.org • http://www.tesol.org/

Publishing Manager: Carol Edwards
Copy Editor: Sarah J. Duffy
Additional Reader: Ellen Garshick
Cover Design: Capitol Communication Systems, Inc.

ISBN 9781931185455
Library of Congress Control No. 2007906105

Contents

EFL Study

Teacher Preparation

Series Editor's Preface

The aim of TESOL's Language Curriculum Development Series is to provide real-world examples of how a language curriculum is developed, adapted, or renewed in order to encourage readers to carry out their own curriculum innovation. Curriculum development may not be the sexiest of topics in language teaching, but it is surely one of the most vital: At its core, a curriculum is what happens among learners and teachers in classrooms.

Curriculum as a Dynamic System

In its broadest sense, a curriculum is the nexus of educational decisions, activities, and outcomes in a particular setting. As such, it is affected by explicit and implicit social expectations, educational and institutional policies and norms, teachers' beliefs and understandings, and learners' needs and goals. It is not a set of documents or a textbook, although classroom activities may be guided, governed, or hindered by such documents. Rather, it is a dynamic system. This system can be conceptualized as three interrelated processes: planning, enacting, and evaluating, as depicted in the figure.

Planning processes include

- analyzing the needs of learners, the expectations of the institution and other stakeholders, and the availability of resources
- deciding on the learning aims or goals and the steps needed to achieve them, and organizing them in a principled way
- translating the aims and steps into materials and activities

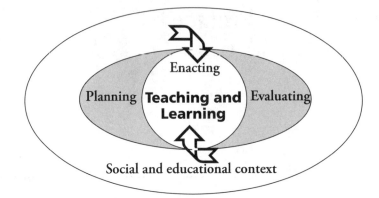

Teaching and learning processes include

- using the materials and doing the activities in the classroom
- adjusting them according to learners' needs, abilities, and interests
- learning with, about, and from each other

Evaluation processes include

- assessing learners' progress toward and achievement of the aims
- adjusting the aims in response to learners' abilities and needs
- gathering information about the effectiveness of the aims, organization, materials, and activities, and using this information in planning and teaching

These processes create a system that is at once stable, rooted in what has gone before, and evolving as it responds to change, to new ideas, and to the people involved. People plan, enact, and evaluate a curriculum.

The Series: Educators Bringing About Change

In these volumes, readers will encounter teachers, curriculum developers, and administrators from all over the world who sought to understand their learners' needs and capacities and respond to them in creative, realistic, and effective ways. The volumes focus on different ways in which curriculum is developed or renewed:

- Volume 1: Developing a new curriculum for school-age learners
- Volume 2: Planning and teaching creatively within a required curriculum for school-age learners
- Volume 3: Revitalizing a curriculum for school-age learners
- Volume 4: Developing a new course for adult learners
- Volume 5: Developing a new curriculum for adult learners
- Volume 6: Planning and teaching creatively within a required curriculum for adult learners
- Volume 7: Revitalizing an established program for adult learners

The boundaries between a program and a curriculum are blurred, as are the boundaries between a curriculum and a course. *Curriculum* is used in its broadest sense to mean planning, teaching, and evaluating a course of study (e.g., a Grade 2 curriculum or a university writing curriculum). A *course* is a stand-alone or a specific offering within a curriculum, such as a computer literacy course for intermediate students. A *program* is all of the courses or courses of study offered in a particular institution or department, for example, the high school ESL program.

The overarching theme of these volumes is how educators bring about change. Change is rarely straightforward or simple. It requires creative thinking, collaboration, problematizing, negotiation, and reflection. It involves trial and error, setbacks and breakthroughs, and occasional tearing out of hair. It takes time. The contributors to these volumes invite you into their educational context and describe how it affects their work. They introduce you to their learners—school-age children or adults—and explain the motivation for the curriculum change. They describe what they did, how they evaluated it, and what they learned from it. They allow you to see what is, at its heart, a creative human process. In so doing, they guide the way for you as a reader to set out on the path of your own curriculum innovation and learning.

This Volume

Developing a new curriculum is a complex process that requires vision, leadership, collaboration, and commitment. The contributors to this volume brought all of these qualities and more to their institutions and learners. In some cases, the writers were charged with developing a curriculum from scratch, while in others they built something new on the foundation of what had been there before. The learners who benefited from these efforts ranged from adults learning computer literacy in the United States and university students in freshman English classes in Japan, to members of the military in the United Arab Emirates and English language teachers-in-training in Brazil. An unintended but important benefit described in many of these accounts is the impact that the development of the new curriculum had on stakeholders not directly served by it, such as other students, teachers, and administrators. The introductory chapter provides a thoughtful analysis of the scope and challenges of curriculum development. Taken together, the chapters in this volume provide a useful blueprint for administrators, teachers, and teacher-educators involved in curriculum development for adults.

Dedication

This series is dedicated to Marilyn Kupetz, a gifted editor, a generous mentor, and a discerning colleague. The quality of TESOL publications, including this series, is due in no small part to her vision, attention to detail, and care.

Kathleen Graves

Acknowledgments

I wholeheartedly thank the contributors to this volume for the time and effort they put into writing these chapters, as well as for the patience they showed during the editing and rewriting process. I am greatly indebted to them for all they have taught me about curriculum development. My deepest thanks and unending admiration go to Carol Edwards and Sarah Duffy for their exemplary skill and professionalism in bringing the book to production. And, of course, I thank Kathleen Graves for giving me the opportunity to take on this project and for her generous advice and support along the way.

Michael Carroll

Creating a New Curriculum: Leadership and Communication

1

MICHAEL CARROLL

Curriculum: A Dynamic Process

At orientation day just before the opening of the new centre, when we were told there was a brand-new curriculum, most people were, on the whole, supportive. Of course some people didn't like the idea that, compared with previous programs we'd taught in, we seemed to be losing some of the freedom we'd come to take for granted. There'd really never been a curriculum to speak of here before, so we were all a bit apprehensive. But overall we were keen to be part of it. It was exciting. There was a lot of energy around on that day. One year down the track, though, there's a much more ambivalent attitude in the staff room. The curriculum turned out to be too prescriptive for some, and not prescriptive enough for others. Some people say it puts so many restrictions on what we can do that we're not really teachers any more, just glorified human tape recorders; others say that if we're going to be given a list of things we have to do in the classroom, we shouldn't have to go round trying to supplement the materials we're given. It's the same with the levels. You hear some people saying it's just too difficult for the students, and then you hear the opposite: It's too Mickey Mouse. The problem is no one asked the teachers what we thought in the first place. If we'd been a bit more involved at the start, we might have had more incentive to make it work instead of complaining or, as some of us did, just ignoring it and doing what we'd always done. Are we better off now than we would have been if we hadn't had the new curriculum? If I have to answer that question I'd say it could have been worse, but it could have been a lot better, too. The students seem to like the idea of an "innovative" curriculum, but whether they are learning more as a result is a question on which the jury is still out.

This ambivalent response from Sandra, an experienced teacher, to an end-of-year evaluation questionnaire touches on several issues that surround the implementation of any new curriculum. As Kathleen Graves points out in the preface to this book, curriculum in its broadest sense is a dynamic process, a social event engaged in by various groups, which brings into contact institutional norms and behaviors on the one hand, and people's ideas about what they think should happen or what they would like to happen on the other. Curriculum, insofar as it is a kind of frame for action, creates spaces for educators to achieve their goals, although at the same time it may place restrictions how they go about doing so. Thus curriculum often generates pronounced feelings of support or antagonism, and because in its implementation it is a living, changing entity, the ways people position themselves in relation to it change as well.

As Sandra implied, although teachers are generally thought to be conservative in professional matters, they are also relatively well disposed towards innovation when they see a need for it. But at the same time, when their view of the need differs from that of the administrators, they are in a strong position to subvert it. Even when looking at curriculum change on a small scale, such as within a single classroom, it is not easy to see how the dynamics between the principal actors might operate. However, the larger the scale of the curriculum, the more difficult it is to both predict and manage the human side of the change. As readers will see in the chapters that follow, most of the contributors to this book grappled with the problem of managing curriculum implementation with groups of teachers, and sometimes other administrators, who often had quite divergent views, although they did so more successfully than the designers of Sandra's curriculum.

Top-Down and Bottom-Up Curriculum

Perhaps the most important way in which curriculum changes vary is whether they originate from the top or the bottom of an organisation. More than 40 years ago, Popper (1962) characterized this dimension of change as a continuum from *utopian* to *piecemeal*. Utopian social designers believe that the initial blueprint is of paramount importance—a specification of what they want to achieve and the most effective way of doing that. Once the blueprint is decided on, they do not expect it to be challenged or amended in any fundamental sense (Sockett, 1976). Piecemeal designers, on the other hand, see the initial blueprint, if there is one, as a starting point, a work in progress, to be worked on by the participants and changed bit by bit so as to become theirs.

In the view of the piecemeal designer, curriculum innovations are most successful when they do not get too far ahead of present thought or practice. As Coulson (1972) pointed out more than 30 years ago, at a time of especially rapid change in British schools, "the teaching profession as a whole, especially the non-vocal majority, are rightly more susceptible to evolution than to revolution" (p. 95). Of course, teachers can and do change their practice, but to varying degrees, like the noncompliant teachers Sandra referred to: "In resilient and resourceful ways [they find] that they can continue to do what they have always done . . . regardless of the impositions of policy" (Hood, 1995, p. 32).

Sockett (1976) provides a useful analogy for understanding the utopian-piecemeal dichotomy. The curriculum designer can be thought of either as an aeroplane designer or as an architect. The aeroplane designer must think of every smallest detail and specify every possible use the aeroplane will be put to; once the aeroplane is built, very little can be changed. An architect, on the other hand, has to build into his or her design the possibility for the people who eventually live in the house to use it however they choose. The may build an extension, knock down a wall, redecorate, change the dining room into the living room, and generally make it their home. If teachers and learners feel that their curriculum is like the aeroplane, they may justifiably feel that they have little involvement in it except to play the essentially passive roles of cabin crew and passengers. If they feel that their curriculum is like the house, on the other hand, they are more likely to see it as theirs to look after, to personalize, and to improve.

It is reasonable to say, then, that curriculum innovations will succeed or fail according to the extent to which teachers in particular, and to some extent students, feel that they are meaningfully involved in the process of change (Claire & Adger, 2000; Mackenzie, 2002; Menges, 1997). The chapters in this book describe curriculum innovations that do just this. Bollati (chapter 2); Abreu-e-Lima, de Oliveira, and Augusto-Navarro (chapter 9); and Gommlich, Rilling, and Uhrig (chapter 10) describe how their students' questions and requests led to changes in the curriculum as it was implemented. Likewise, Shannon (chapter 3) attributes the success of a program at the American University of Sharjah to the fact that all the teachers were fully involved in the development of the curriculum and thus came to "own" it. Similarly, Swenson and Cornwell (chapter 6), Heigham (chapter 7), Strong (chapter 8), and Kucia (chapter 5) variously describe programs

Table 1. Four Models of Curriculum Change

(Adapted from Markee, 1997)

Model	Managers	Teachers or learners
Centre-Periphery	• Make proposals • Create detailed syllabus	• Follow syllabus
Research-Development-Diffusion	• Take initiative to seek solutions to known issues • Gather data from teachers and learners • Create syllabus • Monitor implementation, seek feedback, and make adjustments	• Respond to management initiatives • Give feedback • Follow syllabus
Problem-Solving	• Respond to initiatives from teachers or learners • Support curriculum discussion • Approve syllabus • Support implementation	• Take initiative to seek solutions to issues • Elicit support from management • Create syllabus • Implement curriculum
Linkage	• Take initiative • Encourage teachers and learners to seek solutions • Support and take part in curriculum discussions • Approve syllabus • Support implementation	• May take initiative • Take part in curriculum discussions • Approve syllabus • Implement curriculum

in which staff involvement in the original design and ongoing development was crucial.

A different way to frame the utopian-piecemeal dichotomy is Markee's (1997) four models of curriculum change. The *centre-periphery model* is the most top-down. It describes the traditional situation in which managers, whose authority is derived from their position in the hierarchy, determine changes centrally and then pass them on to teachers to implement. In this model the teacher's role is simply to carry out instructions from above in a more or less mechanical way, hence the name: They are peripheral to the design process. This model seems to have been in place at Sandra's institution, referred to in the opening paragraph. A variation on this model is the *research-development-diffusion model,* in which the instigation for reform and the locus of decision making remains in the centre, but the change agents' authority lies in their expertise in curriculum matters, and the flow of information from all parts of the organisation is seen as an important part of the process. This model is theory driven and rationalistic, and it assumes that rationally justified changes will inevitably be embraced. Therefore, it often pays insufficient attention to the implementation stage because overreliance on the "rightness" of the design fails to consider the relationships between the various people involved.

The *problem-solving model* is a more democratic model in which the impetus for change comes from problems and issues identified within the organization, primarily from teachers themselves. It is therefore a bottom-up approach and is often realised in small-scale action research projects. This model is widely favored in recent work on curriculum change, but it has significant obstacles, most notably that it demands more time, commitment, and skills than many teachers are willing or able to provide. Thus Markee (1997) proposes the *linkage model,* which recognises the complexity of real-life teaching situations and is flexible enough to allow for not only top-down initiatives, and the support that can come with them, but also bottom-up feedback, amendments, and involvement in decision making, particularly at the implementation level. This model underlies most of the program innovations described in this book, and it is indeed the most practicable for large-scale programs where some degree of central initiative is essential, but where diversity of teacher views is likely to be most pronounced.

This volume therefore takes the linkage model as the most realistic model for effectively implementing curriculum change. Although it is true that much of the research shows that top-down curriculum changes, particularly those with an exclusively centre-periphery orientation, are the least likely to result in lasting changes (Markee, 1997, p. 64), clearly there are situations that require centrally led initiatives. The dangers of such initiatives being rejected or subverted, though (Gibbons, 1982), point to a need for serious consideration of how changes are communicated, especially to teachers, and the extent of support mechanisms and feedback responsiveness. This planning for communication is a theme that runs through this volume and is especially highlighted by Shannon (chapter 3) and Strong (chapter 8).

Markee (1997) also discusses a *social interaction model* cutting across the other four—not a model of change initiation as such, but one of how the process of change works. In this model, the diffusion of change is seen fundamentally as a matter of communication. The implication for curriculum innovators is that communication networks need to be planned for rather than simply left to chance.

Teachers' willingness or unwillingness to change is not the only reason effective communication is necessary. If teachers are excluded from all involvement in the direction of the change processes, they may in fact be not so much unwilling as unable to implement it effectively. For instance,

Brundage and McKeracher (1980, pp. 21–31), in an article dealing with adult learning styles, make the following points:

- Adults learn best when they are involved in developing their own learning objectives that are congruent with their self-image.
- Adult learners react to experience as they perceive it, not as the teacher presents it, and they learn best when the content is personally relevant to them.
- Adults learn best when they have learned how to learn.

Mackenzie (2002) suggests that it is useful to see teachers as "learners of our teaching-learning context" (p. 224). Taking this idea one step further and thinking of curriculum change as a learning activity for themselves, teachers might rephrase Brundage and McKeracher's (1980) points as such:

- Teachers learn new ways of teaching best when they are involved in developing their own objectives that are congruent with their image of their classrooms.
- Teachers react to experience as they perceive it, not as the curriculum manager presents it, and they learn best when the curriculum content is personally relevant to their experiences.
- Teachers implement changes best when they have learned how to implement changes.

In other words, if managers of top-down curriculum changes recognize teachers' crucial role in implementation, they must take responsibility for supporting teachers through implementation by listening to and acting on their concerns.

Leadership and Communication

The nine accounts in this volume cross a variety of educational contexts around the world. Some programs were built entirely from scratch, where no program at all existed before (Bolatti, chapter 2; Shannon, chapter 3; Turner & Phillips, chapter 4; Kucia, chapter 5; Gommlich, Rilling, & Uhrig, chapter 10), whereas others arose out of situations in which the developers looked critically at existing programs and, rather than tinkering round the edges, decided to scrap them entirely and rebuild from the base up (Swenson & Cornwell, chapter 6; Heigham, chapter 7; Strong, chapter 8; Abreu-e-Lima, de Oliveira, & Augusto-Navarro, chapter 9). The contributions are roughly divided into three sections: university or vocational preparation, English as a foreign language in compulsory university English programs, and teacher preparation. The unifying theme of all these chapters is that the importance of one or more people with a strong vision of what the program might be, as well as effective communication among the various stakeholders, cannot be overemphasized.

At Black Hawk College (Bollati, chapter 2), the confluence of an innovative dean, a globally minded president, and an ESL coordinator with clear goals kick-starts the process that transforms ESL from a back-door part of the campus to a key part of the college's identity. Bolatti began by noticing a group of potential students who should have been served by the college but were not; she realized that even a modest level of support would have a significant impact on the quality of their lives. In a persuasive example of the idea that small, local changes can lead to greater benefits than originally envisaged, as this program developed it became apparent that the increased involvement of these new students in the life of the college was having a positive internationalizing effect on the wider life of the college itself. Similarly, Kucia at Albany Park Community Center (chapter 5) and Swenson and Cornwell at Osaka Jogakuin College (chapter 6) created new programs motivated by a concern to fulfill key parts of their institutions' central missions. At Osaka Jogakuin this meant creating a curriculum that fundamentally challenged the dominant model in Japanese universities by integrating not only the various English language courses, but also the content courses taught in Japanese, so that the whole university program addressed the college's aim of deepening students' understanding of themselves and the world around them. At Albany Park it meant identifying a fundamental cause of disenfranchisement among the college's catchment population—low computer literacy aggravated by language barriers—and working with staff who were not accustomed to considering issues of language literacy to devise a program that would empower those students.

By not only setting up a new curriculum, but doing so within a brand-new university, Shannon (chapter 3) realized from the start that the key to success would be the staff. He deliberately built systems of committees that involved staff at every stage of the process. Turner and Phillips (chapter 4) did this also, and they took care to maintain those systems even when they encountered clashes of personalities and philosophies, bringing in external advisors to help the committees resolve problems. Like Kucia, Turner and Phillips, working within the Military Language Institute in the United Arab Emirates, found themselves having to work with people who may never before have had to think about issues related to language education.

Both Heigham (chapter 7) and Strong (chapter 8), like Swenson and Cornwell, were charged with creating new, more effective language programs in Japanese universities with entrenched systems and ideas about language education. They had to deal not only with teachers who had varying types of past experience and current aims, but also with administrations in which, although English is seen as important, it is nevertheless thought of as only a part of the institutions' business. Both Heigham and Strong encountered structural problems, such as Japan's part-time teacher system, and realized the importance of space and the physical environment in facilitating the changes they wanted to make. Heigham instituted a clever, efficient system of developing materials: Each teacher wrote one unit of work, which was then shared with the other teachers in the program, resulting in a more diverse range of materials than one person alone could have produced. Strong decided that the seemingly small matter of getting a mailbox installed was worth fighting for, both as a symbol of his ability to get things done and as an essential component of a communication system.

At the Federal University of São Carlos, Abreu-e-Lima, de Oliveira, and Augusto-Navarro (chapter 9) also found themselves challenging established ways of doing things. In addition to having to persuade their colleagues in different departments of the value of considering new methods of organizing teacher education, they had to overcome their students' resistance to unfamiliar ideas. By contrast, Gommlich, Rilling, and Uhrig (chapter 10), despite the fact that they were designing a program to run in two countries, faced relatively few problems apart from a few hiccups in some students' cultural adaptation.

Tradition and Innovation

All of the social aspects regarding how a new program comes into being, how it is communicated to the various players, and how it changes as a result of interaction between people underlie the whole enterprise, and can make or break it. However, the heart of any curriculum is the actual nuts and bolts of what goes on between teachers and students in the classroom. Yet this is a contested area on two counts. First, there is the problem of teacher authority. Teachers have responsibility for what goes on in their classrooms, and therefore the authority to manage it. Programs involving coordination between many classes inevitably face the problem that, at some level, many teachers simply do not want to cede this authority. Second, there is conflict about what the content—the nuts and bolts—should be. Many discussions described in this volume hinge on the competing claims from what might be called *traditionalists* and *innovators*. In many educational institutions, particularly universities and colleges where English is a foreign language, the teaching of English has traditionally been the preserve of departments of English literature. Faculty members in these departments are often highly skilled users of English, particularly as readers and writers, and overwhelmingly knowledgeable about the mechanics of the language.

Learning English themselves through literature and intensive, dedicated study, they form a special group of highly motivated and disciplined faculty, many of whom often have a narrow view of language learning that does not fit well with the characteristics of the majority of learners.

Similarly conflicting ideas often exist in institutions in English-speaking countries, where the traditionalists may be administrators or academics from other fields. Superficially, teaching a language is a straightforward, uncomplicated activity in the minds of many administrators and non-TESOL academics and is thus undervalued as an area requiring expertise. Just as many lay people believe that they know all about education on the grounds that they once attended school themselves, so many believe that they know all about language learning because everyone has learned a language at least once, even if it was only their first language.

Conflicts over what should be included in the curriculum can result in compromises, as when Heigham (chapter 7) pragmatically accepted fewer classes than she would have liked for her Communicative English Program. But they can also result in greater clarity of objectives, as when she realized the need to more forcefully explain the rationale for *extensive* reading to students and teachers who had prior experience only with *intensive* reading. This need to explain to outsiders the purposes and rationales of curriculum structures is a thread that runs through all the chapters in this volume, and it is clearly a crucial aspect of curriculum development. Strong (chapter 8) also had to convince his colleagues of the benefits of parts of his program (e.g., streaming) that were conventionally frowned upon in his institution. The issue for Abreu-e-Lima, de Oliveira, and Augusto-Navarro (chapter 9) was achieving a balance between academic content on the one hand and teaching and communication skills on the other. Having to find a compromise between two initially opposing philosophies led them to a methodology that integrated them in a way that may have been more effective than either side had foreseen.

Conclusion

The innovations described in this book's chapters have all been successful in many ways. Each has resulted in improvements in the quality of language education and in opportunities for the students fortunate enough to have been involved. They are not perfect, of course, because curriculum design is not a science, nor is it a perfect art. To the extent that curriculum design is a social process "vested in the . . . values and beliefs of individual teachers [and learners]" (Tripp, 1987, p. 7), each curriculum is different from any other. They are, though, exemplars of what effective curriculum development can look like. Teachers of adult language learners, whether formally responsible for curriculum development or not, will find in these pages many familiar issues related to their own institutions. Seeing how the authors conceptualized and dealt with these issues will, I hope, help readers formulate ideas, proposals, and solutions for their own working environments.

As these chapters demonstrate clearly, curriculum development cannot be simply imposed from above; rather it depends absolutely on the people who implement it. Planning and purposes are important, but as Hargreaves (1997) puts it, "teachers cannot be *given* a purpose: purposes must come from within" (p. 107). If this book helps teachers articulate purposes that are meaningful for them in their own contexts, then all of the work that has gone into the book will have been well worthwhile.

University and Vocational Preparation

From Back Door to Center Stage: The Evolution of an ESL Program

2

ANNE BOLLATI

When prospective students first enter the Black Hawk College campus in Moline, Illinois, in the United States, they are greeted by a sign welcoming them in different languages, and when they leave, they are thanked for their visit in as many languages. Upon entering the lobby of Building 1 of this comprehensive community college, which houses the administrative offices, the library, and computer labs, among other services, these students find a rack full of information about the college's international programs, information about featured countries, and periodicals from all over the world. In the bookstore, they can purchase a mug decorated with the flags of different countries that says, "Black Hawk College: The World is Our Campus." Looking at the cultural events calendar, these students discover activities that take place during International Education Week in the fall semester and the International Festival in the spring semester. Upon registering, they find two awards that are available specifically for international students: the International Student Achievement Award and the International Student Scholarship Award. They also find a brochure inviting them to become mentors to new international students along with the *English as a Second Language Newsletter* that is produced once each semester by students in the advanced ESL Program and sent to faculty, students, staff, and the community. In the Student Government Association, the Theatre Department, the Music Department, the Tutoring Center, athletic teams, vocational programs, and transfer programs, prospective students find classmates who come from as many as 20 different countries.

During their first visit, new students see that Black Hawk College lives its core value of respect and appreciation for diversity. In preparing the report for a visit from the Higher Learning Commission, a committee wrote that "the College has a strong infrastructure to support the current and future international student base in its exemplary ESL programs and in its International Student Advisor" (Black Hawk College, 2003, p. 7). International programs, most especially the ESL programs, are now center stage at Black Hawk College. However, 14 years ago, that wasn't the case; 14 years ago, the academic ESL Program did not exist.

The Motivation for the Program

In 1989–1990, the college's administration was grappling with finding a way to serve one major constituent group in the community: second language learners, international students on student visas, as well as immigrants who wanted to enter vocational and academic programs at the college. At that time students could take Adult Education-ESL, and once they completed that program, they were placed in developmental, precollege preparatory classes with native speakers or in the General Educational Development (GED; high school equivalency) classes. Both placements created more problems; neither fully prepared students to enter their chosen academic or vocational programs. The developmental classes did not focus on the language development that second language learners needed, nor did the instructors have the academic preparation to create a curriculum to meet their special needs. And the GED instructors were not able to provide the intensive language practice that the ESL students needed. As a result, many students within the community were not served and were not able to meet personal and professional goals, and many ended up dropping out of college.

In 1991, through the intervention of the farsighted dean of liberal arts and public service, who was promoting international programs on campus, and the arrival of a new president with a global perspective, I was hired as an ESL instructor to teach two sections of developmental English. The dean asked me to formulate a proposal for a bridging program for second language learners that I would coordinate once it was accepted by the administration.

The challenges related to the creation of this program were great. The general atmosphere of the college was still quite provincial. The "community" of the community college was the local area, not the global community. And most administrators were unwilling to commit funds to the development of a program not meant to serve the traditional populations.

Therefore, the academic ESL Program was born with little moral or financial support.

Early Challenges

FINDING ACCEPTANCE IN THE COMMUNITY

My first challenge as the new ESL coordinator was to find a way to work within an unwelcoming community. I was assigned to an office with a full-time English instructor who did not want to share space, and I was placed in the contentious English, Philosophy, and Foreign Language Department, which was so embroiled in politics that any decision about the program would be endlessly debated by people who knew little to nothing about ESL. Realizing the fruitlessness of the situation, I deliberately changed the working circumstances. I was able to find an empty desk, a file cabinet, and metal shelves in the part-time Reading Department faculty office area. From this home base, I worked with the dean to change departments—to become a member of the Public Service Department, which allowed the ESL Program to have autonomy under the umbrella of a department. I could now begin to collect the necessary materials, catalogues, and books without infringing on another faculty member's space, and I was also able to make my own decisions about how to develop the curriculum without having to gain the approval of a cumbersome department.

However, I still had to maintain credibility with the English Department. Doing so was essential to the survival and growth of the ESL Program because that department would judge the students according to its own standards in order to allow them to transfer into credit-bearing English classes. All students in the developmental English classes had to write an acceptable paragraph graded by full-time English faculty before being admitted to English 101, Freshman Composition. Because the English Department had a well-organized developmental English component taught by open-minded and knowledgeable faculty members, I arranged to have the advanced-level ESL students participate in the "exit" paragraph process. I also sent the ESL students' compositions to the English Department to be graded by the faculty. The English faculty were impressed by the clarity of the ESL students' writing. Their passing rate was and has continued to be close to 100%. By not being afraid to be judged by the standards set in the English Department, the ESL Program gained the respect of an influential and powerful group on campus.

It was also important for the students in the program to find acceptance on campus. This goal was easily met because of the small group of phenomenal students who made up the first academic ESL Program. When the librarians needed help, one of the Vietnamese students took the job and more than met their expectations. Other students were placed in the Admissions Office and the Dean's Office. When the staff interacted with these students, barriers broke down easily and quickly. When the International Student Achievement Award was established to provide a scholarship of 3 credit hours to international students, there was a ready supply of international campus workers who needed to provide the 30 hours of community service required to maintain the scholarship. The establishment of the International Student Association also helped international students gain acceptance; the student members became part of the Student Government Association and sponsored well-organized public events. They established the International Festival that takes place every April and raises money for the student-initiated international student scholarship. This event attracts more than 1,000 members of the community to campus and showcases the students' food, music, dance, and handicrafts. After 14 years on campus, international students are an "expected" part of the student body, and faculty members regularly contact the ESL Office to ask for international speakers and conversation partners.

FINDING FUNDING

Finding funding for the program was a daunting task. Because the college had not yet made a commitment to international education, the dean had found the money to hire me as the ESL coordinator through the Carl Perkins Grant, one of whose objectives was to provide access to equitable education for students with limited English proficiency. However, because the grant was meant to serve students in targeted vocational programs, I had to make sure that all the ESL students were enrolled in at least one vocational course. Therefore, in the early days of the program, I had to spend a great deal of time helping underprepared students pass a keyboarding class and helping the class instructor understand how to incorporate these students into her class with minimal disruption. During the 4 years that the program was funded through the Perkins Grant, I had to attend meetings and complete paperwork that were not relevant to ESL. After the program became established on campus and the administration began to see its value to the campus, the college assumed full financial responsibility for my salary and, eventually, for the program.

Because funding was extremely limited, it was necessary to develop a curriculum that would serve the needs of the students but would also be economical and efficient. I had to carefully assess the existing resources on campus and make strong connections to them. Black Hawk College already had a well-established Adult Education ESL (AE-ESL) Program and a well-organized developmental English program, so I only had to develop a series of intermediate and advanced ESL classes to create a bridge between these two programs. While designing the new curriculum, I formed an ESL consultant committee of faculty members from both groups. Because they were regularly informed about ESL course developments, these faculty members became partners, not adversaries, in the process. In addition, I kept in contact with the college's bilingual counselor, who made regular visits to students in the AE-ESL Program. She became an integral part of the recruiting process for the academic program. She helped AE-ESL students organize their lives so that they could participate in the new program that required tuition payments, homework, and reliable transportation. Because of her cultural sensitivity and her knowledge of available financial resources, she was key to helping students succeed in participating in this tightly structured academic program.

FINDING SPACE

Finding space on campus for the newly developed classes was another challenge. The eight classes that made up the core of the ESL Program needed to meet every day, which meant that they did not fit the college's scheduling pattern for Monday-Wednesday-Friday or Tuesday-Thursday classes. On top of that, the ESL classes needed to be scheduled between 9 a.m. and noon, the most sought-after time slot, to accommodate students who generally worked late afternoon through early morning and were accustomed to attending class at this time in the AE-ESL Program. The scheduling coordinator and I met regularly to monitor classroom space, and we finally came up with a split schedule for most of the classes. Students would go to one classroom on Monday, Wednesday, and Friday and to a different one on Tuesday and Thursday. Although at the beginning it was difficult for students to remember which room to go to on a given day, they adjusted to the schedule and became a familiar sight to both faculty and students in all four buildings on campus. Each semester I met with the scheduling coordinator to find additional space because no classrooms could be assigned to the ESL Program. On the positive side, the students were not marginalized in one corner of the campus; however, on the negative side, the program was often assigned the least desirable classrooms on campus. Over the past 14 years, additional classroom space has been added to campus, and the ESL Program has been granted some designated classrooms that are spacious and modern.

FINDING INSTRUCTORS

Another major difficulty that has continued to plague the program since its inception is the hiring of qualified ESL instructors. The college is located in the Quad Cities, four small cities on the western border of Iowa and

Illinois. The college is 3 hours away from Chicago and 1 hour away from the University of Iowa, so there is no regular pool of instructors who have training in ESL because those who have the required qualifications tend to find jobs in these other areas. Also, for the ESL Program's first 6 years, the college would not allow the hiring of a full-time faculty member. Therefore, in addition to teaching and performing all the administrative duties, I was continually engaged in faculty training and development. I had to find faculty who were willing to extend their training in reading, writing, or foreign language to ESL. After hiring the new part-time faculty members, I helped them plan their lessons, visited their classes, and provided workshops for these newcomers to the field. After teaching for the program for 2 or 3 years, these instructors had the necessary skills and training to find full-time work in the field, and they often did. So the cycle would begin again. In 1997, the college approved the hiring of one full-time ESL instructor. Although this alleviated the problem, it did not solve it. Finding qualified part-time instructors is still my most challenging and time-consuming duty.

In one attempt to solve the instructor crisis, I developed a course in teacher training (LIB 250). The objective of this course was to familiarize new teachers with the field of TESOL through a series of readings, observations, and teaching practices with the hope that it would produce a pool of trained faculty for the ESL Program. However, most of the candidates for this course were students interested in teaching English for short periods of time in foreign countries. Another attempt to attract part-time instructors involved applying to become an institution able to issue J visas, U.S. government visas for visiting scholars. If such an application were granted, Black Hawk College would be able to invite international scholars to teach in the ESL Program and to study at the same time. However, due to changes in personnel in the International Office, this effort has not yet borne fruit, but holds the promise of a positive international exchange and a solution for the staffing of the summer ESL Program.

Another effort that holds promise for solving the staffing problem is the assignment of specific ESL courses to full-time faculty members in the English Department. One full-time reading faculty member has taught the intermediate reading course, and another has taught the advanced writing class. With some in-house training and training through the TESOL association, these faculty members have begun to provide stability and expertise to the program while expanding their professional credentials. Another positive option has been the hiring of retired faculty members interested in teaching smaller classes with international students. Finding qualified part-time faculty will always be an issue, but there are more options now than there were at the beginning of the program.

MAINTAINING EQUITABLE TUITION

Administrative decisions made to facilitate the establishment of the ESL Program have created problems for the "mature" program. To keep tuition reasonable for international students, who had to pay the out-of-state rate, the ESL classes were assigned 4 credit hours (3 lecture hours and 2 lab hours, which are counted as 1 credit hour) even though the students attended five classes per week. Instructors were compensated at a rate of 4.6 credit hours. This arrangement worked for the students and the college alike until the hiring of a full-time faculty member who needed to teach 15 credit hours each semester. A variety of compromises have been made with the administration over the past few years, including the assignment of a special project to the full-time ESL faculty member. However, none of the proposed solutions has been satisfactory to the college or to the faculty member. Therefore, the administration has accepted a proposal to change the curriculum to allow each class to be worth 5 credit hours. The cost to the international students will not increase significantly because 1 of the credit hours will be assigned as an online credit.

MEETING STUDENTS' NEEDS

The ESL Program was originally designed to meet the academic needs of the resident ESL population who needed more rigorous training in English than could be provided by the AE-ESL Program so that they could access vocational and transfer programs. However, the program soon confronted the need to accommodate the requirements of the students with F-1 visas (granted to international students for full-time study in the United States), who were beginning to arrive at the college. I was faced with the challenge of meeting the needs of two completely different populations within the same program and in the same classes. I had to design the program around both groups' need for academic English, but make it flexible enough to meet the different logistical needs of each group.

The resident population was a working population with limited time and limited resources. Therefore, they could not attend classes for 5 to 6 hours a day, as required by an intensive ESL program. They also needed financial assistance to pay for classes, materials, and books. The F-1 students, on the other hand, had plenty of time to study because they were not allowed to work and needed to be engaged in full-time academic study (i.e., at least 12 credits).

To develop a coherent program, not just a series of classes, for both groups, I consulted the guidelines for intensive ESL programs established by the National Association for Foreign Student Affairs (NAFSA; Barrett, 1982). Among the nine common features listed was a core curriculum that recognizes the four language skills (listening, speaking, reading, and writing) taught at beginning, intermediate, and advanced levels. In accordance with the guidelines, during an orientation program at Black Hawk College, students are tested and placed in an appropriate level and introduced to the important support services.

During the 1991–1992 academic year, the core curriculum of the academic ESL Program was created, passed by the college's Curriculum Committee, and approved by the Illinois Community College Board. This curriculum consisted of two levels: intermediate ESL (ESL 061, 063, 065, 067) and advanced ESL (ESL 071, 073, 075, 077). Each level had four classes addressing the needs of a particular skill area but also encouraging comprehensive language practice. Because the AE-ESL Program (New Arrivals and Levels 1–4) met the needs of beginning-level students by stressing basic vocabulary development, survival skills, and conversation, I did not develop another beginning level. During the 1992–1993 academic year, a transitional ESL class (Level 5) that stressed reading and writing was added to the AE-ESL Program to better prepare that program's students for the academic ESL Program. In 1998–1999, another class was added to the intermediate level, ESL 070, Pronunciation and Conversation. The current structure of the ESL Program is illustrated in Figure 1.

The curriculum has been designed so that the advanced level builds carefully on what was taught at the intermediate level. Table 1 shows the

Table 1. Skill Building and Levels of Articulation

Skill Area	Content
Grammar	Noun phrase, verb phrase, complex sentence, sentence combination
Writing	Sentences, paragraph development, essay, documented essay, research paper
Reading	*Text structure:* textbook chapters, short stories, short novels, essays, newspaper articles, magazine articles *Thematic units:* popular choice, liberal arts, science *Vocabulary:* active vocabulary, vocabulary in context, roots and stems *Library:* Quad-Linc books, Info-Trac periodicals, Internet search engines, computer, word processing, WebBoard, CD-ROM software, Web
Speaking	Question/answer, small-group discussions, panel discussions, public speaking, debating, conversational English functions, pronunciation, vowel sounds, consonant sounds, suprasegmentals
Listening	Aural discrimination, short lectures, long lectures (short propositions and guided fill-ins)

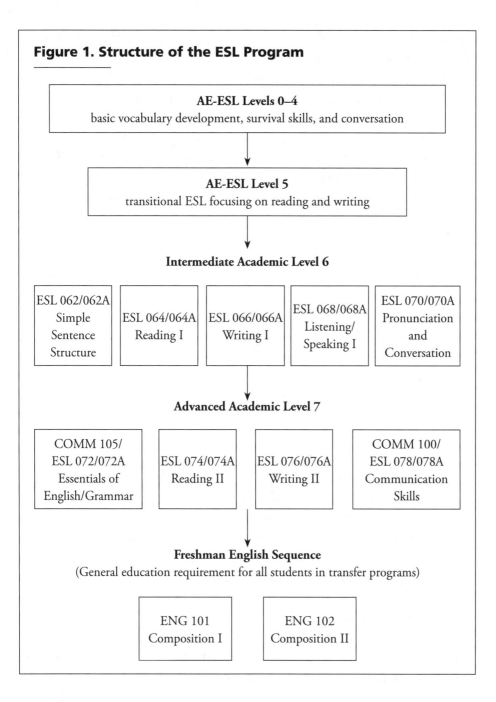

Figure 1. Structure of the ESL Program

AE-ESL Levels 0–4
basic vocabulary development, survival skills, and conversation

AE-ESL Level 5
transitional ESL focusing on reading and writing

Intermediate Academic Level 6

ESL 062/062A Simple Sentence Structure	ESL 064/064A Reading I	ESL 066/066A Writing I	ESL 068/068A Listening/ Speaking I	ESL 070/070A Pronunciation and Conversation

Advanced Academic Level 7

COMM 105/ ESL 072/072A Essentials of English/Grammar	ESL 074/074A Reading II	ESL 076/076A Writing II	COMM 100/ ESL 078/078A Communication Skills

Freshman English Sequence
(General education requirement for all students in transfer programs)

ENG 101 Composition I	ENG 102 Composition II

academic orientation of the program and the progression of skills through each language area.

As stated earlier, it was necessary for this curriculum to meet the needs of the resident students as well as the international students. Through the sequencing of courses and good advising, the program has proven flexible enough to create a positive learning experience for both groups of students.

During the fall semester, the ESL Program offers Reading and Writing classes at each level; the third class is Listening/Speaking. In the spring semester, Reading and Writing are offered again; this time, the third class is Grammar. In the summer, during a 6-week session in which class time is doubled, Grammar and Listening/Speaking classes are offered. Because each class is worth 5 credit hours, the international students can meet their visa requirements by taking all three courses. For each class, a student is given a minimum of 2 hours of homework, so students are able to fill their days with English study. Also, because classes are offered year-round, students can move through the program quickly and advance to the academic majors in a time frame ranging from one semester to two semesters and a summer, depending on their placement scores.

To attract the resident (part-time) students, the courses had to be scheduled either in the morning or in the evening to accommodate their work schedules. The courses also had to be delivered without any break so that students could complete them before going to their jobs. Because each course assigns at least 2 hours of homework, these working students rarely can take more than one course at a time. However, those who decide to take two can do so and still get to work on time. In designing the courses, I made sure that they received college-level developmental course designations from the Illinois Community College Board, which is a requirement of the financial aid programs, so that resident students could receive aid while enrolled.

The structure of this curriculum is seamless in that students can enter at any point and proceed without encountering obstacles. If students enter the ESL Program through the AE-ESL Program, they are given the Combined English Language Skills Assessment and placed in one of the first five levels of the program, which are administered by AE-ESL. Or, if they are assessed as having advanced skills, they are sent to the academic ESL Program. If students enter through the academic ESL Program, they are given the Michigan Test of English Language Proficiency and either placed in Level 6 or 7 or directed to the AE-ESL Program (if their scores are not high enough). Once in the system, they move to the next level through successful class completion and teacher recommendation. Students prove that they are ready to move out of the ESL Program by completing class and portfolio requirements and taking the exit writing exam given by the English Department. Due to coordination among faculty and staff in the AE-ESL Program, the ESL Program, and the English Department, students are placed correctly and understand what is required to move to the next level.

The ESL Program that has evolved cannot be considered an intensive English program because it does not meet the number of contact hours required by the *TCA Standards for Intensive English Programs* (TESOL Commission on Accreditation, 1998); Black Hawk College's ESL students take a maximum of 12 credit hours, as opposed to the 15 hours required by the TCA Standards. However, the program is a comprehensive one that meets all other requirements outlined by these standards that promote best practices.

Milestones in the Development of the Program

The program described in this chapter is the product of a 14-year evolution that involved not only the development of a curriculum but also the development of student services and the hiring of necessary personnel. The history of the development is highlighted in Table 2 and can be divided into three distinct phases of development.

During Phase 1, from 1991 to 1994, all of the basics were put in place. The core curriculum for the academic ESL Program was developed, basic student services were created, and a small staff was hired. Phase 2, from 1994 to 2000, involved great growth and development in both the curriculum and student services along with the staff needed to support this growth.

Table 2. ESL Program Milestones

| Academic Year | Milestones | | | |
	Curricular Addition	Administrative Addition	Staff Addition	Student Services
1991–1992	• Curriculum development approved by Curriculum Committee	• International student admissions requirement established		
1992–1993	• Level 5 ESL class established		• Part-time international student advisor hired • Part-time ESL instructors hired	• International Student Association organized
1993–1994	• ESL graduation ceremony held			• First International Festival held • International Student Scholarship Fund established

continued on p. 24

Table 2 (continued). ESL Program Milestones

Academic Year	Milestones			
	Curricular Addition	Administrative Addition	Staff Addition	Student Services
1994–1995	• Special program for Japanese agricultural specialists established • LIB 250 teaching internship established			
1995–1996	• First evening class offered			• International Student Scholarship Award administered
1996–1997				
1997–1998			• Full-time ESL instructor hired • Full-time international student advisor hired	• Student emergency fund established • Formal international student orientation program established • International student mentor program established
1998–1999	• Pronunciation and Conversation class added • ESL lab established • Business English class offered	• ESL program Web site created		

continued on p. 25

Developing a New Curriculum for Adult Learners

Table 2 (continued). ESL Program Milestones

Academic Year	Milestones			
	Curricular Addition	Administrative Addition	Staff Addition	Student Services
1999–2000	• ESL orientation program offered			
2000–2001	• WebBoard introduced to Reading and Writing classes			
2001–2002	• ESL Portfolio process started	• Academic credit granted for ESL 071 and ESL 077 • ESL Program became part of English Department		
2002–2003	• Laptop granted for Writing II			• Rebuilding for Peace Scholarship started • International Education Week established
2003–2004	• First set of online course corequisites passed by Curriculum Committee			
2004–2005	• Final set of online corequisites passed by Curriculum Committee			

Phase 3, from 2001 to 2005, was a time of maturation for the program. By 2005, the curriculum was fully developed, with online components, and student work was assessed through the portfolio process. Services for international students and resident students alike met all their academic and social needs because there was adequate staff to ensure the quality of the services.

CURRICULAR MILESTONES

The curriculum of the ESL Program developed in direct response to the needs of the community. After the basic curriculum was established in 1991–1992, the AE-ESL coordinator and I discovered that students in the AE-ESL Program were still not prepared for the rigors of the comprehensive curriculum. Therefore, in 1992 a new level was added to the AE-ESL curriculum—Level 5. In this course, students concentrated on academic reading and writing skills. The instructor introduced more advanced sentence structures and some work with library research. Trips were planned to the main campus, where the AE-ESL students took a tour and visited a class in the academic ESL Program. After the trip, students who were interested in continuing their education could meet with the bilingual counselor to arrange financial aid, transportation, and work schedules. The Level 5 instructor and I remained in close contact, and the seamless curriculum, which connected the AE-ESL Program and the academic ESL Program, was created. The addition of this class was key to the ESL Program's success. It helped students develop necessary English skills and stabilize their life circumstances so that they could participate in the program that required intense and prolonged attendance at school.

In 1993 I decided to formalize graduation from the program with a ceremony to which the deans and the administration were invited. This was an important step because it legitimized the program on campus and publicly acknowledged the achievement of the students who completed it. During the ceremony the students gave speeches that reflected on their life experiences and their experiences in the ESL Program, and the administration was deeply moved and impressed by the spirit and the accomplishments of the students. The addition of this ceremony marked the end of the first phase of development.

The next 2 years represented expansion and experimentation with the curriculum. Word spread throughout the international community in the Quad Cities that students could continue to study academic ESL during the day. The evening students in the AE-ESL Program who wanted to study beyond Level 5 asked to have the same opportunity. Therefore, the ESL Program began to offer one Level 6 course each semester in the Tuesday-Thursday format. Even though the offerings in the evening program are still limited, they continue to be a bridge for students who need to improve their skills before beginning academic and vocational programs.

Two special programs were added to the curriculum during these years. In an effort to develop a pool of qualified instructors for the ESL Program and in response to calls from the community for TESOL training to work overseas, I created a class to familiarize students with the field of TESOL and with instruction in both an AE-ESL program and an intensive English program. The course provided a series of readings in all skill areas, observations at all levels of the ESL Program, tutoring, and guided teaching. This course, which can be taken for 1–4 credits and is tailored to students' needs, created the realization on campus and in the community that TESOL is a profession that requires professional training. It can be offered during any semester and, as of 2005, has been offered five times. It has not provided the pool of part-time instructors, as originally intended, but it has provided a service to people in the community.

The specialized ESL program offered for members of the Japanese Agricultural Association during the summer of 1995 brought enough income to refurnish the ESL office and give it a professional appearance. At that time, the international student advisor was Japanese and was a member of that organization. Some of the members expressed interest in visiting organic farms in the United States, hoping to also learn a little English along the way. Thirteen students from ages 13 to 76 arrived in Kewanee, Illinois, and for 6 weeks traveled to hog farms, Amish farms, and herb farms and studied basic English conversation. This program was successful because of the international student advisor's personal connections. Although it was only offered once, it was a good recruitment tool for the ESL Program: In the years that followed, the children of several of the participants came over to attend Black Hawk College.

Over the next few years the curriculum matured, and in 1998 a new course was added to the intermediate program in response to requests from international and resident students alike for instruction in pronunciation and conversational English. ESL 070, Pronunciation and Conversation, is the least academic of all the classes in the program. Students learn segmentals and suprasegmentals while exploring the Quad Cities, meeting U.S. counterparts in the cross-cultural communication classes, and learning to communicate with natural expression. This class has provided many opportunities for students to be involved on campus and in the community.

The curriculum has evolved over time to respond to students' needs and to changes in course delivery. During the past 5 years, due to the growth of technology on campus, the curriculum has come to incorporate technology as a tool for instruction. By writing a proposal to the dean, who set aside special college funds for technology, I was able to get the necessary equipment to establish a lab with collaborative workstations. These consist of tables at which two to three students can work at a computer that has Internet access, CD drives, and microphones. The lab is located in a separate area in the Independent Learning Center so that students can use it after class and on weekends. Many new software programs were ordered to give students individual practice in all skill areas. These programs not only provided instructors with new resources to include in their curriculum, but also provided the opportunity for language practice to community members who could not participate in the ESL Program.

Students were introduced to online instruction through the addition of asynchronous discussion boards that were incorporated into the Reading and Writing classes. In Writing classes, students began to post their weekly journal entries to the discussion board. In Reading classes, students conducted Internet searches and commented on readings on the discussion board. Also, after writing a proposal for technology funds that were available through another college grant, I was able to obtain laptops for students in the advanced Writing class.

The use of technology continues to evolve within the ESL Program. The curriculum has experienced a major renovation during the past year and a half. The full-time instructor and I created an online component that is a corequisite for each class in the program; it will help the ESL students develop the skills necessary to access college-level classes offered in all formats.

MILESTONES IN STUDENT SERVICES AND STAFFING

The evolution of the curriculum was paralleled and supported by the evolution of student services and staffing. During the ESL Program's first 5 years, many new instructors had to be hired to teach the classes in the comprehensive curriculum. As mentioned earlier, the continual training of these part-time instructors placed enormous demands on my time and affected program stability. Therefore, after I had spent 5 years lobbying, the administration agreed to hire a full-time ESL instructor in a tenure-track position. In doing so, the administration made a commitment to the growth and expansion of the program.

During the first year of the program, I was both academic advisor and international student advisor. I developed the admissions policy for the program and learned to work with students who were in the country on I-20 visas. However, as the ESL Program expanded, I informed the dean that if the college wanted to increase the F-1 student population, an international student coordinator needed to be hired. The dean of liberal arts and public service found resources to expand the hours of the Japanese language instructor, who then became the part-time international student advisor.

Through his knowledge, wisdom, and connections in Japan, the new advisor helped expand the number of international students from 1 to 30—roughly one third of whom were from Japan. He provided legal support to students and established the necessary housing and host-family programs. Through the hiring of the new international student advisor, the ESL Program was able to serve not only the resident population but also the F-1 population.

The 1997–1998 academic year was one of growth and expansion for the International Office. When the part-time advisor decided to return to Japan, the college further committed itself to international education by hiring a full-time international program coordinator. With additional time and funding, new programs were established to serve students. The orientation for international students was expanded to include many faculty members and staff, and a mentor program was established to form bonds with local students. International Educational Week activities, the International Holiday Bazaar, and the expanded International Festival became anticipated events on campus. The international programs were now fully integrated into the life of the college.

The International Student Association played an important part in the internationalization of Black Hawk College and gave credibility to the ESL Program. In 1992 four students and I brainstormed ways to make the international presence known to the college community. Those beginning days were full of fun as they all cooked together, traveled together, and presented programs as part of the college's Lunch and Learn Series. As the number of students increased, they became bolder and more determined to help each other. They decided to begin an International Festival to raise scholarship money to help resident students who did not qualify for financial aid. The first festival was a labor of love. Students volunteered to dance, sing, and prepare food, and approximately 300 people attended. News about the exciting event spread, and the next year brought more student and community involvement and more scholarship money. Each year it became more organized and developed into a showcase for the international and resident student populations. After a while, the Student Government Association and the college decided to contribute funds to support the festival, which provided the ESL Program with a significant amount of money to offer in scholarships to local students. The students decided to offer the scholarships to pay for half of one ESL course to needy students. This money has helped a large number of students take the first steps on campus and has encouraged them to take the risk involved with coming to school. Those who received the scholarships became willing participants in the following year's festival. The event today is huge; it attracts more than 1,000 people to campus and raises significant amounts of money to help attract and retain students.

With the development of the scholarship for local students taken care of, I needed to find a way to get financial support for the international students on F-1 visas, who had to pay much higher out-of-state tuition. Because the college already offered full- and part-time scholarships for art, theatre, and athletics, the dean was willing to extend the scholarships to all F-1 students who had earned an equivalent of a C+ average at either the high school or university level in their home countries. These students would receive a tuition reduction of 3 credit hours in exchange for 30 hours of community service each semester; they would work in all departments on campus and in the community. This award increased the international student visibility on campus and created bonds with faculty and staff, who learned to understand and appreciate diversity. In 2002 another scholarship was created through money earned at the International Holiday Bazaar. This scholarship, Rebuilding for Peace, is open to resident as well as international students who propose a project that will increase intercultural understanding on campus. The first recipient created a photo display that challenged the campus community to confront the stereotypes they held about different cultures. It traveled to both campuses and all of the college's outreach sites.

ADMINISTRATIVE MILESTONES

Several key administrative decisions have helped establish and stabilize the program. While I was creating the program, I was also given the responsibility to propose the admissions requirements for international students. I encouraged the college not to institute a Test of English as a Foreign Language (TOEFL) requirement but to have on-campus testing to determine English proficiency. Therefore, the ESL Program could accept students with any level of English preparation and help them develop the necessary proficiency for academic or vocational programs. While in the program, the students could prepare to enter academic programs at Black Hawk College. Those who wanted to transfer could prepare for the TOEFL while attending ESL classes or academic classes by using material available in the ESL lab.

In 2001–2002 the new college administration decided to change the organizational structure on campus, including the academic departments. The placement of the academic ESL Program was again an issue. Should it be part of the AE-ESL Program or the English Department? I wrote a detailed memo to the vice president of instruction with citations from several TESOL publications that encouraged granting academic credit for advanced courses in ESL programs. Because the instruction and the direction of the academic ESL Program was more in line with that of the English Department, the ESL Program was placed in that department.

One of the most important benefits of placement in the English Department is that academic credit has been granted to the advanced ESL

Grammar class and the advanced Listening/Speaking classes. The chair of the English Department and I studied the ESL curriculum and found that there was an equivalence between these two ESL classes and the English Department's Communication 100 and Communication 105 classes. Working through administrative channels, the college created two ESL sections of these courses, to be taught by ESL instructors. Another benefit of placement in the English Department is the ability to share full-time faculty members, which has provided another much-needed source for qualified ESL instructors. The barriers between traditional English instruction and ESL instruction have disappeared, and the credibility of the ESL Program has been fully established.

Program Evaluation

The ESL Program has been deeply involved in the movement to assess student learning. The instructors and I have been invited to attend all the workshops and training opportunities available to the faculty and staff, which has led to the ESL instructors adding classroom assessment techniques to all the classes. In addition, students must now meet a portfolio requirement to graduate from the ESL Program. Students must not only complete reading, writing, and oral presentation sections for their portfolios, but also write a reflection letter on their goals, their language development, and the ESL Program. After the portfolios are completed, I classify and categorize the students' comments, which have proven to be invaluable in helping to change and strengthen the program. Because of these comments, the program orientation has been shortened, homework assignments within levels have been consolidated, and technology continues to find its place.

The students' comments attest to the success of the program. Students appreciate the ability to expand their language skills and feel proud of their accomplishments. Cande, a mother of two from Mexico who went on to become a dental assistant after graduating from the program, ended her portfolio with this statement:

> When I started in the Outreach Center, I quit a couple of times because I was confused and frustrated. I did not think I could learn English. However, I stayed here until I achieved my goal. I did not quit, and I am proud of myself because I have finished my ESL classes.

Conclusion

The ESL Program met with considerable challenges in the beginning. Changing the climate and solving the problems of scheduling and space became possible because the program had two powerful allies who were able to gather the necessary resources. The college's president was determined to open the doors of the college to the world, and the dean of liberal arts and public service had the necessary experience and administrative clout to break down barriers created by faculty and staff opposed to the college's new direction. The Black Hawk College of 14 years ago was afraid to acknowledge diversity; the Black Hawk College of today embraces, celebrates, and even brags about it.

The ESL Program has been successful because its development has taken into account the students' academic and personal needs. It has not developed in isolation, but has reached out to the college community and has become a respected program. The program meets the needs of the international community that has established itself in the Quad Cities and acknowledges the administrative constraints of Black Hawk College while referring to the best practices established by NAFSA and TESOL.

By responding to the needs of the students and maintaining awareness of the political developments on campus, the ESL Program and the international support programs that entered the campus through the back door now stand at center stage.

Engulfed in the Gulf: Procedures and Complications in Starting an Intensive English Program in the United Arab Emirates

3

JOHN SHANNON

Imagine that you have just arrived at a new university, one that has been open for only one semester. The university is in an EFL context, and you have been hired to serve as the director of its intensive English program (IEP). You discover that the program has two official levels into which students enroll and that there are nine sections total: five in Level 1 and four in Level 2. During the first week of classes, students are streamed into the nine sections based on their language ability. This streaming procedure is unwritten and not made explicit to the students. Nevertheless, they quickly come to partially understand it, leading to problems such as numerous student pleas to be moved to a higher section.

You also discover that the IEP has no mission statement and no written curriculum. In fact, you find that the courses offered in the program have largely been built around a comprehensive textbook series, which covers the four language skills and grammar separately. The faculty who had started teaching the previous semester simply did not have enough time to devise, develop, organize, and implement an entire program in the 3 weeks between their arrival and the first day of classes, thus the textbook-as-curriculum program. You are now in charge. What do you do?

The Motivation for the Program

I faced a similar situation when I was asked to take over the IEP at the American University of Sharjah (AUS), in the United Arab Emirates, at the start of the spring semester in 1998. One difference was that I was already the chair of the nascent English Department at AUS, and I assumed the role of acting director of the IEP while remaining chair of English.

Although the IEP had approximately 100 students, 12 faculty members, and adequate facilities for a start-up operation in the spring of 1998, many changes were needed. I felt that the most pressing need was to develop a written program curriculum, complete with a mission statement, core program goals, course descriptions, and objectives for each course. All of this, to my way of thinking at the time, needed to be made explicit because students were confused about their level in the program and instruction was not based on coordinated objectives. The program lacked a sense of cohesion and a clear vision for its future development.

The Curricular Context

FALL 1997

AUS was built in the desert roughly 8 miles from the center of the city of Sharjah. It was situated at the end of a grand boulevard that was lined with the men's and women's campuses of both the University of Sharjah and the Sharjah Higher Colleges of Technology. The five separate campuses together made up what became known as University City. None of the campuses was open for classes prior to the fall of 1997.

In September 1997 there was still no access to AUS on paved roads, and other than a cargo airport nearby, there was very little else in the area around University City. The campus itself was a construction site, with approximately 6,000 workers in yellow or blue uniforms covering the grounds. Drilling, moving earth, pounding dirt, and polishing stone were the routines of the day. Sand and dust were everywhere. Grazing camels even made regular rounds on what has since become known as the Academic Plaza.

Most of the new faculty (the pioneers) of AUS arrived in Sharjah around September 15, approximately 3 weeks before the start of classes. Faculty housing was not yet ready, so all AUS faculty members (a total of about 30 for the entire university) were housed in hotels in Sharjah. Because the university was on the outskirts of the city and because faculty had no transportation (and the taxi drivers had not yet heard of AUS), all preparations had to be done at the hotels. Around September 25, faculty members were able to move into their housing units on campus. The trip to housing was done on dirt roads.

The IEP was originally housed in the English Department. The director of the program reported to the chair of English, who in turn reported to the dean of the College of Arts and Sciences. The dean did not arrive until November 11. By that time there had already been two acting deans.

The initial design of the program was organized by outside consultants who were on-site prior to the arrival of the IEP faculty. They devised the program with two levels in order to make registration easier (i.e., students only had to be placed into one of the two levels). Streaming could then be done after student registration and placement testing. The streaming process consisted of giving students diagnostic tests during the first week of classes and then using the results holistically to reshuffle them into sections graded by proficiency level, with higher sections indicating stronger language skills (i.e., Section 2 stronger than Section 1, Section 3 stronger still, etc.). Thus, students in Level 1 Section 1 were the weakest in the program in terms of English language proficiency, and students in Level 2 Section 5 were the strongest.

Students in Level 1 received 20 hours of English instruction a week (4 hours a day, 5 days a week). These students needed general English; their vocabulary was weak, and their ability to form complete sentences in English was limited. Had they taken the Test of English as a Foreign Language (TOEFL), the vast majority of them would have scored below 400.

Students in Level 2 received 10 hours of English instruction a week and were allowed to take two university courses. To be in this level, they needed a TOEFL score between 450 and 499 or its equivalent based on results from the English Entrance Exam provided by the American University of Beirut. In fact, only 15% of the students had such a score; the rest were placed in Level 2 based on results from an additional placement test or due to the streaming process. Although they represented the strongest students in the program, the language proficiency of the vast majority of them would have put them below the 450 mark on the TOEFL.

During the first semester the IEP offered few computing, recreational, or library facilities for the students. This lack of facilities placed an additional burden on teachers, who did their utmost to provide quality instruction even though resources were limited.

The IEP was a large program in relation to the rest of the university: 174 of the 280 university students were placed into the IEP, and 12 of the 30 university faculty members were IEP instructors. Because it was such a significant program within the university, it was imperative to move it directly under the auspices of the dean of the College of Arts and Sciences.

Having the program within the English Department meant that, prior to being sent to the dean, all requests, requisitions, proposals, and so on first had to be approved by the chair of the English Department, which was a much smaller unit consisting of only four faculty members. Delays inevitably occurred, and these delays led to frustrations for the IEP director.

As a result, the director and I (as chair of English) petitioned the dean to allow the IEP to become a separate unit within the College of Arts and Sciences. At first we encountered reluctance to change the structure of the college, but a new building was soon going to open, and it would ultimately be large enough only for the IEP. It suddenly made sense to separate the IEP and English Department administratively as they prepared to separate physically, with the IEP going to a building of its own. Making the IEP an autonomous unit within the College of Arts and Sciences was a major coup for the program. It meant that from that point on, the administrative chain of command went from the IEP director to the dean, with no third party in between.

LEADERSHIP ISSUES

In the program's first semester, the establishment of systems was largely top-down. The upper administration established university-wide systems, and department heads created procedures within their respective units. The first steps toward doing this in the IEP were articulated in a memo written by the program director on September 21, 1 week after the faculty had arrived. The memo outlined 28 issues that were not being handled systematically. The issues encompassed serving the students (e.g., placement testing, registration, exit criteria), serving the faculty (e.g., recruitment, professional development, performance evaluation), and serving the program (e.g., scheduling, budgeting, planning).

Recognizing the deficiencies was not enough, however; the director also needed to establish systems that would not conflict with either the constraints of the available physical facilities or the overall framework of how business was conducted at the university. That was no easy task. For the first couple of weeks, the faculty did not have functional computers or telephones, so communication within the program and among the various departments on campus was done primarily by word of mouth. There was not even a system to inform faculty members of new developments in the program and on campus. The initial solution was to use plastic trays as mailboxes for each instructor. In that way, at least written correspondence could be distributed to all concerned parties.

Another issue that required the director's leadership was finding ways to create appropriate roles for faculty within the program. The director accomplished this in part by forming the following committees: Computer

Lab Development, Curriculum and Materials, Faculty Applications Review, Faculty Evaluation, Hospitality, Professional Development, and Scheduling. The formation of these committees began the process of giving the faculty a voice in program operation.

The Process of Redesigning the Program

At the start of the spring 1998 semester, the director of the IEP resigned. In fact, he resigned on the very first day of classes. Because I was serving as the chair of the English Department at the time and seemed like the most logical person for the IEP job, I was appointed acting director of the IEP for the remainder of the academic year. I thus led both units during the spring semester.

The delivery of the textbook-based curriculum during the spring semester was mainly the same as it had been in the fall. However, the greatest new task became curriculum development with an eye toward restructuring the program for the following academic year. To that end, all previous committee work was suspended. Those interested in continuing their former committee responsibilities were able to do so on a voluntary basis only, but all IEP instructors were required to sit on a newly established curriculum committee. My rationale was that the development of the program was our top priority and everyone's input was important in the process. The goals of the committee were to produce written statements on the program's mission, overall goals and values, vision for the future, and full course descriptions (i.e., syllabi for every course taught). The end result was to be a restructured IEP that better met students' needs.

The work of the new committee began with a questionnaire asking faculty to describe what they perceived to be the needs of their students. The faculty then participated in a SWOT analysis, an assessment of the program's **S**trengths, **W**eaknesses, **O**pportunities, and **T**hreats, to determine the IEP's current status (Hecht, Higgerson, Gmelch, & Tucker, 1999) and its possible directions for the future (see Appendix A). This analysis yielded a great deal of information.

The program's strengths included a faculty with diverse backgrounds, pedagogical styles, and previous experience in Arab countries; an externally beautiful campus; adequate resources; competent and helpful support staff; coeducational classes; and students with relatively good skills.

The weaknesses included the systems for student placement and grading, a perception that the program was TOEFL driven, students whose expectations were unreasonably higher than their abilities, lack of a written curriculum, and no course descriptions. In addition, there were no language/video labs or self-access facilities, no academic tutoring/writing lab, and an underdeveloped professional library. Furthermore, student motivation was seen as low, and there was confusion over the two-level system, especially with regard to registration.

The opportunities included funding for conferences and professional development, participation in program building, and research support from the library. Additionally, there were materials development opportunities, interactions and collaboration with other AUS departments, and in-service workshops with faculty from University City. Finally, faculty had the opportunity to meet and become friends with people from different cultures, learn about Arab people and the Arabic language, and serve as pioneers in the desert.

The threats included the perception of the IEP as a TOEFL-driven program, misconceptions of our product by students and parents, and being an American university in an EFL setting (as opposed to in a country where English is the native language of the majority of speakers). Other threats included the cost of the program, the historically low price of oil at the time due to an oil glut on the market, competition from other tertiary institutions, the relatively low rate of student success in the program up to that point, and the lack of a minimum language requirement for acceptance to the university (i.e., all otherwise accepted students could study in the IEP no matter how poor their English skills were).

At the end of the SWOT analysis, we worked on a statement concerning our future goals for the program. Our vision, or 5-year plan, was to go from an IEP to an English for academic purposes program with more experiential and enrichment activities. We also wanted to develop a learning/self-access center, provide students with more exposure to English, and increase the diversity of the student body. As program director, I took it upon myself to write the first draft of the mission statement and distribute it to the faculty for their comments. Our collaboration during the spring 1998 semester resulted in the following mission statement:

> *English is the medium of instruction at the American University of Sharjah and therefore, competence in that language is a prerequisite for student success. The mission of the Intensive English Program (IEP) is to prepare learners to enter the university and excel as students. The main goals of the program are to increase students' language proficiency to a level suitable for study in courses taught in English and to enhance their academic skills in order for them to function successfully in first-year coursework. (American University of Sharjah Catalog, 1998, p. 42)*

We also worked on developing course descriptions with specific objectives for each course offered (see Appendix B for a sample course description). This was done by organizing the faculty into subcommittees for each of the language skills (reading, writing, listening, and speaking, as well as grammar). And we had a subcommittee that worked on developing a self-access program, which would provide a fifth hour of instruction for the students each day. The result of our efforts was a proposal for a new IEP, whose ownership would be in the hands of the faculty who molded it.

REORGANIZING THE IEP

The proposal was to change the number of levels from two to five. Levels 1–2 would focus on general English, and Levels 3–5 would be more academic in nature. Throughout the program, however, two goals would guide everything: to improve students' language proficiency and to prepare them to be successful students in an English-medium university.

Under this proposal, students in Levels 1–4 would receive 20 hours of English language instruction a week plus 5 hours of self-access time in one of three labs (reading, video, and computer). In effect, they would study English 25 hours a week. Level 5 students would receive 15 hours of English instruction and would be allowed to take one introductory university course (e.g., Math 001 or 101, Physics 001 or 101). Table 1 shows a breakdown of the different levels.

For the proposal to become a reality, it had to be addressed to the entire faculty of the university at two general assemblies. Each assembly involved a thorough discussion of where we were in the curriculum development process and our justification for wanting to create such a program. These assemblies provided us with a forum in which to educate our colleagues in other academic disciplines about second language education and its importance at a university where virtually all students had learned and were continuing to learn English as a second or foreign language. We took center stage in our efforts to radically reshape what was at that time by far

Table 1. Structure of the Proposed IEP

(*American University of Sharjah Catalog*, 1998, p. 43)

Level	Instruction	Self-Access	Total	Placement	University Courses
1	20 hours	5 hours	25 hours	Diagnostic Test	0
2	20 hours	5 hours	25 hours	TOEFL 400	0
3	20 hours	5 hours	25 hours	TOEFL 425	0
4	20 hours	5 hours	25 hours	TOEFL 450	0
5	15 hours	0 hours	15 hours	TOEFL 475	1

the largest program on campus. By the end of the semester and with the endorsement of the dean of the College of Arts and Sciences, the proposal was approved by the chancellor, and we were in business with a new IEP for the 1998–1999 academic year.

REVISING ASSESSMENT PROCEDURES

The major assessment issue had to do with exiting the program. The TOEFL requirement for matriculation was 500, but the Institutional TOEFL had never been administered on campus, and we decided not to give it at the end of the first semester. The first director of the program was not familiar with the regional administering agency of the exam (AMIDEAST) and instead developed three criteria for students to matriculate: an average grade of B or higher in IEP course work; a score of 3 or higher on the Written English Test, an in-house equivalent of the Test of Written English (TWE); and a score of 145 or higher on an in-house English proficiency test (EPT). Grades were based on criteria spelled out in the course syllabi (e.g., a combination of results on quizzes, exams, assignments, and projects), and the final grade was obtained by computing an average of the grades for three Level 1 courses (Reading/Writing, Core, and Seminar) and two Level 2 courses (Advanced Reading/Writing and Seminar). The EPT was designed by the program director as a TOEFL equivalent, although no statistical data suggested a positive correlation between them. Using the three criteria as yardsticks, 90 out of 172 students (approximately 52%) met the requirements and matriculated into the university to begin their first-year studies the following semester. The results were unsatisfactory because we felt that students were not adequately prepared for full-time studies in English. In other words, our language standards for matriculation were not high enough.

We were certain that the "successful" IEP students from the fall semester would suffer as full-time undergraduates. After much thought and discussion, we decided to eliminate the three criteria for matriculation used in the fall and instead administer the Institutional TOEFL on campus. Only by getting a score of 500 or higher would students be able to matriculate. Our goal at the time was to raise the university's language proficiency standards and make it more difficult to exit the IEP. At the end of the spring semester, 31 out of the 97 IEP students (approximately 32%) scored at least 500 and matriculated into the university. In comparison to the 52% who matriculated in the fall, it was evident that it had in fact become more difficult to exit the program and that our standards had indeed risen.

Using only one criterion for the spring semester had a profound, mostly negative effect on the students, but we felt that maintaining a firm stance was the best position to take. We needed to use an external, internationally recognized proficiency test to ensure that students achieved a minimum level of English language proficiency prior to starting their full-time studies. We continued to use the criterion of scoring at least 500 on the TOEFL for two reasons: First, although low, it represented a bare minimum proficiency level for students to have an opportunity to succeed, and second, it was the highest score that we could reasonably expect our students to obtain. We would have preferred a higher requirement, such as 550 on the TOEFL, but we realized that far too many students would be placed in the IEP from the outset and remain there as language learners for multiple semesters or fail altogether.

Another assessment issue that we faced during the spring semester involved student placement. As we developed the curriculum, most instructors preferred to set a minimum TOEFL requirement (e.g., 400, 425) for entrance into the IEP. Doing so would have almost certainly allowed us to become a 1-year preparatory program. As a new university, however, we needed to bring in as many students as possible; disqualifying them on the basis of language proficiency was counterproductive to the effort to expand the student body. Our job was to address their English needs in the IEP; unfortunately, we would not be able to meet the needs of many of them within 1 year, especially those who entered with a sub-400 TOEFL score. Even if they gained 50 points on the TOEFL each semester, they would need three or more semesters to reach 500. Nevertheless, we had to accept these students with weak English skills and do our best to prepare them for study at AUS, even if it meant having them in the IEP for three or more semesters. Although our vision for the future was to set a minimum TOEFL requirement for admission, for the time being we had to work with all students who were otherwise qualified for study at AUS.

MAKING POLICIES

In addition to developing the curriculum and devising new assessment procedures, we needed to establish policies and procedures for the program. The most pressing issue was the lack of a university attendance policy. Without a policy in place, student attendance was very poor. Classes of 14 students regularly had only 5 or 6 who showed up. Nevertheless, lessons had to be planned for the entire class in the event that all students did attend. Student absences were demoralizing to faculty and frustrating to students who attended. In addition, the ones with poor attendance started exhibiting behavioral problems as they fell further and further behind the others. Still, because there was no official attendance policy, students could and did flaunt their ability to miss classes. I will never forget a discussion I had with an IEP instructor who told me that a few of her students came to her prior to the start of their 1 p.m. class and asked her if she wanted any food from a local McDonald's. They were going there to get lunch and would arrive in class whenever they arrived there (i.e., very late if at all). The teacher simply told them that they would be marked absent, which they were. Unfortunately, the only consequence that the students were faced with was missing the activities that day and whatever subsequent impact that would have on their grade in the course. That consequence was not enough to persuade them to attend and take their classes more seriously.

The crux of the problem was that students with attendance problems did not give enough merit to the relationship between attending class and learning the language. They wanted a TOEFL score of 500 or higher but were not sufficiently participating in class activities, paying attention to their instructors, and doing their assignments for that goal to become a reality. In sum, they were not willing to take responsibility for their own language learning, and it was apparent that they could not be helped if they did not attend their classes. As a result, an attendance policy for the program was articulated and proposed for the fall of 1998 (see Appendix C for the complete policy statement). The policy stated that students had to attend 90% of all IEP courses. All absences, excused or not, would be counted. We did not want to be involved in bargaining situations, so we proposed a strict attendance policy that did not leave room for exceptions. For us, an absence was an absence was an absence. Failure to maintain the required 90% attendance rate for any reason would result in an administrative removal from the course with a failing grade.

The attendance policy was endorsed by the dean, approved by the chancellor, and ultimately made university policy, though later revised to 85% required attendance. This issue was not specific to the IEP; it was a university-wide problem, and the efforts and ideas of IEP instructors led the way in overcoming it for the entire university.

Another policy that was implemented at the start of my tenure as acting director of the IEP had to do with the flow of information within the program and among departments in the university. The plan was simple. All requests of a professional nature from IEP faculty would first go to the acting director. If approved, they would go on to the dean or to the appropriate department. This system centralized all requests, with the key word here being *system*. Prior to its implementation, there was no administrative system for making requests or for addressing concerns, so faculty, staff, and administrators would go directly to other university leaders (e.g., the directors of purchasing, information technology, and admissions; the registrar; the dean; even the chancellor). In most cases, the next link in the tacit chain of command was being skipped. We thus needed to implement a formal system to regulate the flow of information from the program to other units on campus. This new system increased the workload of the administrative staff, but it also led to better accountability in the program and ultimately to greater efficiency. Nevertheless, although it improved the flow of information upward within the university hierarchy, it did not give voice to faculty concerns, comments, and issues that would be heard directly by the university's upper administration. Such a system was still a few years away, finally appearing with the advent of the elected AUS Faculty Senate, which first convened in January 2000.

Curriculum Development Encapsulated

In the spring of 1998, the curriculum development project of the IEP at AUS achieved success for three reasons. First, its completion was predicated on contributions from all members of the faculty; it was thus an inclusive undertaking with all faculty involved in the decision-making process. In fact, their ideas, creativity, and enthusiasm formed the basis for all that we did. By the end of the process, they had ownership of the program; they believed in it and knew that the result of their efforts was a program that would much more effectively meet the needs of the students.

An added outcome of being inclusive was the development of teamwork within the program. When dealing with groups of people, cooperation is necessary to make changes work. It was especially important that, throughout the process of curriculum development, the individual instructors worked together to make the program successful. It was at this time that *I* was replaced by *we*. Instructors had already had sufficient time during their first semester to adapt to the immediate classroom context at AUS. What they needed was to become a part of something bigger. Getting them to cooperate and collaborate built the *esprit de corps* of the program and provided them with a feeling of ownership and a sense of responsibility for the program's successes and failures.

From an administrative perspective, being inclusive also involved being a bridge builder within the university and being willing to adapt to different ways of doing things. At AUS, there were administrators and support staff from various countries who had different cultural backgrounds and divergent work ethics. Yet somehow we all had to work together for the greater good of the university. I thus felt that it was extremely important to get to know as many of them as possible. In fact, during that first year I regularly ate lunch with colleagues from university services. Our networking together at lunchtime bonded us, building essential ties that enabled us to communicate our needs to each other in an informal setting.

Second, the curriculum project was successful because we simplified our procedures and systems as much as possible. For example, the establishment of the interoffice communication system, whereby all requests had to go first to the program director, centralized the flow of information, allowing the acting director to take responsibility for such requests. At the same time, it relieved faculty from having to follow up on requests and gave them more time to focus on the more important task of building the program.

We also simplified our work by continuing to use a skills-based textbook series as the primary source of instruction while the curriculum was being created. Although the textbook series that we used was ultimately not selected for continued use the following year, it was nonetheless a valuable source of information and activities for the classroom. Additionally, its use freed up a great deal of time for curriculum development and other important administrative duties (e.g., student assessment, new faculty and student orientation).

The final reason that our project was successful was patience. We prioritized the creation of systems and then proceeded one step at a time, without pushing the university system too hard or too fast during the first year. For example, computerized grading procedures could not be introduced the first year because our computers and technical support were not sufficient at that time. By the second year, however, we were keeping student records electronically, something that was simply not possible during the curriculum development process.

Being patient also meant avoiding comparisons to other, usually well-known programs during start-up. I often had to remind myself and the faculty that a new program could not be expected to run as efficiently as an established one. This point may seem obvious, but it was not at all obvious to some during our first year of operations. A frequent complaint was that we were not doing things the way they were done back home at University X. An appropriate and fairly common response was to note that the creation of an IEP was a process, and the first steps were the most difficult. Keeping that in mind obviated potential frustrations as they surfaced.

Finally, exhibiting patience meant understanding that the great changes being proposed would not be implemented until the following year and that the ad hoc program would continue until we finished our curriculum work. It also meant that we had to pay attention to the immediate needs of the students, faculty, staff, program, and institution even though our long-range vision was to change the way we responded to those needs. Knowing that we were creating something special did not alleviate the difficulties we had during that first year, but being patient certainly helped. In many ways it was the key to our success.

Conclusion

At the time of this writing, the IEP at AUS was in its eighth year of operation. Since the groundbreaking work done in the start-up year, the program has continued to develop in ways that were intended to meet the changing needs of the university's students. For example, it has become a six-level program with credit-bearing course work. Placing new students into levels involves an analysis of test scores on three measures (the TOEFL, the Michigan Test, and a TWE-like exam), with the first week of classes reserved for additional diagnostic testing to determine the appropriateness of each student's placement. Students in the lowest levels of the program study together until midterms, at which time they are reevaluated and streamed into new sections by proficiency level for the remainder of the semester. Reading and writing skills are now integrated into one course at the highest and lowest levels of the program, but not in between. Additionally, students can no longer take regular university courses while enrolled in the IEP; instead their focus is solely on learning English while preparing themselves for first-year studies.

In many ways, the 5-year plan articulated in the spring of 1998 has become a reality. The program is much more academic in nature, and the self-access component has continued to develop in ways that better meet the students' language learning needs.

In the future we would like to see the university TOEFL requirement raised from the current 500 to 530, which would enable us to do more English for specific purposes work with higher level students. We would also like to establish a minimum TOEFL score of 400 for entry into the program. Doing so would eliminate the two lowest levels of the program and give the remaining IEP students a much greater opportunity to successfully exit the program within one academic year. These two issues are related to policy, but they would both have a dramatic impact on the curriculum in ways that would make the program stronger.

The process of curriculum development and revision is neverending. What was once thought to be in the best interests of the students and the program may later be seen as ineffective, inappropriate, or inefficient. Time is the best assessment tool because it holds the answers to all of the key questions. Our curriculum project in the spring of 1998 allowed us to reshape the IEP. Its impact is still being felt today as the program continues to grow and develop.

Appendix A: March 8 Memo on Curriculum Development

I would like each of you to think about the items listed below. By briefly discussing them, we will be setting our schemata, so to speak, in relation to the discussion of vision, mission, and values that will follow.

Student goals
Students' educational backgrounds
Age/level of maturity
Need for orientation/advisement
Educational/academic needs of students
Student strengths and weaknesses

ISSUES FOR DISCUSSION

SWOT Analysis: What can we say about our program in regard to the following items [one example was given in each area]:

1. *Strengths*: Qualified and experienced faculty
2. *Weaknesses*: Two-level, multiple-section program is confusing to students
3. *Opportunities*: Professional growth through regional conference attendance
4. *Threats*: Unknown quality of AUS may inhibit students from enrolling

Vision for our IEP (5-year plan): Recognized as the leading IEP in the region

Mission Statement: What we do now. More information to follow.

Core Values: What we are committed to and what we believe in.

We are committed to open and fair communication in our interactions with each other and the students.

Appendix B: Sample From the IEP Reading Curriculum for the 1998–1999 Academic Year

The fundamental goals of the reading skills component are twofold: to improve student reading comprehension and to increase student reading speed. These goals will be met through the extended practice of a variety of reading skills within a diverse range of text forms and genres. Students will also gain an understanding of, and appreciation for, the importance of reading both inside and outside academic settings.

NOVICE LEVEL

Students at this level have limited proficiency in reading but should be able to interpret clearly written language in areas of practical need and for survival in an English-speaking classroom.

Objectives

- Develop basic reading skills such as identifying topic, and main and supporting ideas
- Identify cohesive and coherence structures (transition, topic sentences, and linkages)
- Find the meaning of unfamiliar vocabulary from context

ELEMENTARY LEVEL

Students at this level learn to understand the main ideas in simple texts dealing with a variety of topics in familiar language situations, and show some ability to find meaning from context in simplified prose.

Objectives

- Predict the topic, focus, and meaning prior to reading thoroughly
- Skim and scan
- Understand the main and supporting ideas
- Identify cohesive and coherence structures (transitions, topic sentences, and linkages)
- Develop the ability to recognize collocations of key words
- Use a simplified English-English dictionary

INTERMEDIATE LEVEL

Students at this level should be able to read with full understanding connected texts dealing with topics about which the reader has interest or knowledge.

Objectives

- Make inferences about author, topic, meaning, and purpose
- Identify word definitions from context
- Develop the ability to summarize and paraphrase portions of the text
- Identify fact versus opinion
- Understand the purpose and tone of the text
- Identify word definitions from context

ADVANCED LEVEL

Students at this level should be able to read longer prose texts of many paragraphs in length and show a reading ability approaching readiness for academic work.

Objectives

- Understand textual organization (explanatory, descriptive, process, cause and effect, comparison and contrast, persuasive, argumentative)
- Recognize, identify, and evaluate the author's arguments
- Determine the author's bias
- Identify Latinate and Greek affixes
- Develop the ability to outline texts

BRIDGE LEVEL

Students at this level should be able to follow essential points of unadapted written discourse in areas of specific interest and knowledge with the ability to understand conceptually abstract and linguistically complex texts of the type found in university classes.

Objectives

- Further refine the objectives of the four preceding levels
- Competently use a college-level English-English dictionary

Appendix C: IEP Attendance Policy

(*American University of Sharjah Catalog*, 1998, p. 43)

ATTENDANCE/DISCONTINUATION

Classes meet daily, Saturday through Wednesday. Because of the intensive nature of the program, regular attendance in all courses is expected, and as a matter of policy, students are required to attend at least 90% of all IEP courses. If a student fails to maintain regular attendance in a particular course, he or she will be given a warning (at approximately the eighth absence in a five-hour per week course). Upon the fourth absence after the warning, the student will be withdrawn from the course. Also, an absence, whether excused or unexcused, is still an absence. Missing 12 class meetings is grounds for withdrawal from the course.

LATENESS

Classes begin on time, and students are expected to be in class on time. Students who arrive late disrupt whatever activity is being performed. Three occasions of tardiness count as one absence.

The Development and Features of a Multidimensional Curriculum With Integrated Assessment

4

JEAN TURNER AND JON PHILLIPS

Current thinking and research indicate that a good curriculum meets the needs of students, promotes the learning of valuable knowledge and skills, is motivating to students, and satisfies the concerns of those who are invested in students' learning, including students, teachers, and school administrators. Instructional programs in which the learning activities and assessment practices are integrated in a meaningful, structured manner can better serve students because effective assessment promotes the learning of valuable and valued skills, is motivating to students, and is beneficial to the quality of instruction (Messick, 1994; O'Malley & Pierce, 1996). True integration of curriculum and assessment is not achieved, however, through simply adding assessment practices to classroom activities. Integration requires the thoughtful collaboration of those developing the curriculum and assessment. This chapter describes the process and product of such an endeavor.

A direction that has been vigorously pursued in curriculum design is the notion of task-based learning, frequently complemented by an experiential, process approach (Budd & Wright, 1992; Kohonen, 1992; Kumaravadivelu, 1991; Prabhu, 1987). Tasks, as noted by Long and Crookes (1992), "provide a vehicle for the presentation of appropriate target language samples to learners" (p. 43). Ideally, a thorough needs analysis is conducted to identify the specific language-use situations that learners will encounter. Examining and classifying the results of the needs analysis leads to the pedagogic tasks that are the foundation of the learning activities (Jordan, 1997; Long & Crookes, 1992).

Assessment practices have evolved with the task-based movement, resulting in more frequent use of tests that require students to perform realistic tasks as the basis for assessing their developing skills (Norris, Brown, Hudson, & Yoshioka, 1998). At the same time, curriculum and test development specialists have been encouraged to integrate learning activities and ongoing assessment in the classroom (Genesee & Upshur, 1996; O'Malley & Pierce, 1996). When measurement is ongoing and nonintrusive, a better sample of student learning is achieved—a more complete picture of what students have learned. Students benefit from more frequent feedback on their successes and shortcomings, and teachers can fine-tune their instructional plans, enhancing learning opportunities.

The Curricular Context

The integrated curriculum and assessment program described here was developed by the academic staff of the Military Language Institute (MLI) of the United Arab Emirates (UAE). Like any well-conceived instructional program, the curriculum addresses the needs and concerns of students and stakeholders in the students' learning. Its design took into consideration the conditions and constraints at the MLI. Because an instructional program is best understood when one has a clear picture of the educational environment, we preface a discussion of the features and development of the MLI curriculum with a description of MLI students, administrative structure, and teaching staff.

The MLI offers intensive English language instruction for enlisted personnel and officers who are assigned by their military command to learn English. Some MLI students are preparing for study at UAE or foreign universities, some expect to attend vocational programs abroad, and some are required to study English to enhance their performance in their current and future job assignments. All MLI students have a minimum ninth-grade education and basic literacy in English, as determined by an initial screening test. Students are generally assigned to the MLI for 9 months.

The MLI has both a military and an academic administrative structure. The commandant is responsible for the operation of the school, and academic concerns are handled by the academic director and staff. Working collaboratively with the commandant, the academic administration is responsible for planning and overseeing the curriculum and assessment, pedagogical technology, and in-service faculty training and evaluation.

The school employed about 60 teachers during the time that the curriculum was developed, all of whom were native speakers of English, had degrees in applied linguistics or a closely related field, and had at least 3 years' teaching experience. The staff included four bilingual advisors who were native speakers of Arabic, certified teachers of English, experienced in teaching in the Arab world, and experienced in working with people from the United States.

The Process of Designing the Program

The directive for the academic administration during the initial 3 years of its contract was to create and implement an innovative curriculum and a comprehensive assessment plan to measure the effectiveness of the MLI language training. This directive included recruiting qualified teachers, establishing a computer-assisted language learning (CALL) component of the curriculum, and developing the facilities needed to implement and support the new curriculum. In the first year, while the administration worked on such tasks as developing the facilities, a cohort of approximately 100 students entered the MLI and studied in a general English development program supported by the Spectrum series (Warshawsky & Byrd, 1996).

In the second year, with the facilities and policies established, the academic administration began to plan the development of what is referred to as the Core Curriculum (the Core). The academic director proposed that the Core be developed by MLI teachers with input from three short-term, expert consultants (ECs)—one each in technology, curriculum, and curriculum and assessment. (We were the EC in curriculum and assessment [EC-C/A] and an on-site academic administrator designated as the Core coordinator, respectively.) The academic administration and interested teachers conducted a thorough needs analysis that addressed four areas:

1. What are the intended purposes of instruction? What do students, unit commanders, teachers, and administrative staff members expect students to achieve, given what is known of the students' characteristics and the learning environment?

2. What are students' academic experiences in their first language and in English? How do students' previous academic experiences impact their learning of English at the MLI? What are their strengths and limitations with regard to life experiences and cross-cultural interaction?

3. What do students need to know about and be able to do in English?

4. What parameters for curriculum design are presented by the military environment?

Information from a variety of sources was examined. These sources included a teacher survey (see Appendix A) and two student surveys, one for students entering the MLI English program and one for students who had completed the program (see Appendix B for English translations). Additional sources included interviews with unit commanders, reviews of training materials, visits to Ministry of Education schools to observe students and meet with teachers, and consideration of the initial students' entry and exit proficiency levels and rates of progress.

One of the issues that emerged in the process of conducting the needs analysis was that many students had not previously participated in similar information-gathering activities and had difficulty articulating their needs. This problem was addressed by translating the surveys into Arabic and training the bilingual advisors in techniques that facilitated data collection and analysis. The bilingual advisors conducted an orientation for each class to explain the reasons for conducting a needs analysis and to help students understand how to express their thoughts and opinions. Before asking students to complete the surveys, the advisors led a discussion of the questions and the students' ideas. Because the survey data were in Arabic, compiling and analyzing the results required that the bilingual advisors be trained to identify in the data the professional and personal situations in which the students needed to use English. The advisors then translated the compiled results into English.

Meeting with the unit commanders responsible for identifying the military personnel to receive language training was an especially critical component of the needs analysis. The focusing questions for these meetings were "What are the language learning expectations for the individuals selected for the MLI?" and "What is the basis for selecting the individuals who are sent?" While meeting with the unit commanders to collect information on their needs, it became clear that the units often lacked clear criteria on which to base their selection decisions. As a result of these meetings and discussion of the findings with the MLI military administration, criteria were established, a more effective student intake system was developed, and a process was established for prioritizing the population to be served by the MLI. A literacy assessment was developed for intake screening to ensure that candidates accepted for study at the MLI would have proficiency in reading and writing English at a minimum of the Novice-Low level, as described in the guidelines for proficiency published by the American Council on the Teaching of Foreign Languages (ACTFL; 1986). It was also decided that potential MLI students would take as a screening and placement measure the Secondary Level Proficiency Test (SLEP; Educational Testing Service, 1980).

The newly established prioritization system included consideration of candidates' ranks and needs, with the first priority being officers slotted for future training or education that required English and the second priority being enlisted personnel with similar future assignments. Space permitting, enlisted personnel who had not yet been slotted for future training that required English but who met the basic selection criteria would be accepted for study.

The development of the Core began with a meeting of the three ECs and the academic administration (the academic director, the Core coordinator, and the two additional members of the academic administration). The EC in technology focused on matters related to incorporating the CALL aspect of the curriculum. The EC in curriculum and the EC-C/A met with the academic director, the Core coordinator, and teachers to begin designing the Core. Outcomes of these meetings included determination of the Core objectives and formation of a steering committee.

The steering committee consisted of five teachers, a bilingual advisor, the Core coordinator and the two other academic coordinators, and a military administrator. The teachers, who were selected based on interest and experience, received full release time from their teaching duties for the duration of their involvement.

Working with the Core coordinator, and based on advice from the EC-C/A, the committee defined three important features of the Core:

1. emphasis on increasing students' awareness of learning processes and how language can be used for communicative functions
2. use of computer technology to enhance learning
3. integrated assessment

The committee also decided on the modules' duration and topics as well as how students at different proficiency levels would be placed into the program. Additionally, it developed the overall framework of objectives for the Core and designed an assessment plan that would accommodate the needs and constraints imposed by the military nature of the school. These points are summarized in the following discussion.

MODULE TOPICS AND STUDENT PLACEMENT

The committee determined that the Core would include 12 three-week topical modules, broken into four terms (see Table 1). Some of the topics (e.g., travel, sports) were identified through the needs analysis; some (e.g., military, environment) were mandated by the military administration.

As noted earlier, a literacy test and the SLEP were introduced as screening and placement measures. Initially, the only students placed into the Core were those with SLEP scores of 37 or below. These students were sorted by score into three proficiency groups: those with scores between 20 and 25, 26 and 31, and 32 and 37. To the extent possible, students were placed into their MLI classes with others in their proficiency group. Students with scores higher than 37 were placed into high-level courses.

Table 1. Core Topics

Term No.	Module No.	Topic
1	1	Myself
	2	Family
	3	Home
2	4	Food
	5	Health
	6	Travel
3	7	Shopping
	8	Cars
	9	Military
4	10	Sports
	11	Environment
	12	United Arab Emirates

In the first trial of the Core, all students used the same modules, although teachers were encouraged to tailor assignments to the level of their specific classes. For example, in writing a biography, a high-proficiency class with SLEP scores between 32 and 37 would be expected to write more complex sentences than a low-proficiency class, but both classes would complete the same task.

After the initial trial, the decision was made to place low-proficiency students into the first module, so they would complete the entire set of 12 modules. Middle-proficiency students were placed into the 5th module, so they would complete 8 modules. High-proficiency students were placed into the 9th module, so they would complete only 4 modules. After completing a sequence of 4 modules, students retook the SLEP, and those with scores of 37 or higher could advance to a high-level course. Class membership in the Core was shuffled after every 4 modules based on the students' performance on the SLEP.

DEVELOPING THE CORE OBJECTIVES

The academic director provided strong leadership for the steering committee's development of clear program goals and objectives for the Core and also for establishing a coherent framework for planning the course. This leadership was of critical importance in meeting benchmarks for completing planning tasks and establishing a participatory process for discussion and group decision making.

The process of developing the Core objectives began with a series of meetings to review the MLI mission statement already in place and to revise it based on the experience of the first year, the information gained in the needs analysis, and the vision for the new program. At the end of each of these meetings, the secretary posted the minutes and the modified version of the mission statement on the intranet and requested input from each participant. After reaching consensus on revision of the statement, the team began working on the program goals, taking into account the students' needs, the institution's policies, and the manner in which the teachers conceptualized content. As noted previously, the steering committee had made a decision to base the Core on the ACTFL (1986) proficiency guidelines. The committee also agreed to emphasize the development of all four language skills. The committee knew from the initial year's experience that students entering the Core would have proficiency levels ranging from Novice-Low to Intermediate-Mid on the ACTFL scale, with the majority at the lower end. It proposed that the four skills should be integrated and practiced intensively and that there should be focus throughout the Core on grammatical, functional, and strategic aspects of language development. As they conceptualized how to incorporate these three aspects into the general Core goals, the team considered the following points:

- *grammatical level*—MLI students at low levels of proficiency tend to have picked up many words and structures by virtue of the country in which they live. This prior learning should be incorporated into the course, but emphasis must be placed on relearning the language. With a small, focused body of grammatical material, accuracy should occupy the same place as fluency. Accuracy is important because what students learn, or relearn, is a foundation for later learning.
- *functional level*—English is used in many different settings in the UAE. As citizens of that country, MLI students may often be called upon to use the language in real-life situations. The Core can and should reflect this reality. Modules should include series of simple, practical language-use situations. Through this approach, and because of the large amount of English spoken and used in the UAE, students can begin to use the language in real-life situations with greater ease and accuracy. Oddly, English proficiency will allow them a greater degree of inclusion in the day-to-day workings of their own country. Small successes on this functional level may increase their motivation for learning English and their confidence in using it.

- *strategic level*—Because the Core students are studying a second language in an intensive program, emphasis should be placed on helping them become more effective learners. The first elements should help them understand what learning is and how they learn. The next should involve introducing, practicing, and re-presenting strategies and practices that will help them learn more effectively.

Program objectives were derived from general program goals through careful consideration of the question: "What do students need to learn or do to achieve these goals?" Over the course of meetings and discussions, the steering committee established the objective categories. (Table 2, on pp. 58–59, displays the original Objectives Grid for Module 4.) The categories include the four skills, learning and study skills to help learners become aware of their strengths and overcome their weaknesses as learners, vocabulary development as it relates to specific module topics, cultural aspects of language and behavior, and computer use (because the mandate was to offer instruction through the latest in instructional technology). These categories are discussed in more detail in the next section of this chapter.

After identifying the major categories, the committee worked on developing specific instructional objectives within each category. The description of the ACTFL Intermediate-High level was an important resource in this activity because Intermediate-Advanced is the target proficiency level for exiting the Core.

With assistance from the EC-C/A, the team outlined and identified in syllabi grids the specific objectives for each module topic. The grids then served as the basis for conceptualizing and formulating modules projects.

FRAMEWORK FOR THE CORE OBJECTIVES

The Core is multidimensional and procedural (Prabhu, 1987), with a focus on fostering meaningful communication. The instructional objectives reflect what graduates generally need to do in English, both within and outside the workplace, and are distributed across nine categories: Functions, Listening, Speaking, Reading, Writing, Grammar, Computer Skills, Learning Skills and Strategies, and Cross-Cultural Goals (see Table 2 for these categories as applied to a particular module).

One of the major purposes of English language instruction at the MLI is to develop the students' ability to use English in their academic, professional, and personal lives; therefore, learning activities are constructed around realistic tasks that require the learning and practice of important language skills and knowledge. The Functions category reflects this emphasis. It is expected that students' ability to use English will improve across the four modalities and that their level of grammatical accuracy will improve as well. These goals are reflected in the Listening, Speaking, Reading, Writing, and Grammar categories.

The needs analysis revealed that computer-based technology intrigued MLI students and provided a natural means for them to communicate in English. Activities in the Computer Skills category are intended to increase students' computer skills and to enhance language learning through the students' attraction to technology.

The needs analysis also indicated that some MLI students lacked the critical thinking and study skills necessary for success in an intensive program such as the Core and other instructional programs to which graduates of the MLI might be assigned. The Learning Skills and Strategies category includes aspects of the Core that are intended to address this possible shortcoming.

Finally, the Cross-Cultural Goals category was created for two reasons. First, due to the nature of their jobs, members of the UAE military are likely to come into contact with people from other countries, such as military advisors, instructors, and visitors. UAE military personnel serve as unofficial ambassadors of their culture and society and, as such, benefit from a greater awareness of the unique contributions that one's country offers to the global community. A second, related reason is that English is often used in these interactions because it is the language that the visitor and the Emirati share.

Each Core module employs a task-based approach, which focuses on typical classroom tasks and how they might be taken beyond the classroom to the learners' other language-use environments (Skehan, 1996). The learning activities in each module are centered on three projects: one focused primarily on the development of writing skills, one focused on the development of oral skills, and one whose focus varies across the modules. The projects are designed to facilitate students' learning of the skills and knowledge presented and practiced in the lessons.

Table 2 displays the original objectives grid for the fourth module, Food (Military Language Institute, 2001b). The oral skills project requires students to create an infomercial by working in groups of three to create a virtual storefront. The groups prepare and perform a role play between a shopkeeper and two customers (although this project was later modified to require a Microsoft PowerPoint presentation instead of a virtual storefront due to limitations in storage space for students' digital files). The writing skills project requires individual students to write a description of how to make a local food dish or drink. The third project incorporates both writing and speaking; it is another group project that requires students to create a menu and a role play in which they demonstrate their ability to interact using the skills and information they learned in the module.

Though later in the chapter we discuss more thoroughly the

Table 2. Objectives Grid for Module 4: Food

(Military Language Institute, 2001b)

Project 1: Prepare a virtual storefront and a role play	Project 2: Write a process paragraph about preparing food	Project 3: Create a restaurant menu and a role play
Functions		
• Ask for and give opinions • Ask about prices • Shop for food	• Describe making a food item • Describe food items	• Order food • Ask for and give opinions
Listening		
• Understand core vocabulary and structures in context	• Comprehend details from short process monologues	• Understand basic questions and responses • Understand core vocabulary in context
Speaking		
• Use core vocabulary and structures in context	• Give instructions • Describe food items	• Interact in a social setting • Make a simple presentation
Reading		
• Understand and recognize common affixes and parts of speech • Understand ingredients on packages	• Comprehend simple recipes	• Comprehend simple instructions • Understand descriptions of menu items
Writing		
• Use and spell core vocabulary accurately • Use core structures appropriately • Use basic punctuation • Write sentences	• Use and spell core vocabulary accurately • Use core structures appropriately • Use basic punctuation • Write a process paragraph	• Use and spell core vocabulary accurately • Use core structures appropriately • Use basic punctuation • Write sentences and questions
Grammar		
• Present tense • Count and mass nouns • Quantifiers	• Imperative • Time and sequence words	• Request modals • Adjective forms of nationalities

continued on p. 59

Developing a New Curriculum for Adult Learners

Table 2 (continued). Objectives Grid for Module 4: Food

Project 1: Prepare a virtual storefront and a role play	Project 2: Write a process paragraph about preparing food	Project 3: Create a restaurant menu and a role play
Computer Skills		
• Access and use server activities • Use Microsoft PowerPoint	• Search Web for pictures and download them • Use Microsoft Word • Insert pictures into Word document	
Learning Skills and Strategies		
• Work collaboratively • Plan, organize, and deliver presentation • Manage time • Meet due dates	• Work independently • Manage time • Meet due dates	• Work collaboratively • Plan, organize, and deliver presentation
Cross-Cultural Goals		
• Compare customs and eating habits • Offer food and so forth to foreigners	• Compare customs and eating habits • Offer food and so forth to foreigners	• Compare customs and eating habits • Offer food and so forth to foreigners

modifications made to the Core as a result of the trials that were conducted, it is important to note here that in addition to changing the first project to incorporate PowerPoint slides, the second and third projects were modified as well. Feedback from students and teachers after trialing the module highlighted the fact that young men in the UAE do very little cooking and eat out frequently in restaurants where English is the language shared by customers and restaurant staff. The original second project was therefore replaced by the original third, which requires students to create and perform role-play interactions in restaurants. A new third project was designed with a focus on writing skills. For this new project, a restaurant review, the objectives for the original second project were adopted with revisions that reflected the change from describing a process to preparing a review.

INTEGRATED INSTRUCTION AND ASSESSMENT

The program's assessment plan had to meet military and pedagogical concerns; therefore, it includes both internal and external assessment. Internal assessment is tied directly to the Core instructional objectives, and external assessment involves proficiency testing, that is, the measurement of skills and abilities not directly addressed in the curriculum.

Internal assessment has three components. The first component is Module Tests of specific aspects of the Listening, Reading (including vocabulary), and Grammar objectives. (See Appendix C for general test specifications and example items from the revised Module 4). The Module Tests were developed by the Core team based on general specifications prepared by the EC-C/A. During the needs analysis year of operation, following prior practice, all objectively scored assessments had been marked by military personnel to ensure test security and impartiality and fairness for teachers and students. As the program and its number of students expanded, the bilingual advisors began assisting the military personnel. While the Core was being developed, the Core coordinator worked with the military testing officer to establish testing procedures that would meet the satisfaction of the military command; specifically, it was resolved that two teachers would be responsible for scoring and would check one another's scores. Teachers would not be allowed to score their own students' tests.

The second component of internal assessment is performance, or project-based, assessments. In the process of learning how to do the projects, students complete work that is incorporated into their portfolios, which are assessed by their teachers. Teachers give feedback and grades on specified aspects of Computer Skills, Learning Skills and Strategies, and Cross-Cultural Goals.

The final projects themselves are evaluated by an assessment team. The team's efforts focus on the goal of the Functions category, although included in the ability to perform the functions are aspects of Speaking, Writing, and Grammar. The team's work ensures reliability of scoring because team members undergo rigorous training and continuous monitoring. In addition, assessment of the projects by the team rather than by the students' teachers promotes impartiality while protecting teachers from accusations of unfair grading.

External assessment is conducted through the SLEP. In addition to serving as a screening and placement measure, the SLEP is administered to students after the completion of four modules and again when they complete the Core program. Scores on this test are not included in students' grades, but they represent a standardized measure that can be used to show accountability to outside individuals and agencies.

The needs analysis indicated that MLI students, many of whom had been somewhat unsuccessful in their earlier language studies, would benefit from having clear goals, small units of instruction, and frequent feedback on their progress. These instructional features might be even more important for MLI students than for students with stronger academic backgrounds and skills. To stay engaged in learning, MLI students need to know precisely what is expected of them and how specific classroom activities facilitate their learning. The Core accommodates these needs by integrating instruction and assessment practices and by presenting the goals for each module in the module introductions. Appendix D contains the initial pages from the first module, *Myself* (MLI, 2001c), which illustrate the development team's general approach. Each module begins with a statement of what students will learn in the module, a summary of the three projects, and a description of how students' work will be assessed. The introductory page of the fourth module, *Food* (MLI, 2001b; see Figure 1 on the following page), shows how this information is presented.

The assessment team evaluates the projects according to two criteria: form and content. Form relates to accuracy of structures, punctuation or pronunciation, and, in the case of written projects, accurate spelling of vocabulary. Content relates to length, organizational structure, task completion, and accuracy of vocabulary. In the introduction to the task and in the checklist for completing it, students are presented with information about these criteria (see Appendix E).

In the original design of the modules, there had been some differences in the percentage weightings across the projects in various modules. These differences reflected the individual authors' ideas about the importance of the components of a type of project. After the initial trial of the Core modules, the percentage weightings for projects were set according to type (oral, written, or a combination utilizing computer skills). Standardizing the percentage allocation yielded equally useful scores and facilitated the assessment team's work because it scored the projects using a locally developed software program on the MLI intranet.

Evaluation of the Curriculum

The first four modules were developed by the steering committee. In creating them, the committee resolved issues regarding module sections and format, layout concerns, and general policy issues, although the initial development work did not occur completely smoothly. Individual teachers chose a module topic from the list according to their interest and experience and took responsibility for developing a module according to the framework. In several cases, teachers had previously developed materials on these topics and had firm ideas about how the materials should be assembled and what would work. As they began trying to fit what they had previously done into the framework they had agreed upon, they discovered that they had to modify their materials and ideas. Based on their experience, several teachers proposed to extend the modules that they were working on from 3 to 6 weeks; others insisted that the agreed-upon framework must be followed.

The committee broke down into two cohorts: One intended to use the

Figure 1. Introduction to the Food Module

(Military Language Institute, 2001b)

What Will You Learn?

You will learn to...
- ask and answer questions about food prices
- describe how something is made
- order food in a restaurant

You will also learn...
- how to work with pictures on computer
- how to organize your learning

Your Projects

Supermarket TV Commercial	**Restaurant Role-play**	**Restaurant Review**

Your Grade

Items		Points	Your Score
Projects	Supermarket TV Commercial	20	
	Restaurant Role-play	15	
	Restaurant Review	20	
Learning	Binder Maintenance	15	
	Preparation Materials		
	Linking of Projects		
	Grammar and Vocabulary Log		
Module Test		30	
Total		100	

framework, and the other believed that the quality of the materials would be improved by deviating from the framework. In this academic culture, where the administration had promoted collaboration and decision making through consensus building, the committee was unable to proceed. Some members resigned, and the project fell behind schedule. The EC-C/A was asked to return to help the group get past its personality and pedagogical issues and, in her role as an expert and an outsider, to meet with the committee and the administration to facilitate resolution of the communication problems that had arisen. Ultimately, several members of the original group were offered other responsibilities, such as developing orientation materials to familiarize the teachers with the new curriculum, and new members replaced them.

The steering committee members returned to their tasks and, using the framework, completed the first four modules, which served as a model for the teachers who volunteered to work on the remaining modules. The teachers who took on responsibility for developing module materials were also given release time to complete the task.

The modules were completed over a period of 12 months. The first four modules were piloted with two classes (25 students total). Each class was taught by a team of two teachers, allowing the teachers ample time for providing feedback to the module authors. In a series of site visits, the EC-C/A reviewed the first four modules and advised on procedures for piloting the materials. She also assisted in establishing guidelines for scoring the module projects. In a final visit, after these four modules had been piloted, she reviewed the assessment team's policies and procedures and assisted the Core coordinator in developing a procedure for the review and revision of subsequent modules despite pressure from the military administration to publish the modules as soon as each was completed.

After the initial small-scale trial, the Core replaced the Spectrum-supported curriculum, with the understanding that all Core materials would be trialed during the academic year. In this larger trial, 170 students (14 classes) were taught by 21 teachers. The Core was also trialed at Zayed Military College, a military preparatory school, where 14 classes were taught by 14 teachers. These trials allowed participants to assess the effectiveness of the new curriculum and to identify and address its shortcomings as well as its strengths.

A curriculum revision team was established, and an electronic tracking system was created for teachers' feedback on module content, format, and other features. A centralized teachers' site was maintained on the MLI server, where teachers could submit suggestions and comments. Systemic procedures were developed for teachers to submit supplemental materials that they had developed for teaching the modules. The centralized site enabled them to share their lesson plans and computer-generated activities with one another, providing a forum for sharing ideas and eliminating unnecessary duplication of effort. Teachers also used the intranet as a way to get feedback on shared ideas.

Supplementary materials were organized by module, project, language category, module page number, instructional objective, and proficiency level (Novice-Low to Intermediate-Low, based on the ACTFL [1986] proficiency guidelines). After supplementary materials were trialed, some were incorporated into the revised modules, and some remained available as resources. The curriculum revision team was responsible for reviewing the teachers' feedback on each module. If recommendations were made to replace or add module materials or activities, the team reviewed the teachers' supplementary submissions to determine if they were suitable for inclusion in the module before creating new materials. This policy gave teachers a voice in the ongoing revision and refinement of the modules.

After each module had been piloted and revised, it was printed and made available as a Teacher Manual and as a Student Book. The manuals and books were also uploaded onto the server with accompanying sound and video files. In addition, a group of teachers developed an online video library, an extensive project that entailed producing or locating appropriate materials, obtaining permission for their use, creating materials to facilitate using the video clips as appropriate supplements to the Core, and establishing online interfaces.

During the trial period of the new curriculum, several shortcomings were identified and addressed, and strengths verified.

AREAS OF CONCERN

Four primary areas of the curriculum that needed additional attention were identified. The first was related to the fact that MLI students' past learning experiences had encouraged them to be passive learners; their classes prior to attending the MLI tended to have been teacher fronted, and memorizing material to pass tests had been the most important target. When the students reached the MLI, they expected the teachers to "give" them the language and to teach to the tests. The students needed to be taught how to learn in the new curriculum. The teachers had varying degrees of success in helping them understand how to do this, and some students were resistant to trying new learning strategies. Throughout their studies, students received clear descriptions of the program goals and expectations for their learning as well as regular formative feedback to help them see their progress, but they also needed a comprehensive orientation to the new curriculum. The orientation that was put in place was composed of three principle components.

First, all students attended an hour-long assembly on the first day of class in which the student affairs officer, a member of the military administration, delivered in Arabic a welcome message and program orientation. The Core coordinator worked closely with this officer to train him in all aspects of the course and provided a course description document that was translated into Arabic and presented in the student handbook given to each new student.

Second, in the first class meeting, teachers provided a hands-on orientation to the course and distributed student books. Teachers also led students through a number of activities designed to acquaint them with the roles of the student and the teacher, the projects, and how students would be evaluated. The teachers distributed binders to the students, guided them through labeling the organizers, and provided them with sample vocabulary and grammar log sheets. In addition, a bilingual advisor visited each class on the first day to answer in Arabic any questions the students might have.

Third, the CALL teachers provided a standardized orientation to using the computer, including information on hardware, software, and using Microsoft Word. The orientation activities during these first 3 days of classes also helped students with some of the set-up tasks for the projects to be completed in the first module.

A second area of concern was that certain activities and projects did not work as intended—they were confusing, were too difficult to implement, or simply did not promote learning of the targeted skills and abilities. The changes to the Module 4 projects discussed earlier are typical of the kinds of modifications that were made. Additionally, some modules lacked sufficient material for 3 full weeks of instruction. Problematic activities had to be replaced, and additional material had to be prepared; once developed, all of the new material had to be piloted again.

The third area of concern had to do with the expectations of the MLI military administrators. Although they were pleased with the student assessment results, they thought that the materials might be too easy. The curriculum materials were developed for student success; they presented students with clear, finite objectives in each module and provided sharply focused instructional activities. The majority of students achieved high scores on the projects and module tests, but because the military administrators did not fully understand the curriculum design, they assumed that if most students performed so well, the modules must be too easy. Their concerns were addressed from three perspectives. First, much time was spent explaining to key members of the military administration the principles underlying the approach to learning promoted by the new curriculum. The individualized nature of the program was also explained, that is, that students are evaluated according to the learning objectives included in each module, not against one another or against a standard outside the curricular objectives. Second, the assessment procedures for the projects were reviewed and scoring was tightened to present a greater challenge to the more proficient Core students. Third, the EC-C/A conducted a complete item analysis of each module test. Guided by the outcomes of this analysis, she revised the tests to make them more challenging. The content and response options of items that the analysis had shown to be easy were closely examined and revised to present a greater challenge to students. All of the questions were changed from three-option to four-option multiple-choice to reduce possible guessing (see Appendix C for examples of questions from Module 4).

The final area of concern was also related to assessment. As described earlier, the student projects were assessed by a team rather than by the students' teachers. Some teachers and students complained that the scores on the projects did not provide sufficient feedback about the students' progress and learning. The assessment team responded by developing an online feedback system that addressed this problem.

STRENGTHS

Once the Core materials were used in the classroom, teachers recognized certain strengths. They could see that, based on higher levels of student involvement in the projects, these projects were more effective in promoting student learning than the previous language program had been. Students did not simply memorize material to pass a test; they practiced and used language in meaningful ways.

Additionally, the instructional objectives seemed to target useful, manageable skills and knowledge and were accessible across the range of students' proficiency levels. The materials seemed culturally appropriate and linked to the known world of the students. The fact that the CALL lab tasks were directly linked to the module projects appeared to increase the students' motivation to complete the tasks, and student performance on the projects and tests indicated that the tasks accomplished their purposes. Finally, the internal and external assessment scores met the demands for accountability as expressed by the MLI administration.

Conclusion

The development of the Core was a significant endeavor that took place while the school increased in size from a student population of 100 to 400 and the administration and faculty were involved in the creation of new facilities, development of new policies and procedures, teacher recruitment, and in-service training.

The needs analysis provided multiple perspectives on the students' previous academic experiences and their language interests, needs, and goals. Examination of this information led to the development of objectives grids, which guided the development of the three projects that form the foundation of each module. The modules include multiple integral assessments designed to promote, support, and monitor students' learning of valuable and valued skills on an ongoing basis. In short, the directive for the Core curriculum appears to have been met: The curriculum reflects the language learning needs of MLI students and includes a comprehensive plan for monitoring and evaluating students' progress and the degree to which they attain specified skills and knowledge.

The development of the objectives grids was an essential element in creating the Core, but two additional elements were critical. The first was the collaboration and support of the academic and military administrations, and the second was the efforts of the team members themselves and the professional development support that they received.

From the outset, the military administration was committed to establishing an effective language program through collaboration with the academic administration. The director's professional qualifications and vision were respected, as he respected and appreciated the commandant's guidance in military concerns and continued support and enthusiasm for the project. The Core coordinator ensured that the goals of the project were met despite the lengthy development process and the number of people involved. He also ensured that the essential steps of trialing and revising the materials were achieved. And despite the MLI teachers' professionalism, the development and implementation of the Core required many of them to adopt ideas about language learning and teaching that they had not previously considered. Ongoing meetings facilitated by the coordinators, the participation of external consultants, and institutional support for attending and participating in regional and international conferences facilitated the teachers' modification of their practices to reflect and support the principles of the task-based process approach that the Core embodies.

Appendix A: Teacher Survey

Please take some time to reflect on and respond to these questions as thoroughly as you can. The information will be used as we design the new curriculum.

What levels have you taught? _____ Officer _____ Enlisted

Note: If you have taught officers and enlisted classes, please note to which group you are referring as you answer the questions.

Your students as people

- What life experience do they bring to the class?
- What are some characteristics of your students that you have noticed in your day-to-day and other interactions with them?
- What are some of their interests? What are some things they are not interested in?

Your students as students generally

- What study skills do you think they have? What study skills do you think they lack?
- What are some of their beliefs about learning and teaching?
- What types of learning appeal to them? What types of learning do not appeal to them?

Your students as language learners

- In what skill areas are they most proficient? Least proficient?
- What kinds of activities "work" for you most often? Which ones don't work?
- What language-learning strategies do they use? What language-learning strategies do they need?
- What kinds of language experience do they bring to class?
- What is important to them as language learners? How do they believe that learning "happens"?
- What "kinds" of English do your students need?

Appendix B: English Versions of Student Surveys

SURVEY FOR STUDENTS ENTERING THE MLI ENGLISH PROGRAM

Work-related

Listening/Speaking
How often do you speak or listen to English at work?

Always _____ Sometimes _____ Never _____

What do you speak or listen to at work? Please be specific.

Writing
How often do you write English at work?

Always _____ Sometimes _____ Never _____

What do you write at work? Please be specific.

Reading
How often do you read English at work?

     Always _____   Sometimes _____   Never _____

What do you read at work? Please be specific.

Outside of Work (Speaking/Listening, Reading, Writing)

- At home with servants or repairmen
  How often do you use English at home?
  What skills do you use at home?
  How do you use these skills?

- At businesses (repair shops, supermarkets, stores, etc.)
  How often do you use English at businesses?
  What skills do you use at businesses?
  How do you use these skills?

- Restaurants
  How often do you use English in restaurants?
  What skills do you use in restaurants?
  How do you use these skills?

- At Etisalat, banks, etc.
  How often do you use English at these places?
  What skills do you use at these places?
  How do you use these skills?

- For travel
  How often do you use English for travel?
  What skills do you use for travel?
  How do you use these skills?

- With the media (TV, radio, the Internet, etc.)
  How often do you use the media in English?
  What skills do you use with the media?
  How do you use these skills?

- With people generally
  How often do you use English with people generally?
  What skills do you use with people generally?
  How do you use these skills?

SURVEY FOR GRADUATES OF THE MLI ENGLISH PROGRAM

Directions: In order to improve the MLI English Language Program, we would like information about your use of English. Please answer the following questions completely and accurately.

Military Branch _____ Unit _____

Job Title _____

Job Responsibilities (Please list at least five specific tasks expected of you in your job):

When you entered the MLI, what level did you begin at? _____

When you left the MLI, what level did you leave at? _____

Section 1: Use of English in your job

1. Since leaving the MLI, have you used English **in your job**?

   ☐ Yes, I have.   ☐ No, I haven't.

(If you answered "Yes, I have," go to Question 2. If you answered "No, I haven't," go to Section 2.)

2. What English language skills have you used?

   ☐ Listening/Speaking   ☐ Reading   ☐ Writing

3. If you have used **Listening/Speaking Skills** in your job:

   How often have you used English in your job:

       Always   Sometimes   Rarely

   Who have you talked to?

   What have you talked about?

   Give specific examples of how you have been required to use English for speaking and listening in your job:

4. If you have used **Reading Skills** in your job:

   How often have you read English in your job:

       Always   Sometimes   Rarely

   What have you read?

   Give specific examples of the kinds of materials that you have been required to read in your job:

5. If you have used **Writing Skills** in your job:

How often have you written in English in your job:

> Always   Sometimes   Rarely

What have you written?

Give specific examples of the kinds of writing you have been required to do in your job:

Section 2: Use of English in your life outside of your job

1. Since leaving the MLI, have you used English **outside of your job**?

☐ Yes, I have.   ☐ No, I haven't.

(If you answered "Yes, I have," go to Question 2. If you answered "No, I haven't," go to Section 3.)

2. If **Yes,** check the topic areas where you use English and answer the questions.

At businesses (repair shops, supermarkets, stores, banks, Etisalat, etc.)

How often do you use English in these situations:

> Always   Sometimes   Rarely

Give specific examples of how you use English in these situations:

At home (servants, repairmen, etc.)

How often do you use English in these situations:

> Always   Sometimes   Rarely

Give specific examples of how you use English in these situations:

Media/Entertainment (newspapers, magazines, radio, TV, cinema, videos, music, Internet, computer software, etc.)

How often do you use English in these situations:

> Always   Sometimes   Rarely

Give specific examples of how you use English in these situations:

Restaurants

How often do you use English in these situations:

> Always   Sometimes   Rarely

Give specific examples of how you use English in these situations:

Travel (airports, hotels, travel agents, travel situations, etc.)

How often do you use English in these situations:

     Always   Sometimes   Rarely

Give specific examples of how you use English in these situations:

Other Topic Areas (i.e., doctors, foreign friends, foreign business acquaintances)

How often do you use English in these situations:

     Always   Sometimes   Rarely

Give specific examples of how you use English in these situations:

Section 3: Your ideas about the MLI English Language Program

1. Studying at MLI helped me increase my confidence in using English.

   Strongly Agree   Agree   Disagree   Strongly Disagree

   Comments:

2. I was able to practice and improve my English when I studied at MLI.

   Strongly Agree   Agree   Disagree   Strongly Disagree

   Comments:

3. My MLI teachers used many different activities to help me learn and practice English.

   Strongly Agree   Agree   Disagree   Strongly Disagree

   Comments:

4. My MLI teachers encouraged me to practice my English and participate in class activities.

   Strongly Agree   Agree   Disagree   Strongly Disagree

   Comments:

5. I made a strong effort to improve my English when I studied at the MLI.

   Strongly Agree   Agree   Disagree   Strongly Disagree

   Comments:

6. If there were a course available, I would study at the MLI again.

    Strongly Agree   Agree   Disagree   Strongly Disagree

    Comments:

7. When I use English for my job or outside of my job, I use what I
    learned at the MLI.

    Strongly Agree   Agree   Disagree   Strongly Disagree

    Comments:

8. My English listening and speaking skills improved because I
    studied at the MLI.

    Strongly Agree   Agree   Disagree   Strongly Disagree

    Comments:

9. My English reading skills improved because I studied at the MLI.

    Strongly Agree   Agree   Disagree   Strongly Disagree

    Comments:

Appendix C: General Specifications for the Module Tests and Example Items From Module 4

[Asterisks indicate a correct answer.]

GENERAL STATEMENT OF PURPOSE

Each module has a Module Test which is administered by the military
administration. A module's Module Test is intended to measure the extent
to which the students have mastered specific learning objectives for the
module, those not measured through the projects. Each module test
includes four sections:

1. a listening section, measuring the students' mastery of the module's
    listening objectives
2. a reading section, measuring the students' mastery of the module's
    reading objectives
3. a section intended to measure the breadth of the students' mastery
    of the core vocabulary
4. a section intended to measure the breadth of the students' mastery
    of the core structures

The total test has 50 multiple-choice items. Each item is worth one point.
The items are distributed across the four sections as follows:

Listening = 12
Reading = 12
Breadth of Vocabulary = 14
Breadth of Structures = 12

The total time allowed for the pilot Module Test is 2 hours. The scoring of all items is done using a key. (The correct response to an example item is indicated by an asterisk.)

LISTENING SECTION (12 ITEMS IN TOTAL)

The listening section of the Module Test is intended to measure students' mastery of the specific listening objectives listed in a module's Objectives Chart. There are three listening texts with 4 items each. The texts represent the types of texts that students encounter in a specific module. The listening texts are audiotaped and the items are both heard and read. All listening texts and items are delivered in a natural, but slower than typical rate, with no contractions. Each passage has 4 questions intended to measure main ideas and details that reflect a module's topics, core vocabulary, and core structures.

Listening text features:
Length: 40 seconds or less
Topic: determined by the module topics & tasks
Types of names: half of the names are Emirati, half are Western
Rate: slowed, but natural. No contractions.
Source: written by test development team, though may be adapted from authentic material

Listening item format: All items are multiple-choice with four options. The stem of the item is in the form of a question. Items are based on main points and important details in the passage that reflect the topics, core vocabulary, and core structures of the module. The information needed to answer an item correctly is salient when the text is heard (that is, salience in the script is not sufficient; the information must also be salient when the script is performed). Incorrect options are derived from the content of the passage. To reduce memory as a factor in measuring listening, students hear the questions (but not the options) before they hear the passage. They then hear the passage. Then they hear the first question and have 15 seconds to choose the best answer from the options presented in their test booklet. Then they hear the second question, and so on.

Example Listening Passage & Items (from Module 4: Food)
Listen and choose the best answer. Fill in *a, b, c,* or *d* on your Answer Sheet.

Listening 1   Rick is talking with a shop assistant in a supermarket. First, you have one minute to read all the questions and choices.

Now listen to Rick talk to the shop assistant.

Rick: Excuse me, where are the tomatoes?

Shop Worker: They're here by the lettuce.

Rick: By the lettuce? Oh, yes. I see them. How much are the tomatoes?

Shop Worker: They are 4 dirhams a kilo.

Rick: I'd like 2 kilos.

Shop Worker: Here you are.

Rick: Thanks. Also, do you have any onions?

Shop Worker: Yes, we do.

Rick: How much are they?

Shop Worker: They're on sale. They're only 2 dirhams a kilo.

Rick: Two dirhams? That's a good price. Give me 3 kilos, please.

Shop Worker: Here you are.

Rick: Do you have any green peppers?

Shop Worker: Yes, we do. They're right here.

Rick: They don't look very fresh, but those carrots look good. Give me a kilo of carrots.

Shop Worker: One kilo. OK. That will be 4 dirhams for the carrots.

Rick: OK. That's all. Thank you.

Now answer the questions.

Where does Rick find the tomatoes?
- a.   next to the onions
- b.   near the mushrooms
- c.   next to the lettuce*
- d.   near the carrots

How much does Rick spend for onions?
- a.   3 dirhams
- b.   4 dirhams
- c.   8 dirhams
- d.   6 dirhams*

What is the condition of the green peppers?
- a.   They are not fresh.*
- b.   They look good.
- c.   They look greasy.
- d.   They are frozen.

How many carrots does Rick buy?

    a. 1 kilo*

    b. 2 kilos

    c. 3 kilos

    d. 4 kilos

READING SECTION (12 ITEMS IN TOTAL)

The reading section of the Module Test is intended to measure students' mastery of the specific reading objectives listed in a module's Objectives Chart. There are three reading texts with 4 items each. The texts represent the types of texts that students encounter in a specific module. The items are intended to measure main ideas and details that reflect a module's topics, core vocabulary, and core structures.

Reading text features:

Length: 100–300 words (Modules 1–4)

Topic: determined by the module topics & tasks

Types of names: half of the names are Emirati, half are Western

Source: written by test development team, though may be adapted from authentic material

Reading item format: All items are multiple-choice with four options. The stem of the item may be in the form of a question or an incomplete sentence. Content items are based on main points and important details in the passage that reflect the topics, core vocabulary, and core structures of the module. Incorrect options are derived from the content of the passage.

Example Reading Passage & Items (from Module 4: Food)

Read and choose the best answer. Fill in *a, b, c,* or *d* on your Answer Sheet.

Restaurant Review—The Maharaja Palace

    The Maharaja Palace is a new Indian restaurant in Dubai. You can find it in the Crowne Plaza hotel. The food there is a little expensive, but it is very delicious. The inside of the restaurant is beautiful, too. The tables and chairs are nice and comfortable, there is a large family section, and you can watch the chefs as they are cooking. Their most famous and popular dish is their special Tandoori chicken. Everybody also loves the *naan,* or Indian bread. You can order it in garlic, butter, or regular flavor.

    The service is very good. A waiter came to my table almost every 5 minutes. My main dish came in only 10 minutes. I had the chicken curry with rice. My friend ordered the vegetable Maharaja with garlic *naan.* We enjoyed our meal very much.

One problem I had was the price of the drinks. If you go, only order water, because other drinks are too expensive. Also, much of the food is spicy. For some people, it will be too spicy. I don't like spicy foods, so I told the waiter and the chef prepared food that was not spicy. One last thing—there is no buffet on the weekends.

However, these problems aren't too bad. I like very good food and nice service, so this restaurant is a good choice for my family and me. We will go at least one time a week. Try it sometime yourself. But be sure to call ahead for reservations on the weekend evenings. It can be very busy at that time.

Review by: Mr. Paul Watkins

What are two of the more popular things on the menu at this restaurant?
    a. the chicken curry and the Tandoori chicken
    b. the vegetable Maharaja and the rice
    c. the Tandoori chicken and the *naan**
    d. the vegetables and the chicken curry

According to Paul, what is the best list of **good** comments about this restaurant?
    a. the price of the drinks, the *naan*, and the service
    b. the service, the taste of the food, and the inside*
    c. the Tandoori chicken, the spicy food, and the buffet
    d. the buffet, the service, and the price of the drinks

According to Paul, what is the best list of **bad** comments about this restaurant?
    a. expensive drinks, bad service, and the inside
    b. the taste of the food, no buffet, and the waiters
    c. the price of the water, the greasy food, and the reservations
    d. no buffet, expensive drinks, and spicy foods*

What can we say about Paul's review of this restaurant?
    a. He does not like the restaurant because of the spicy food and the prices.
    b. There are some things he doesn't like, but he thinks the restaurant is very good.*
    c. He likes the restaurant because of the buffet and the price of the food and drinks.
    d. He does not like the restaurant because he needs reservations on the weekend.

BREADTH OF VOCABULARY SECTION (14 ITEMS IN TOTAL)

The breadth of vocabulary section of the Module Test is intended to measure the breadth of students' mastery of the core vocabulary for a module. Vocabulary items to be included in a test are taken from across the major categories in the core vocabulary list.

Breadth of Vocabulary item format: The breadth of vocabulary items are multiple-choice with four options. There are two types of items. In type one, the examinee sees a picture and chooses the correct word for the pictured object. In type two, the examinee is presented an incomplete sentence and chooses the best word to complete the sentence given the context. Options are derived from the core vocabulary list and are plausible, but incorrect.

Example Vocabulary Item—Type 1 (from Module 4: Food)

Choose the word that matches the picture. Fill in *a, b, c,* or *d* on your Answer Sheet.

Item number X.
a. some carrots*
b. some bread
c. some grapes
d. some butter

Example Vocabulary Item—Type 2 (from Module 4: Food)

Choose the best answer to complete each sentence. Fill in *a, b, c,* or *d* on your Answer Sheet.

I need to see _____ so I can see the prices and what kind of food I can order at this restaurant.
a. a bowl
b. an atmosphere
c. a menu*
d. an appetizer

BREADTH OF STRUCTURES SECTION (12 ITEMS IN TOTAL)

The breadth of structures section of the Module Test is intended to measure the breadth of students' mastery of the core structures. The items to be included in the test are taken from the explicit grammar points included in the Objectives Chart and practiced in the module. The module and learning objectives are reviewed to identify the 5 or 6 most critical aspects of grammar taught in the module. A test includes at least 2 items for each critical area.

Breadth of Structures item format: The breadth of structures items are multiple-choice with four options. The items are linked by content and presented in the form of a dialogue. Each item is a sentence or question such as might have appeared in the module. The incorrect options are modeled on errors that students typically make with the particular construction.

Example Breadth of Structures Items (from Module 4: Food)

Saif and Ahmed are ordering food at a restaurant. Choose the best answer. Fill in *a, b, c,* or *d* on your Answer Sheet.

Waiter: Good evening, gentlemen. _1_ your order?
  a. May I take*
  b. May take
  c. Could take
  d. Would I take

Saif: Yes, I'd like the grilled hammour and _2_ french fries, please.
  a. one
  b. any
  c. some*
  d. a

Waiter: I'm sorry, sir. We don't have _3_ french fries at the moment.
  a. one
  b. any*
  c. some
  d. a

Saif: No french fries? That's strange. Okay, I _4_ the fried rice, then.
  a. have
  b. having
  c. will having
  d. will have*

Appendix D: Example Pages From
Myself, Student's Book 1

(Military Language Institute, 2001c)

What Do You Know?

Task 1 Write the number of the word in the box below where it belongs
on the form.

1. Pager Number	10. First Name	19. Telephone Number
2. Gender	11. Rank	20. PO box
3. Military Number	12. Mobile Number	21. Signature
4. Date of Birth	13. Today's Date	22. Unit
5. Last Name	14. Date of Issue (Passport)	23. Nationality
6. Hobbies and Interests	15. Marital Status	24. Branch
7. Place of Birth	16. Names and Ages of Children	25. City
8. Passport Number	17. Country	26. E-mail Address
9. Place of Issue (Passport)	18. Middle Name	

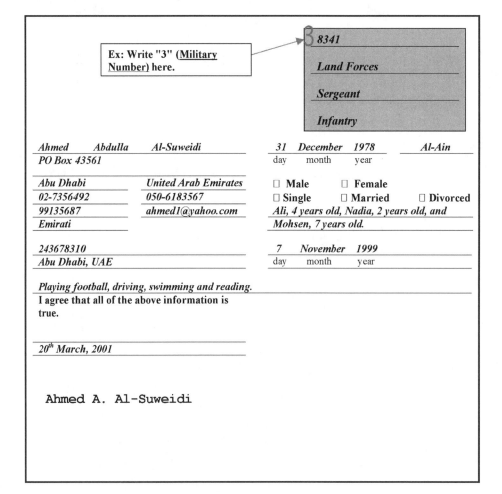

Vocabulary

Task 1 Read the Exit Card and tell where each of the words below should be.

United Arab Emirates
Ministry Of Interior
General Directorate
For Naturalization And Residence
Department of Naturalization
And Residence ....
Exit Port : ....
Leaving For : ....

Purpose of Departure :
1. Employment   2. Tourism
3. Treatment   4. Study
5. Transit   6. Permanent
7. Others   Departure

EXIT CARD

Full Name : .... Father's Name : .... Family Name : ....

Nationality : .... Sex :   1- Male   2- Female

Passport No. : .... Date of Issue : ....

Place of Issue : .... Occupation : ....

Date of Birth : .... Place of Birth : ....

Address In The U. A. E.

Emirate : .... City / Village : .... Zone : .... Street :...............
Tel. No. :............... P. O. Box :...............

Accompanied By

Name	Date of Birth	Sex		Name	Date of Birth	Sex
1...............	....	....	4...............	....	....	....
2...............	....	....	5...............	....	....	....
3...............	....	....	6...............	....	....	....

For Official Use Only

File No. :............... Date of Departure : .... Flight No :...............

Signature Passport Officer ....

Please Surrender This Slip Upon Departure
Number of Companions : ....

1. What is *Emirati*?_____

2. What is *Al-Kaabi*? _____

3. What is *soldier*?_____

4. What is *Al-Ain, UAE*? _____

5. What is *31 July, 1970*? _____

6. What is *male*? _____

7. What is *02-643-8979*? _____

8. What is *Ali Salem Al-Kaabi*? _____

Task 2   Match the words and phrases with their definitions by writing the correct letter in the blank. Look at the forms on the previous pages to help you.

_____ Exit Port   a. PO Box + City + Country

_____ Place of Birth   b. When you were born

_____ Occupation   c. Another word for "job"

_____ Leaving for   d. When your passport was made

_____ Date of Birth   e. Saeed Sultan Ali Al Blooshi
                               (What's *Sultan*?)

_____ Street Address   f. Where you are leaving from

_____ Nationality   g. Where you are going

_____ Father's Name   h. Khalidiya/32nd Street/Abu Dhabi,
                               for example

_____ Date of Issue   i. Emirati or American, for example

_____ Mailing Address   j. Where you were born

Listening

Task   Listen and fill in the form with the correct information.
           Part 1 / **Part 2**

Gulf Times Subscription Form

Full Name: _____

Address: _____

Home Telephone Number: _____

Mobile Number: _____

Job: _____

Job location: _____

Marital Status: _____   Children: _____

Hobbies: _____

Languages: _____

1. His name is Ahmed Abdulla Al-Suweidi. _____

2. He is 30 years old. _____

3. He lives in Abu Dhabi. _____

4. He is from Fujairah. _____

5. He is married. _____

6. He has three children. _____

7. He is in the UAE Air Force. _____

8. He is a colonel. _____

9. Now, he studies English at the MLI. _____

10. He likes to study languages. _____

11. He speaks Arabic and a little English. _____

12. He likes Japanese and Chinese food. _____

13. He likes football and boxing. _____

14. He drives a Toyota Corolla. _____

Appendix E: Introductory Page and Checklist From *Family, Student's Book 2*

(Military Language Institute, 2001a)

PROJECT 2: BIOGRAPHY

A biography is something that you write about another person. A good biography describes the person and brings him to life. This is a written project. You will choose a relative to write about. You will then decide what to write about that person. You will open a word processor file and save it using the person's

name. You will write and save your biography on the computer. You will check it several times and make changes to it.

Your Grade for the Biography (20 points)

About the Project

This project is 20% of your grade. You will write on the computer and revise your work. Your writing must be easy for your teacher, class-mates and others to understand.

Form (30%)
a. Write at least 15 sentences.   • 20 points
b. Use capital letters and periods. Spell words correctly. • 10 points

Content (70%)
a. Organize your writing in a clear sequence.   • 20 points
b. Use Core vocabulary and grammar correctly.   • 20 points
c. Complete the task.   • 20 points
d. Demonstrate originality.   • 10 points

What Did You Learn?

Task 1   Write down 5 new **Adjectives** and 5 new **Nouns** you learned in this section.

Task 2   Write down five new sentences or questions with the words you learned.

Task 3   Biography. Read the sentences. For the ones you did or know, put a □. For the ones you didn't do or don't know, or are not sure of, put a ✕.

_____ I wrote at least 15 sentences.

_____ I spelled words correctly.

_____ I used correct capitals and punctuation.

_____ I used the grammar and vocabulary that I learned in class correctly.

_____ I corrected my paper and revised it at least once.

_____ My biography was easy to understand.

_____ I used the computer to write this.

_____ I enjoyed writing about my relative.

_____ I feel more confident about writing in English.

Please Don't Shake the Mouse: A CALL Curriculum for Adults With Zero and Low Levels of Computer Literacy

5

AUDREY KUCIA

Aminah always wore a wide grin and a beautiful silken head wrap in a deep eggplant or seawater blue. She was a middle-aged Ethiopian refugee who had raised three children, but she had only 2 years of formal education. She came to the Albany Park Community Center (APCC) to become literate, learn English, and acquire skills for greater success in U.S. society. Confronted with a computer for the first time in her life, Aminah did what seemed natural: She picked up the mouse and began shaking it. Soon her neighbors followed suit, and the computer-assisted language learning (CALL) lab teacher was faced with a group of North African and Middle Eastern immigrants and refugees who, although well intentioned, lacked basic computer literacy. Students shook and squeezed mouses and inserted floppy disks upside down, backwards, and, on a few memorable occasions, into CD-ROM drives. One of the first directives that the CALL lab staff incorporated into the introduction to the computer literacy program was "Please don't shake the mouse."

Some people may take for granted their ability to use a computer. Every day, they use computers at work and school. They encounter computers at the library, in museums, and in government buildings. Although learning a new program or application may cause anxiety, most people do not have to think about using the keyboard or mouse. Many may not even remember when they first learned to use a mouse. However, for an adult student encountering a computer for the first time in a second language learning context, picking up the mouse and shaking it might seem as intuitive as gliding it across the mouse pad and clicking one of its buttons seems to someone else. The CALL lab staff at APCC found that they could not take for granted that students had fundamental computer skills. These fundamentals became the foundation of a computer literacy program developed for adult ESL students.

Grant monies made it possible for the CALL lab staff to purchase more computers and software, thus enabling the development of this program. The staff created the program to develop students' computer literacy and to equip them to use technology to study English. The goal of the CALL lab's curricular activities was for students to engage in self-directed technology use and independent use of skills practiced in CALL lab sessions.

The Digital Divide

Lack of computer literacy produces a "disenfranchised underclass, just as surely as if they could not read or write" (Fiser, 2005, p. 115). The United States has a *digital divide*, a gap between those who do and do not have access to computers and the Internet, as noted in an October 2000 report by the U.S. National Telecommunications and Information Administration (NTIA). In the United States, the digital divide results in the further disadvantaging of lower income groups. The NTIA found that access to and use of technology fell with falling income levels. In 1998, in homes with an annual income of $75,000, 80% had computers, and 60% used the Internet. In homes with an annual income between $25,000 and $30,000, fewer than 40% had computers, and fewer than 20% had Internet access. In households with an annual income below $15,000, computer ownership was 15%, and Internet use just 10% (NTIA, 2000). Additionally, White people were more likely than people of color to own computers and have access to the Internet. As Tyner (1998) notes, these disparities in access to computers are a serious problem and reflect fundamental social inequalities.

The Curricular Context

APCC is located in Chicago, Illinois, in the United States, and serves a multiethnic, working-poor population. Many local residents are educationally disadvantaged, and nearly half are foreign born and lack English language proficiency. The development or improvement of English language literacy skills is integral to the center's ESL curriculum. Classes focus on survival English, including language needed for daily activities such as visiting the post office, opening a bank account and using the bank, and grocery shopping.

STUDENTS

The APCC literacy department's ESL classes are offered during the day, in the evening, and on Saturdays. This section focuses on the daytime student population. During the development of this program, the ethnic breakdown of ESL students was approximately 40% Latino, 30% Middle Eastern, 10% South Asian, 10% Korean, and 10% Eastern European. Generally, students were working poor and poor, with 2–5 years of schooling at any point in their lives. Student levels of English proficiency ranged from zero to higher intermediate. Students were divided into five levels:

- Level 1—zero literacy in any language and zero English skills
- Level 2—literacy and low English skills
- Level 3—literacy and low-intermediate English skills
- Level 4—literacy and intermediate English skills
- Level 5—literacy and high-intermediate English skills

Most students had little or no experience with computers. A small number owned computers for their children's education but said they did not know how to use them. The majority of students only had contact with computers at their APCC classes and at the public library.

The ESL classes had an average enrollment of 30 students. The average group size in the lab was 12 students, with one computer per student. Each class was assigned two hour-long sessions each week, but because classes were divided, individual students had a single hour-long session of lab time each week. Some students were frequently absent and therefore received fewer contact hours in the lab. Frequent absenteeism was due to domestic challenges such as child care, pregnancy, household responsibilities, and fatigue from having worked night shifts. Staff suspected that some students had learning disabilities, but the center did not have a social worker at the time of the curriculum's development, and staff drew upon minimal resources in trying to serve these students.

STAFF

The computer literacy program was staffed by daytime and evening computer lab resource teachers and was initiated by these teachers together with the director of the literacy program. Other lab staff included a college student intern and community volunteers.

Many of the ESL classroom teachers held master's degrees in TESOL or a related field, and some had international teaching experience. However, most lacked experience integrating CALL into their lesson planning. Many lacked confidence in their own computer literacy and felt uneasy about using technology to teach others. As similarly noted by J. Harris (1998), teachers cited lack of training and support as chief reasons they had not been integrating technology into their classroom activities. Many perceived CALL as a separate component, distinct from time spent on classroom learning; they felt that CALL was limited to students' time in the computer lab and did not have a direct connection to classroom activities. The affective barriers that hindered student progress also affected classroom teachers, many of whom preferred to avoid technology rather than admit the need to build their skill sets.

EQUIPMENT

A grant for the expansion of the CALL lab and its resources made the development and implementation of a new CALL curriculum possible. Prior to the receipt of the grant, staff had begun work on the curriculum, but a lack of resources challenged its practical application. Staff used grant monies to upgrade equipment, more than double the number of computers in the lab, and purchase English language learning software. The lab was equipped with 15 stand-alone, networked personal computers equipped with headphones and speakers; three networked printers; and two portable stand-alone computers on carts that could be wheeled into a classroom and connected to the network. The lab was also equipped with two laptops and an overhead projector. English language learning software included programs in the following areas: vocabulary, grammar, and listening. The lab was also equipped with two keyboarding programs.

The Motivation for the Program

Concurrent with administrative and staff plans to improve the CALL lab and develop a computer literacy program, student representatives had demanded that computer use be made a greater part of education at APCC. They wanted the center to acquire more computers and lab staff to give students more time and instruction in computer use. Similar to the Chicago elementary school parents in a study by Chen and Dym (2003), APCC students wanted to acquire computer skills in order to help their children with homework, to improve their own English language skills, and to find better employment. The lab staff proposed the development of a CALL curriculum that addressed literacy department goals of improving students' overall literacy, including computer literacy, and English language skills.

The staff considered familiarity with computers and their applications important for students' advancement in their education; access to better paying employment, information, and resources; and community involvement. Staff also viewed computers as additional conduits of English language lessons and practice. To achieve these goals, they planned to expand the English language learning software library and improve ESL teacher comfort and familiarity with computers. Internet literacy was included in the program goals because it was felt that the students were vulnerable to being victims of the digital divide.

The Process of Designing the Program

At first, the staff met with the head of the literacy department about designing a CALL curriculum with greater emphasis on ESL learning goals. However, the needs analysis revealed that students needed to develop basic computer skills before they could independently use software and the Internet. In the needs analysis, the staff assessed what skills students already possessed and determined what skills they would need to achieve eventual independent-use goals, use ESL language learning software, complete word-processing tasks, and use the Internet. Staff also consulted ESL classroom teachers and collected class syllabi so that the CALL lab experience could incorporate and reinforce classroom content. Because student deficiency in basic skills was so great and basic skills would be needed to use software and the Internet, the staff were able to quickly divide the program into three parts: basic computer literacy, software use, and Internet use. All goals depended upon students' ability to use computers, so the staff made basic computer literacy the first component of the program. Because ESL software focused on content studied in class and was more predictable than the Internet, the staff made software use the second component and Internet use the final component. The staff hoped that the program's three-component structure would enable students to use newly developed skills in subsequent sections of the program.

From September 2001 to September 2002, over the course of three terms of instruction, the staff developed, adapted, and evaluated the computer literacy program. Some procedures and materials that were originally developed for the first semester were postponed after review by lab staff and classroom teachers, usually because they had underestimated the time needed to work on basic computer skills. After two terms of use, the staff and classroom teachers agreed on time allowances for each level of the curriculum. At that point, classroom ESL teachers who had been with the center through the history of the new curriculum had built up substantial experience with the program and the staff. Informed by the needs expressed by these teachers, the staff developed a computer literacy curriculum to support, educate, and guide classroom teachers.

In their needs analysis, the staff found that some students had been in the ESL program for several terms, had visited the computer lab multiple times to use English language learning software, but had not learned to use the mouse or keyboard. In the past, to maximize the number of students using the computer lab, students worked in groups of two or three at a single computer. But students with high-level English language skills ended up dominating mouse and keyboard use for several reasons: Some high-level students grew impatient with low-level students and found it easier to do everything themselves; some low-level students insisted that high-level students perform all tasks that required using the mouse or keyboard; and in some cases, high-level students felt that they helped low-level students by modeling mouse and keyboard skills. As a result, low-level students had little or no practice using the mouse or keyboard.

For the new program, lab staff felt that the development of individual computer literacy was best served by having students work on their own, one student per computer station. In the event that students worked in pairs, the staff would monitor them and ensure that each student in the pair spent an equal amount of time using the mouse and keyboard.

Students went to the CALL lab with their ESL classmates; therefore, CALL lab groups were determined by a student's placement in the ESL classes. Generally, all students needed to develop mouse and keyboarding skills, so the staff decided to start all students with basic computer literacy practice. Because general computer literacy was so low, all students benefited from time spent reviewing and practicing mouse and keyboard skills, regardless of their relative strength in comparison to their peers.

For the purposes of this chapter, *computer literacy* is defined as knowledge of the vocabulary and functions of a computer, familiarity with computer applications, and an ability to use a computer and its applications. For the APCC curriculum, *basic computer literacy* was defined as familiarity with the basic parts of the computer and their functions as well as use of the mouse and keyboard. These skills came to be defined as *basic* because they are the minimum requirements for using simple software programs. The second level of computer literacy was defined as the ability to successfully navigate English language software programs as well as familiarity with and ability to use basic word-processing skills. At the third level of literacy, the staff introduced the Internet and included vocabulary and functions of basic Internet applications as students practiced basic skills such as locating and navigating a Web page.

Initial English language content related to computer literacy; however, the staff made an effort to incorporate classroom vocabulary into a software program that students used to practice mouse skills. In the software-use component of the class, classroom language content was incorporated as the topic of software study (e.g., a software unit on the grocery store) and as the topic of paragraphs typed into the word-processing program. The software component's computer language content related to use of software (e.g., *insert a disk, select "food" on the menu, double-click on the food icon, close the program*). In the Internet component, the staff introduced students to new vocabulary for Internet use (e.g., *Web page, search*) and worked with teachers to design activities that focused on classroom content.

LEVEL I: BASIC COMPUTER LITERACY

Introduction to the Lab, the Computer, Its Parts, and Their Functions

Lab staff provided students with a lab orientation that started with a review of rules and procedures. Among the rules, staff requested that students not press the hard-drive power button. In the past some students had a tendency to immediately or repeatedly press this glowing green button. The second part of the orientation reviewed the parts of the computer and their functions.

The staff conducted both parts of the orientation in English, but also used Spanish, Arabic, and Urdu with some groups. They also created multilingual resource sheets for use in teaching mouse skills. For students who had zero English skills, or very low-level English skills and corresponding low levels of education, the staff felt that an English-only environment would not be as beneficial as a positive, affective environment in which students could feel comfortable in their new roles as technology users. In an effort to further lower affective barriers and create a more intimate and supportive learning environment, each student and lab staff member wore a name tag, and staff always addressed students by name.

Mouse Use

In the second part of the basic program, lab staff introduced the mouse and mouse skills (e.g., holding it, manipulating it, clicking, double-clicking, dragging). They used demonstration and pictures to show students how to hold, click, and double-click the mouse, and they encouraged students to practice these skills. As mentioned earlier, students did not instinctively know how to manipulate the mouse; common initial approaches to mouse use included shaking it, squeezing it extremely hard, or holding it too gently.

Lab staff devised three different activities for students' initial mouse skills practice. The first activity involved holding and moving the mouse. Staff directed students to use the mouse to manipulate the screen position of the white arrow (cursor) that corresponds to the mouse. They asked students to use the mouse to touch the four corners of the screen and move in straight lines vertically, horizontally, and diagonally across the screen. After students demonstrated competency in this activity, they moved on to the click and double-click component of the activity. In this component, staff showed students how a single click would highlight an icon on the desktop and a double-click would open a program. After students demonstrated competence in mouse manipulation, click skills, and double-click skills, the staff introduced the second activity.

In the second activity, the staff required students to open a Microsoft Word document that contained a clip-art picture of a cat and another of a mouse. The staff asked students to manipulate the graphic mouse's position on the screen. This required students to click on the mouse, hold the button down, and move the mouse. In the second level of this activity, the staff instructed students to increase the size of the mouse and to decrease the size of the cat. This task required students to click on the graphic once to reveal the black box that framed the graphic. Students then clicked on the box and maintained contact, dragging the box outward to make the graphic larger or inward to make it smaller.

The third mouse skills activity incorporated a review of the parts of the computer. The staff used a crossword-puzzle software program to create an original word-search puzzle using the vocabulary for the parts of the computer. This program allowed staff to later create puzzles using vocabulary studied in classroom lessons. In the program, students searched for the vocabulary in the puzzle. Once students located a word, they would click on the first letter of the word, hold the button down, and manipulate the mouse in order to draw a line from the first to the last letter. After they drew a line between the first and last letters, they would release the mouse button, and the word would change color from the original black to red or gray. If students did not successfully draw their line, the word would not change color. By navigating through the program, including opening the program, opening the word-search component, and choosing the assigned puzzle, students were required to manipulate the mouse and use click and double-click skills.

Keyboard Use

Students usually developed sufficient mouse skills after two or three lab sessions. The staff then introduced keyboard use by helping students develop familiarity with alphabet and numeric keys as well as basic function keys. For this activity, staff used the typing software products MicroType (2006) and Mavis Beacon Teaches Typing (2006). The software helped students learn how to locate and use various keys. Students spent two to three sessions working exclusively on keyboarding skills; as the term progressed and students moved on to higher level skills, the staff gave them supplementary time to further develop keyboarding skills.

Issues Related to Basic Computer Literacy

Lack of experience with computers was a negative affective factor for many students. They generally preferred to avoid computer use rather than admit to or demonstrate lack of knowledge and skill. This anxiety about technology compounded students' affective barriers stemming from second language learning, low levels of education, and, in some cases, advanced age. Lab staff did not initially realize the amount of time needed for development of basic skills and did not sufficiently communicate the importance of this need to teachers at the outset of curriculum development. Also, teachers and lab staff disagreed over how much time should be spent working on mouse and keyboard skills. Small-group meetings, staff meetings, and teachers spending time with students in the lab yielded a consensus that devoting more time to basic computer skills was fundamental for students to eventually attain high-level computer skills.

CALL lab staff and teachers alike desired greater integration of computer skills with classroom content, and although keyboarding practice did not reflect classroom content well, the staff felt that development of this skill would enable students to later work on word-processing tasks first developed in the classroom. At later stages of the curriculum, staff also found it beneficial for students to devote time at the end of an activity to continued reinforcement of basic mouse or keyboarding skills.

LEVEL II: SOFTWARE USE

Navigation of Basic ESL Software Programs

Once students demonstrated adequate proficiency in mouse and keyboard use, the staff introduced software programs with simple interfaces that required minimal movement between screens and minimal optional menus. In piloting the curriculum, staff generally found that the more complicated the interface, the more frustrating the student experience. Students became frustrated because they were apt to stray from the activity or unintentionally shut down or freeze the program by repeatedly clicking on various options and extra menus. One of the programs used at this level, the New Oxford Picture Dictionary (1997), concentrated on vocabulary acquisition, and lab staff used it to coordinate vocabulary study with classroom content. Doing so supplemented content study and achieved a CALL lab goal of having lab activities reflect and reinforce classroom studies.

Additional English language software was used to review vocabulary and present more language learning tasks. Students continued to develop their mouse and keyboard skills while reinforcing classroom content. Lab staff developed easy-to-follow guides to using various software programs, demonstrated software use, reviewed individual software program guides, and gave one-on-one instruction and aid.

Word Processing: File Menu

The staff introduced word-processing software (Microsoft Word) after students had had at least two lab sessions working with vocabulary and task-oriented English language software. The needs analysis of basic word-processing skills and a survey of teachers revealed that students should concentrate on a File-menu skill set. In Microsoft Word, students learned to Save and Save As, Open, Close, and Print. The staff had originally planned for the curriculum to go beyond these basic skills, but they later found that the majority of students needed one or two terms to master and independently repeat them.

Issues Related to Software Use

The CALL lab staff and ESL teachers agreed that word-processing skills were important, but opinions differed regarding how quickly students could progress from basic skills to skills such as inserting pictures into documents. Although the latter skill was not considered particularly challenging, lab staff insisted that students should first master basic skills and show a certain level of word-processing speed before working on a task that required them to insert pictures. Some teachers felt that the "wow" factor of the insert-picture task was justification in itself and that the lab staff were denying students an opportunity to do an interesting activity.

The lab staff questioned the pedagogical value of the insert-picture task because most students had trouble searching for and independently inserting pictures, and the lab staff found themselves doing most of the search-and-insert work. Although students enjoyed having images related to the text in their documents, the activity did not yield much in the way of student practice of computer skills. The lab staff and ESL teachers eventually reached an understanding that before they proposed a new CALL lab activity, teachers would reflect on the pedagogical value of the activity, especially with a view toward learning computer skills.

Another issue related to the lab staff's request that teachers send students to the lab with a completed writing assignment ready to type. Some students arrived with an assigned writing task but had not yet written anything, and they had difficulty both attempting to compose something and typing. The CALL lab environment exacerbated the sensitivities of slower students whose slower progress in language use was exaggerated by their slower progress in keyboarding.

LEVEL III: INTERNET USE

The administration and CALL lab staff set specific objectives concerning eventual independent student use of the Internet. Staff followed the framework described by Sunal, Smith, Sunal, and Britt (1998), wherein teachers incorporate Internet use into the learning culture and teacher-guided Internet use is a step toward students' eventual independent use (see Figure 1 for an outline of the Level III components). At level one, teachers use the Internet to inform lesson plans and gather resources. At level two, teachers share with students materials and resources found on the Internet and use these materials to supplement the classroom curriculum. At level three, students work on the Internet as part of a lesson. At level four, teachers create projects and additions to the curriculum that would not be possible without the Internet. At level five, students direct their own Internet use. At APCC, students, staff, and ESL teachers achieved level four.

Lab staff and classroom teachers worked together to ensure that lab Internet use was supported by classroom warm-up activities, non-computer-based classroom activities, classroom follow-up use of information, and activities completed in the lab session. The staff gave teachers technology workshops on classroom use of portable computer units, laptops, the projector, the Internet, and software. They created an orientation to the lab, its regulations, and its resources for review by teachers and volunteers and gave orientation workshops on existing software resources and new titles being considered for acquisition. Lab staff set up equipment and did troubleshooting for technology use in the classroom. In workshops on best practices, teachers and lab staff shared Internet resources as well as Internet activities they had created.

Figure 1. Outline of Level III: Internet Use

Orientation
1. *Introduction*—description and explanation of Internet
2. *Vocabulary review*

Activities
1. *All Internet*
   a. Web page as content for task completion
   b. Web page as support for content and source of task
   c. Web page as both content for task completion and source of task
   d. Scavenger hunts (includes links to multiple pages to be used to complete a task)
2. *ESL-specific sites*
   a. Web page as source of grammar practice
   b. Web page as source of grammar testing
   c. Web page as sources of reading comprehension activities
3. *Searches*
   a. Use of search engines to locate images

Lab staff developed a Microsoft PowerPoint presentation to introduce students to the concept of the Internet and related basic vocabulary. The staff worked with ESL teachers to create activities that used the Internet as support for classroom content and as a source of content and tasks. Staff showed students how to use search engines to find texts and images and how to search for materials in students' native languages. Staff found that English language searches generally yielded text materials that were too advanced for students, but image searches were more successful. Additionally, the staff and ESL teachers worked together to guide students through creating activities that made use of public resources, such as the home pages of the city of Chicago and its public transportation network.

Students had a high likelihood of error when they typed in complete Web addresses. So lab staff created a system of network folders for ESL teachers, who put links for their class lab activities into those folders. Students would then come in to the lab, access the folder labeled with their teacher's name, and click on links for that day's activities.

There was disagreement among lab staff about the practice of accessing preselected Web pages. Although the staff created the system and appreciated its ease of use for ESL teachers and students, one of the staff members was concerned that students were not practicing the skill of entering Web addresses. However, in their own Internet use, the staff accessed most Web pages through links and spent little time typing in addresses, so they decided that the system was helpful because it encouraged students to practice using links.

Initially, ESL teachers described their goals and discussed content areas with lab staff, and the staff found Internet resources and designed activities for students. Over time, the staff encouraged teachers to find their own content and task resources and to design their own activities. Though some teachers initially protested, with experience, they gained confidence in their ability to combine technology use and materials development. They also shared resources, which helped guide those teachers who were less than enthused about classroom Internet use and the design of lab activities. With each new term, the bank of developed materials grew, as did teachers' confidence and aptitude. Over time, some teachers came to view Internet use as integral to classroom lesson planning.

Tasks could be categorized as focusing on content, task, or both. The staff drew tasks from the public domain or from sources designed for use with ESL students. An example of a public-domain activity was one that focused on understanding nutritional information on food labels and was supported by a visit to ice cream vendors' home pages. The teacher designed a worksheet with questions related to page content and asked students to provide answers based on their review of the Web pages. In another activity, students used a Chicago-area newspaper's classified ads search engine to look for available apartments. Yet another activity made use of an online interactive quiz on the subject of household safety and first aid to support a classroom unit on the subject. In addition, lab staff created support activities for common topics (e.g., learning about Chicago) by creating a scavenger hunt—a worksheet with questions that could be answered by visiting various Web sites.

Students' ESL-specific use of the Internet focused on visits to Web sites, such as *Dave's ESL Cafe* (1995–2007), that offered grammar and reading comprehension quizzes. These activities were especially popular with students who preferred a grammar-centered curriculum.

Issues Related to Internet Use

The staff approached the integration of Internet into the curriculum with not only caution but also mindfulness of the time investment required for students to establish basic skills, comfort, and ease in using ESL language practice and word-processing software. As CALL lab staff and ESL teachers gained experience with student needs and progress, certain questions about the value of introducing the Internet arose. Staff concerns included students' need for further development of basic skills, security, and the anticipation of a great need for troubleshooting.

In working on basic skills and software, students sometimes had a knack for discovering program bugs and manipulating the computer in unforeseen ways (e.g., gripping the mouse so tightly that highlighted images turned rainbow colors and the computer froze) that would shut down their software or freeze the program. These not infrequent incidences were a source of stress for staff as well as students.

Some students had a tendency to click on any and every button and menu option presented by a given interface, which raised a problem. Whereas software programs offered a limited set of options, staff were concerned about students clicking on pop-up windows, sidebar menus, and advertisements on the Web because doing so could make the network vulnerable to viruses. Staff therefore decided to upgrade the lab's virus protection.

One more problem persisted, however. Some sort of Internet policy needed to be developed before students were instructed to use it, but staff, teacher, and administration views conflicted regarding what restrictions to enforce. Some felt the Internet should be used for educational purposes, not personal entertainment. Some were concerned that students who had conservative religious beliefs and lifestyles might be offended by other students viewing, for example, pornographic sites. Others felt that students had a right to use the Internet for whatever they wished, just as they would if they had computers and the Internet in their homes. The administration, staff, and teachers discussed whether one's Web viewing when using a publicly funded facility would be protected by the U.S. Constitution's First Amendment right to free speech.

Everyone eventually agreed that the Internet could be introduced for student use at higher levels of computer literacy (i.e., those who demonstrated competence in Levels I and II). In addition, the staff would introduce students to the Internet through controlled activities and discourage them from clicking on pop-up windows by explaining the risks of doing so. And because the majority of students surveyed had never used the Internet, it was finally decided that Internet use would be structured and that students would only be able to view content on sites selected by the teachers.

Assessment

At the beginning of each level of the program, students were asked to rate their level of skill. After the staff described and demonstrated information and skills, students completed a brief survey that indicated whether they knew the described information and skills and at what level they felt they could use the skills (see Appendix A for an outline of the assessment program for Levels I through III and Appendix B for examples of the student self-assessment survey). After two practice sessions, students were again asked to rate their proficiency, and finally, before moving to the next level, students were asked to rate their mastery of the skills. Low-level students received additional attention, and high-level students were asked to assist them.

Lab staff and teachers met during class breaks and after classes were over for the day to discuss class performance and individual student performance. Student progress was also reviewed in weekly staff meetings. The lab staff felt that communication with classroom teachers was important to further the goal of connecting computer literacy instruction with institution-wide literacy goals. Also, because classroom teachers had greater intimacy with students, they often were able to provide helpful information about whether a particular student was generally slow in the classroom, might have a learning disorder, or was under stress due to personal circumstances. Students often felt more comfortable working with their classroom teachers, so some classroom teachers spent time in the lab working one-on-one with students who had low-level computer literacy.

Program Evaluation

Communication among participants in the program largely influenced how the staff evaluated the success of the computer literacy program. During the time period described in this chapter, evaluation of the curriculum came in the form of meetings between lab staff, the administration, and classroom teachers as well as feedback from students, volunteers, lab staff, and classroom teachers. Lab staff were most concerned with students' ability to acquire skills, build upon acquired skills, and independently repeat skills. Given the students' low levels of literacy and language, the staff evaluated curricular activities based on the appropriateness of language and vocabulary used, with a preference for the most simple and easily understood low-frequency vocabulary.

The staff evaluated students' acquisition of English language vocabulary for computer use through informal quizzes, observation, and one-on-one interaction with students. For English language studied in the classroom, the staff consulted with classroom teachers, students, and volunteers about which software programs provided the best reinforcement. Additionally, as the curriculum for development of computer literacy was being piloted and adapted, staff undertook, modified, and completed a program for classroom teacher computer literacy (see Appendix C for a description of this program). Throughout the development of the student and teacher computer literacy program, lab staff, administrators, and classroom teachers met in workshops, in meetings, and one-on-one to identify technology learning needs, address students' emotional needs, and establish the best approach to teacher technology education.

For the student program, staff felt that all students needed more basic skills practice and that the development of basic skills should be ongoing, but they had difficulty declaring that a certain number of hours of practice would yield mastery of mouse and keyboard skills for most students. The staff felt challenged in evaluating the relative success of instruction because they had no basis of comparison for work with adult learners who had low levels of education and had rarely if ever used computers. Books and research that dealt with introduction to computing were not helpful because they assumed that students had mouse and keyboard skills.

The staff relied on practice and reinforcement of skills and a variety of instructional approaches to address students' different learning styles. For example, with mouse use, staff found that students who did not respond well to written, oral, or demonstrated instructions benefited from one-on-one work in which a staff member or volunteer would initially hold the student's hand on the mouse and guide him or her through the skills to be practiced.

Lab staff also used a variety of approaches in software instruction. They found that software demonstrations to the group supplemented by handouts were successful in helping most students eventually achieve the ability to independently use the software. As with using the mouse, staff found that some students did best when their initial software instruction included repeated individual assistance.

The staff based its self-evaluation on student progress, student feedback, and feedback from teachers and volunteers. The staff were always mindful of students' overall lack of experience with computers and the need to address different learning styles. They evaluated how well students were able to carry over skills learned in one level of the program to the next, and from one school term to the next. At the beginning of the second term, staff asked students to repeat the introduction to mouse exercises that required them to manipulate the mouse directionally, click, double-click, highlight, and drag. Staff also observed how well students were able to perform these same tasks while using the word-search software. For keyboard use, staff asked students to complete the initial evaluation offered on either of the typing programs and noted the ease with which students were able to complete typed assignments. For general software use, they asked students to open, navigate, and use software used in the past. For Internet use, they asked students to access their teacher's folder and open the link for a particular lesson.

For the basic skills of mouse and keyboard use, staff met with ESL teachers and agreed to integrate additional explicit practice of these skills into the last 10 minutes of each lab session. The staff and ESL teachers felt that students had made dramatic improvements from the past, but still needed to reinforce and practice their skills.

Conclusion

After a year of development and assessment, the staff felt that they had completed the framework for the computer literacy program for Albany Park Community Center's adult population of students with zero to low-level computer literacy. In the development of the program, the lab staff realized that nothing should be taken for granted vis-à-vis students' existing knowledge. They found that the most basic skills merited greater time and consideration, teacher education and communication were invaluable, and progressing slowly and using review and reinforcement best served the acquisition of skills.

Acknowledgments

I would like to acknowledge Jeffrey Bright, Hafija Patel, and Mary Anne Seigel and would like to give special recognition to John Kamplain.

Appendix A: Assessment Program

LEVEL I: BASIC COMPUTER LITERACY

Self-Assessment

a. Information and skills are described and demonstrated
b. Students are asked to report whether they know this information and/or possessed described skills
c. After two practice sessions students are again asked to report their mastery of information and skills
d. Before moving to Level II, students are asked to again report their mastery of information and skills

Lab Staff Assessment

a. Low-level students are monitored and given more one-on-one assistance
b. High-level students are asked to aid low-level students
c. Lab staff communicate with classroom teachers about the class's general proficiency and progress as well as that of low-level students

LEVEL II: SOFTWARE USE

Self-Assessment

a. Software use is demonstrated and students are asked whether they can use demonstrated software
b. Students self-assess before moving on to another software title
c. Students self-assess throughout the cycle of their use of word-processing software

Lab Staff Assessment for General Familiarity and Proficiency

a. Low-level students are monitored and given more one-on-one assistance
b High-level students are asked to aid low-level students
c. Lab staff communicate with classroom teachers about the class's general proficiency and progress as well as that of low-level students

LEVEL III: INTERNET USE

Self-Assessment

    a.   Internet use is demonstrated and students are asked how well they can use demonstrated Internet applications

    b.   Students self-assess throughout the cycle of their use of the Internet

Lab Staff Assessment for General Familiarity and Proficiency

    a.   Low-level students are monitored and given more one-on-one assistance

    b.   High-level students are asked to aid low-level students

    c.   Lab staff communicate with classroom teachers about the class's general proficiency and progress as well as that of low-level students

Appendix B: Student Self-Assessment Surveys

Name:

Class:

Teacher:

Mouse Use					
	1st lab	3rd lab	Midterm	9th lab	Last lab
I can:					
Move the mouse in all directions					
Click					
Double-click					
Highlight					
Drag					

Name:

Class:

Teacher:

Microsoft Word					
	1st lab	3rd lab	Midterm	9th lab	Last lab
I can:					
Open Word					
Open a new document					
Save As					
Open a saved document					
Print					
Close Word					

Appendix C: Computer Literacy Program for Teachers

A. Orientation

1. Lab rules and regulations
2. Resources
3. Philosophy and goals for students
4. Familiarity with student level and progress
5. Communication with lab staff

B. Resource Education

1. Orientation to software titles and review of content topics
2. Orientation to new software titles and content topics being considered for acquisition
3. Review of shared Internet activity resources and best practices exchange

C. Technology Use Education

    1. Orientation to portable personal computer setup and use
    2. Orientation to laptop setup and use
    3. Orientation to projector setup and use
    4. Orientation to use of software and Internet in the classroom
    5. E-mails to teachers sharing links to potentially useful Web sites

D. Support for Activity and Materials Creation

    1. Best practice example review
    2. Guidance and feedback with respects to developing or developed materials
    3. Consultation and suggestions for incorporating software and Internet use into existing course plan
    4. Consultation on how to better prepare students for computer lab activities, i.e. prelab lead-ins and postlab reviews

EFL Study

Pulling a Curriculum Together: Addressing Content and Skills Across English and Japanese

6

TAMARA SWENSON AND STEVE CORNWELL

In the mid-1990s, Osaka Jogakuin College (OJC) was faced with several challenges. Although it had established an English program that was well respected throughout Japan, the college was being forced to deal with falling enrolment and the marginalized situation in which junior colleges in Japan found themselves (Kaneko, 1997). In the 1990s the number of college-aged students was falling at such a rate that many institutions of higher education found themselves scrambling for students. At the same time, as higher education became more established, more women began going to 4-year schools rather than junior colleges, which were where women had traditionally continued their education. More than 90% of the students in junior colleges are female (Brender, 2003; Sugimoto, 1997), and at many, including OJC, there are no male students. To further complicate the situation, junior colleges had the image of being finishing schools where women could obtain a little more education before entering the workforce for a few years and then marrying and raising a family. It was against this background of falling enrolment and negative views of junior colleges that OJC considered how it might create a new curriculum to help it remain competitive and continue as a leader in English language education.

At about the same time, changes in Ministry of Education, Science, Sports, and Culture (hereafter the Ministry of Education[1]) policies regarding

---

[1] In January 2001, two ministries were combined to form the current Ministry of Education, Culture, Sports, Science, and Technology (*Monbukagakushô*), now officially

general education requirements at colleges and universities in Japan allowed the OJC faculty to consider broader curriculum changes than had been possible before ("Kokuritsu dai iki nokori," 2003). These changes allowed for a new conceptualization of the curriculum and its individual components. OJC decided to seize the opportunity to create a completely integrated curriculum, linking not only the first-year English courses by themes but also the second-year English courses and the courses taught in Japanese.

The Curricular Context

HIGHER EDUCATION IN JAPAN AND AT OJC

Before describing how the new curriculum was developed, we look at how OJC's system of education is different from those commonly found in institutions of higher education in Japan. Japan's higher education system has long been one in which students spend a great deal of effort preparing for entrance exams, which are the primary way of entering a university (McVeigh, 2002; Schoppa, 1993). Once students are in, at many universities it is accepted that students will not study hard but rather will apply themselves to club activities and part-time jobs (Sugimoto, 1997). It is not uncommon in Japan for teachers to be encouraged to pass students even when they have not been to class or have not turned in assignments (McVeigh, 2002). Additionally, a system of make-up exams exists at many universities so that those students who do not pass a course initially have an extra chance to do so.

OJC has consciously rejected many of these ways of operating. It does not fit the finishing-school image of junior colleges mentioned earlier; instead it tries to encourage the development of women who will participate actively in society. While at school, OJC students must study, must attend classes regularly, and are given many opportunities to reflect on their future in society. They are presented with alternatives to the "study, work, marry, raise a family" scenario that many in Japanese society feel is the only appropriate track for female junior college students.

---

abbreviated as MEXT. Prior to this, the Ministry of Education, Science, Sports, and Culture (*Monbushô*), was called the Ministry of Education or Education Ministry in English-language newspapers and government documents. In this chapter, we refer to it as the Ministry of Education because our discussion of government policies concerns the earlier ministry.

COLLEGE AND CURRICULUM BACKGROUND

To understand how the current curriculum evolved, it is important to look at the background of the school. OJC began as a mission school in the late 1800s, a time when many missionary societies established schools in Japan. It is part of the legacy of the Wilmina Girls' School founded by Presbyterian missionaries in 1884. At the time of the curriculum revisions described in this chapter, OJC was part of a family of schools consisting of a junior high school, a senior high school, and the junior college; in 2004 OJC opened a 4-year university. OJC is now an interdenominational Christian school whose mission and curriculum are interwoven, both helping to define the institution.

OJC's mission declares it to be an educational community based on Christianity whose aim is to "raise up persons who search for truth, respect themselves and others, have the power of insight supported by accurate knowledge and rich sensitivity and participate actively in society" (Souritsu 30 Shunen Kinnen Iinkai, 1998, p. 148; see Appendix A for the mission statement and three pillars of OJC education). The school tries to achieve three main goals through its curriculum and programs: (a) challenging students to strive for a high level of excellence in the English language, their major area of study; (b) helping them broaden and deepen their under-standing of the world as they learn to make autonomous decisions; and (c) helping them develop a clear sense of their worth as a person, a unique individual of immeasurable worth (*Educational Philosophy*, n.d.).

Although OJC can trace its roots back to the late 1800s, it founded the junior college with one major, English, in 1968. At that time, like many schools, it separated English education into the four skill areas, with each English course independent from the others, and all other courses required by the Ministry of Education were taught in Japanese. However, after a series of brainstorming sessions begun in 1979, the faculty arrived at the conclusion that the school needed to be innovative or it would just be another school with an English program (OJJC Karikyuramu Iinkai, 1998). It was at this time that the curriculum began to change from a skill-based one to something new.

At first, changes to the courses and course materials were incremental and not far-reaching. These changes continued until 1985, when a commit-tee was formed and given the task of creating a radically different English curriculum. The resulting curriculum for the English courses was character-ized by integrating the four skills, studying important topics in English, and using materials created specifically to meet the needs of the students (OJJC Karikyuramu Iinkai, 1998). Gone was a curriculum that allowed the English courses to exist in separate, isolated skill areas. In its place was the beginning of an integrated English curriculum.

During the first year, the curriculum focused on six topics: language and expression, women's rights, internationalization and culture, consumer society and advertising, human rights, and social responsibility and awareness (Chihara, 1998) in three classes (reading, oral English, and composition). Because every class covered the same topics during the same 2- to 3-week Integrated Unit period (Figure 1 shows the integrated English curriculum), the teachers for each group of students were able to coordinate coverage in a "first read, then discuss, and finally write" pattern. Ideally, the students read about the topic before discussing it and then wrote about it using the prescribed rhetorical pattern.

This new integrated English curriculum was not static, and the English faculty made regular revisions to the materials (see Table 1). These revisions updated materials, removed areas of perceived or actual bias, and addressed deficiencies that teachers perceived in the curriculum. The read-discuss-write pattern remained unchanged.

During the second year, students selected four one-term, topic-based classes (two for each term). In these classes, they used the skills that they had learned in the first year to study a wide range of topics, from the role of the family and women in the workplace to the language of Mark Twain and issues in the environment. Each teacher prepared a different course, based upon his or her own expertise and interests, to offer students. In addition, all second-year students took a required listening-based course on current events and global issues.

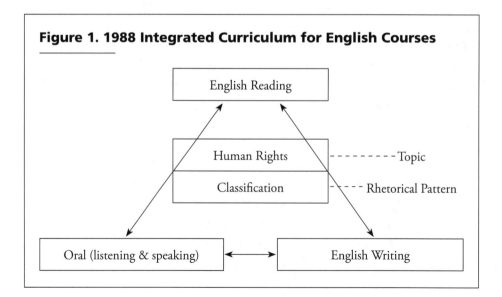

Figure 1. 1988 Integrated Curriculum for English Courses

English Reading

Human Rights — — — — — — — Topic

Classification — — — — Rhetorical Pattern

Oral (listening & speaking) ↔ English Writing

**Table 1. Changes to the Integrated English Curriculum
From 1988 to 1993**

1988		1993	
Topic	**Rhetorical Pattern**	**Topic**	**Rhetorical Pattern**
The world of words	Illustration	Introduction	
How to be a good wife, mother, and woman	Process	Women's issues	Process
Internationalization	Definition	Internationalization and culture	Definition
Prejudice	Classification	Human rights	Classification
Advertising	Compare/contrast	Consumer society and advertising	Compare/contrast
Conformity	Persuasion	Social responsibility and awareness	Persuasion

When the English curriculum went into effect in 1988, it was a huge departure from what other junior colleges were doing. In addition, it a represented the first step in the eventual integration of the entire curriculum along thematic lines. However, the integration of the English curriculum was not matched by a similar integration of courses taught in Japanese, which followed the traditional separation of general and specialized education (e.g., sociology, psychology, physical education, secretarial courses). The English faculty made small revisions in the materials and thematic areas covered, but the English curriculum's basic design remained unchanged. Students studied topics in English, using a content-based curricular model. Yet, by the 1990s, in addition to the societal challenges mentioned at the beginning of this chapter, the course materials had become outdated and the faculty composition had changed, reflecting a higher level of training in teaching English as a foreign language. At the same time, there was growing concern that although the English courses were connected to the school's mission, they comprised too small a percentage of students' total credits (22 of the 62 needed for graduation). Most other courses, aside from those devoted to religious education, were not connected to the college's mission, which is not surprising considering that they had not been designed with the mission in mind. To address all of these concerns, the faculty decided to develop a new curriculum.

The Process of Designing an Integrated Curriculum

INITIAL DEVELOPMENT

Beginning in 1995, the faculty began the process of redesigning the curriculum.[2] The first step was to reconsider the school's mission statement. After several months of meetings, the faculty approved an updated version, one they believed reflected their expectations for a liberal arts education. Once the updated mission statement was approved, the actual work on curriculum revision began.

The faculty made two important decisions at this point, which drove most of the revision process and were essential to the creation of the new curriculum. All courses, whether taught in English or Japanese or offered to first- or second-year students, would address one of the major thematic areas of the curriculum. And although all students would take courses in each thematic area to provide a broad education, they would need to focus on one area in their second year to deepen understanding. These two decisions marked a complete departure from the traditional approach to curriculum development in Japanese tertiary education. No longer was there considered to be a separation between English education and general education. English would be the language of some classes, Japanese of others, with all being directed toward fulfilling the school's mission.

EXPLORING POSSIBILITIES

To begin the revision, the curriculum committee (which consisted of most full-time faculty members[3]) discussed educational, teaching, and testing rationales, along with how placement and proficiency testing could be integrated into the curriculum and what the outcomes of the curriculum should be. In other words, what did we want students to gain from their 2 years at OJC?

As mentioned earlier, one of the motivating factors was not only to integrate the English classes, but also to integrate the non-English classes

---

[2] We were intimately involved with the curriculum project described in this chapter, from planning and conceptualization to the development/setting of what are referred to as the four core units to the actual writing of materials used in the core units for reading, discussion, and writing courses. In addition, we served as liaisons during the curriculum development process and have since led annual material revisions.

[3] Japanese universities and colleges rely heavily upon adjunct faculty. During the curriculum revision period at OJC, the college's English faculty consisted of six full-time native-English-speaking teachers and seven full-time native-Japanese-speaking teachers. The remaining eight full-time faculty members taught general education and specialty courses in Japanese. With approximately 700 students, OJC relied upon approximately 90 adjunct faculty members to teach a majority of the courses.

in the curriculum by having them address the same issues and themes. To achieve this, the curriculum committee began by reviewing the themes that the first-year English courses covered. To do this, the committee was divided into five working groups, each of which dealt with one of the current themes, which at the time were Peace, Self-Expression, Life and Science, Current Society, and Humanities. These groups had three tasks: (a) decide the goals for the theme; (b) determine the second-year courses to offer in the theme area and decide if any current courses, taught in English or Japanese, addressed the theme; and (c) outline the content of the courses taught in Japanese.

Each group spent several meetings working on the first two tasks. One aspect of this work was what we referred to as the *dream plan*. As part of creating the dream plan, group members created key-word cards to indicate the areas they felt the themes should cover. These key words would later become the cornerstone themes for each unit (key words for the Life and Science theme included *evolution, scientific theory,* and *space exploration*). After finishing this brainstorming stage, the groups brought their ideas back to the full committee for discussion and approval. This reporting-back stage was inserted to ensure that study of any one theme would enhance the study of the other themes.

The time spent planning, rearranging, and discussing was essential for the overall success of the curriculum. Without a broad consensus on the goals for instruction and a determination of the types of courses available to students in the second year, the curriculum would not have become the coherent whole we were seeking.

When the revisions began, the faculty planned to implement the new curriculum in the 1997 school year. Originally, we felt that the new themes would basically be variations of the old themes extended into the non-English course curriculum; thus much of the current English course materials could be slotted into appropriate units, and we would not need to write much new material. In a way, we were approaching the new curriculum as a conceptual reworking of the five themes we already had, extending those themes to the second year, and refocusing all other courses to support the English curriculum.

It should be noted that we began to use the term *core* to refer to the thematic units. This was a conscious change because rather than just referring to the content covered, the core concept was seen as a type of major or track for students to pursue. In other words, a student would study all five themes in her first year and then select a theme or core to focus on during her second year. She would then have to take a certain number of courses in that core area. For example, if she became interested in Peace Studies in her first year, she could choose that as her core area, and in her second year she would take at least two of her required four topic-based courses in the Peace core. In addition, she would take courses taught in Japanese that supported her core choice. Thus, by the time she graduated, she would have studied her core area in quite some depth.

ISSUES AND CONFLICTS IN CURRICULUM DEVELOPMENT

By October 1996 work was well underway, with the curriculum committee taking its mandate seriously. The committee considered a wide variety of issues, ranging from how to provide or build schema by providing in-depth coverage of the themes in Japanese to how the curriculum could help students who had difficulty with courses. This last concern was the impetus for many decisions made later in the process. No one on the faculty wanted to pass students who could not do the work, yet they wanted to help those who found their studies difficult. However, as the committee attempted to address all the issues, problems developed, and the new curriculum began to look like an unattainable dream plan made in the best of all possible worlds.

Other issues included whether to maintain all existing special programs (e.g., human rights week, religious retreat), to add courses and themes, to change the academic calendar, and to add a summer session. The idea of adding a summer session, which would give students more opportunities for intensive study and to make up any classes they had failed, soon had to be reconsidered because the committee realized that it would be too difficult to assign faculty or administer summer courses under the school's existing administrative structure. There were also questions about whether students would actually attend summer classes if they were offered, how much it would cost to add a new semester, and how the new academic schedule might conflict with special programs such as human rights week and religious retreat, which were integral to the school's mission, as well as physical education seminars. In spite of problems like this, work proceeded, and most energy was put into linking the cores with Japanese general education courses. However, because of the time involved in addressing the various issues, a decision was made to put off implementing the new curriculum from 1997 until 1998.

In February 1997, with many of the problems resolved, we began looking at actual courses. We had just finished discussions in the fall on issues of identity and diversity. We had talked about students developing social and personal identities and the need to look at interactions both within and between cultures, looking both inward and outward. Changes to general education courses would help support the students' learning in their cores and support them linguistically by allowing them to gain deeper background knowledge in their first language. For example, four new courses that would support the Peace core were suggested: the United Nations; the

World Before the UN; Balance of Power, Peace, and Culture; and Ethnography and Culture. Other courses, including Law I and II, Economics I and II, and Music, were slated for elimination or changed into courses related to specific cores, such as when Law II was changed into International Law, which could then fit into the Current Society core.

As mentioned earlier, we were also considering changing the academic calendar. The primary rationale for doing so was to give students who failed a course the opportunity to retake it in an "extra" term rather than waiting a year for it to be offered again. Waiting a year meant some students would not be able to graduate in 2 years. We were now looking at a calendar that included spring, fall, and winter terms. The new winter term was designed to help students make up classes and focus on electives. It was to be a short, 7-week term of highly intensive classes.

By July 1997, the committee was assigning the topic-based courses to thematic areas. The existing second-year one-term topic classes were being placed into cores. It was while we were working on this that a major change occurred.

A NEW DIRECTION

Up to this point the faculty had been working with the five thematic areas mentioned earlier: Peace, Self-Expression, Life and Science, Current Society, and Humanities. However, in July 1997 the college president requested that the five themes be merged into four so that there would be clearer separation between the areas. This request was a shock to the system. Committee members felt blindsided by the suddenness of the decision and were already stressed out by existing time constraints, which would now be exacerbated. But the committee acknowledged that having only four major thematic areas would allow more thorough coverage of each theme. In retrospect, the decision not only helped focus coverage by eliminating overlap, but also was necessary to focus the curriculum more tightly. The four themes finally settled upon were Peace Studies, Science and Religion, Human Rights, and Crises of Life (environmental and social issues). These became the core units of the new curriculum—themes covered in courses in English and Japanese.

At this point, the curriculum committee asked the liaisons[4] to assign current courses to one of the four cores. By September 1997, the Japanese

---

[4] Historically, the liaison committee supervised annual revisions to English education materials. Each English course has a liaison to coordinate the course, communicate school policy to the teachers, and handle any problems raised by students or teachers. Liaisons are English teaching faculty in charge of all the sections of a course. The liaison committee has eight members, one from each of the following courses: Reading, Discussion, Writing, Phonetics, Grammar, Topic Studies I, Topic Studies II, and Topic Studies III.

courses were being folded into the new curriculum, and decisions were being finalized as to which courses to keep, which to revise, and which to eliminate. One of the causalities of going to a four-core system was that many of the literature and art courses found themselves outside the four thematic areas, a situation that some faculty saw as undesirable and unfortunate.

A modification of the key-word exercise described earlier was conducted; faculty came up with new key words and matched them with cores and course titles. For example, the key words *hunger* and *population* were placed under the Crises of Life (environmental and social issues) core. It was at this time that course descriptions began to be written along a framework required by the Ministry of Education, which included purpose, major content, suggested materials, teaching approach, method of evaluation, and course texts.

In October 1997, the college's president gave the curriculum committee an important reminder. He told them not to lose sight of the fact that all courses were to support content-based English education that would be accessible to the students. He said this because work in some groups had begun to go off tangentially. The group discussing the theme of Science and Religion, for example, had begun spending much of its time considering how to explain the basic concepts of cosmology and the emerging *theory of everything*. Though intriguing, this was not within the basic goal of the theme: to provide students (in English) with an understanding of the impact of science and religion on modern life. The president's timely reminder helped shift all groups back to the dual purpose of the curriculum: learning about core themes and doing so through English instruction.

The committee placed Japanese courses into the cores as well. For example, Foundations of Society I was placed in the theme of Human Rights, providing students with additional schema for material on this topic taught in first- and second-year English courses (see Figure 2).

WRITING INTEGRATED MATERIALS

By the end of October, the committee had agreed upon a framework for all courses, including the course description information that needed to be provided to the Ministry of Education and the overall content goals of each unit. Once these were established, the English teaching faculty, led by the liaison committee, took on the task of writing the curriculum materials for the new cores; they focused on first-year courses. Preparation of the syllabi and materials for second-year courses was seen as a task for the course instructors because, in most cases, only one section of a course would be offered, or the same teacher would teach all sections of the course.

Fortunately, the materials-writing stage did not have to start from

Figure 2. Integrated Curriculum for English and Japanese Courses on Human Rights

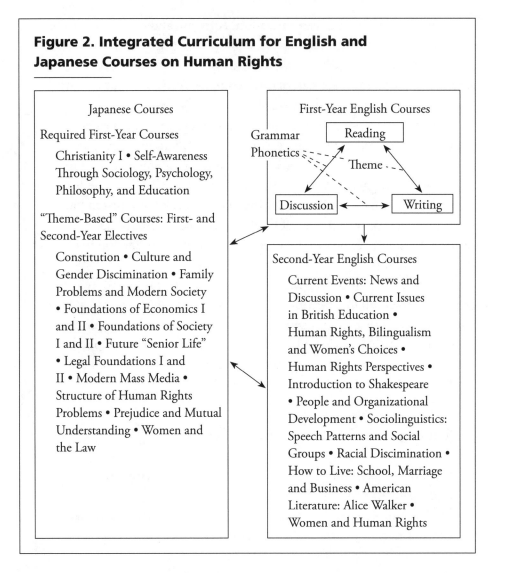

scratch. In 1996, 2 years before the curriculum was finally adopted, faculty members had begun looking at the English education materials in light of the curriculum revisions being discussed at the time. Though the focus areas had been reduced from the original five to four in July 1997, much of the information collected and materials considered remained relevant to the final four topics, which aided the writing process greatly.

By the fall of 1997, with the themes settled, the liaison committee was able to consider what the first-year English course content goals should be for each core, the order in which the topics should be introduced in the first year, and the rhetorical patterns of English writing that should be connected to each core. Historically at OJC, rhetorical patterns have played a significant role in both the reading and the writing programs, with students studying how to organize various types of paragraphs and essays (e.g., illustration, process, categorization, compare and contrast, persuasion) by analyzing examples in reading class and then writing their own drafts in writing class. Two concerns drove this part of the revision process: making sure the English language materials were linguistically appropriate and making sure they fulfilled the theme goals.

The liaisons decided on the following order and matched rhetorical patterns: Peace Studies was paired with illustration and process paragraphs, Science and Religion with classification and the basics of essays, Human Rights with compare/contrast and cause/effect, and Crises of Life (environment and social issues) with persuasion and the basics of research papers. Once this decision was made, all English teaching faculty began writing and revising materials. Two working groups were formed to develop materials for the first two units.

The faculty assigned to write materials for each unit had to not only create activities suitable for reading, discussion, and writing classes, but also make sure the activities could be used by learners with a wide range of proficiencies. Whenever possible, the reading materials were supposed to use the rhetorical patterns assigned to the unit. In addition, each unit was supposed to include

- two or more videotaped lectures
- four paragraphs for each rhetorical pattern (Unit 1)
- three or more essays for each rhetorical pattern (Units 2–4)
- vocabulary lists, comprehension worksheets, discussion questions, and quizzes for each paragraph, essay, or lecture
- model outlines or organizational questions for the paragraphs and essays
- explanations of the rhetorical patterns
- survey and gap activities for discussion
- other materials as deemed necessary to provide 5 weeks' worth of materials

The group members were also requested to locate three or four textbooks that could be used as course readers in addition to the common materials. Individual course instructors could then select one text from among these.

This process did not go as smoothly as we had envisioned because the writing of materials was added to other duties, and deadlines came and went without the required materials being completed. At this point, we realized that, without help, not all of the materials would be ready on time and requested that the college hire materials writers to work on the second-term materials (the Human Rights unit and the Crises of Life unit). These writers were asked to review the materials made for the two core units already completed and to use them as a template for creating materials that met content and linguistic goals.

PROBLEMS IN THE WRITING PROCESS

The writing process was not without its problems, including lack of time, a small faculty, failure to set specific goals for materials prior to preparing them, differing philosophies of education, and a general feeling of pressure and stress because of all of the above.

Lack of time was immediately felt. Because of the desire to implement the new curriculum with the beginning of the 1998 school year, once basic decisions were made, the faculty were under extreme pressure to complete the materials by the print deadline of early March. The pressure was especially acute because of OJC's preference for providing a *turnkey* curriculum by giving teachers almost all the materials they would need for the first-year reading, discussion, and writing courses. The materials in the original integrated English curriculum from 1988 amounted to about 100 pages for discussion, reading, and writing courses, with the bulk used in discussion. Only the reading course regularly used commercially available texts, selecting topic-related readers for each unit. Writing teachers were provided with less material, but also had less time, meeting only 2 hours a week rather than 3. Though we were not starting from scratch, in the fall of 1997, when faced with the need to write and revise material for a new curriculum, it felt as if we were.

Additional problems were the small size of the faculty, the lack of experience in materials writing, and the shortness of the deadline for completing the materials. All English language instructors, native speakers of English as well as native speakers of Japanese, found themselves expected to develop materials regardless of their previous experience. Because of this, the drafts often considered well written by our colleagues were frequently far above the linguistic ability of the target learners.

All of these problems caused us to commit a cardinal sin in materials writing—we began writing materials before setting specific content goals. Failure to set goals resulted in the generation of a great deal of material that on one level met the overall curricular goals, but that on another level, that of daily use, lacked cohesion. For example, writers for the Peace Studies unit generated materials ranging from the organization of the United Nations and conflict resolution stages to the Nobel Peace Prize process and famous peace activists such as Gandhi and Martin Luther King, Jr. All were related to the overall topic of peace, yet no conversation had taken place about which specific goals should be covered. Although this has been rectified to some degree, the initial result was a collection of materials that were poorly sequenced and unfocused.

Coupled with these problems was the human element. Fortunately, all teachers at OJC are committed to giving students the best education possible; however, differing philosophies of education led to some lively exchanges of opinion. For example, teachers differed on what weight should be given within the materials to content coverage versus skills training. Another difference of opinion dealt with the amount of ambiguity acceptable in various questions, activities, and procedures. For example, should vocabulary be actively taught, or is it something more passive that students could learn on their own?

All of this contributed to a general feeling of pressure and stress within the faculty, which has slowly dissipated. Our experiences with the writing of this curriculum have led us to value the importance of scheduling sufficient time for revisions and clearly articulating goals before beginning to write any materials.

THE FINISHED CURRICULUM

The "finished" first-year curriculum consists of four units spread out over two terms, covering topics in reading, discussion, and writing classes at approximately the same time. Ideally, the rhetorical pattern and content topics are first introduced in reading, covered again in more detail in discussion, and written about in writing. The actual teaching of a unit generally proceeds as in the following example from the unit on Peace Studies. In reading class, students are introduced to the general concepts of peace studies, and the rhetorical patterns are covered. They read an illustration paragraph on Nobel Peace Prize winners. Then, during the same week, in discussion class, they receive further exposure to the topic, completing a gap activity about Nobel Peace Prize winners and discussing their accomplishments. In writing class, they continue to study the rhetorical patterns and use them to write a paragraph, due in the middle of the unit, about a person who promoted peace. In this way, materials are integrated and themes recycled across the curriculum (see Appendix B for examples of reading, discussion, and writing activities). The curriculum themes and rhetorical patterns are displayed in Table 2.

Table 2. Curriculum Core Themes and Rhetorical Patterns

Unit	Core Themes	Rhetorical Pattern
1	Peace Studies	Illustration, process
2	Science and Religion	Classification
3	Human Rights	Compare/contrast, cause/effect
4	Crises of Life (environmental and social issues)	Persuasion

In their second year, students select courses from among the four cores. These courses, which are generally referred to as Topic Studies I and II, are designed to deepen students' understanding in their chosen area of study. Both involve writing a short research paper with appropriate use of academic citations as well as reading and having discussions about the topic. All students also take a current events listening course, called Topic Studies III, in which they study current news using broadcast and print sources.

Evaluation and Subsequent Revisions

All of the courses described in this chapter use assessment criteria that are set by the liaisons depending on the specific needs of the course. These criteria, along with suggestions for teaching the courses, are listed in the college catalog that teachers receive during orientation. For example, the discussion course assessment criteria for the first term are as follows: class work 60%, Unit 1 project 20%, and Unit 2 project 20%. By setting clear assessment criteria, the liaisons intend for students to be evaluated similarly within and across the sections of a course.

Regular evaluation of units and courses has always been an important aspect of the OJC philosophy. Even before this curriculum was adopted, at the end of each unit students filled out questionnaires asking how well they felt they had learned the unit topics and how they felt about the materials (see Appendix C for an example of a current student evaluation form). Following the implementation of the new curriculum, however, the full- and part-time faculty were also surveyed about the materials and invited to a special lunch meeting to discuss how the materials could be improved.

The feedback from faculty and students helped us determine what needed to be immediately revised for the 1999 school year. Since then, we have held regular sessions with teachers to get their assessment of the materials as well as other aspects of education at OJC. In addition, each course has an e-mail list that teachers can use to ask questions, share classroom suggestions, or, if there is a problem with an activity in the materials, post a notice.

Conclusion

Curriculum revision is an ongoing process. Each year since the current curriculum's inception, the faculty have revised and rewritten materials. Goals have been clarified for the overall units. Materials have been added, deleted, and rewritten so that they more closely meet the learners' English language levels. Our most recent revision has been to focus on the vocabulary necessary for academic success (Coxhead, 2000).

At each stage, we have strived to improve the curriculum materials while maintaining our adherence to the three goals of the curriculum, which bear repeating here: (a) challenging students to strive for a high level of excellence in the English language, their major area of study; (b) helping them broaden and deepen their understanding of the world as they learn to make autonomous decisions; and (c) helping them develop a clear sense of their worth as a person, a unique individual of immeasurable worth (*Educational Philosophy*, n.d.).

Appendix A: Mission Statement and Three Pillars of OJC Education

MISSION STATEMENT

This school is an education community based on Christianity. Our aim is to raise up persons who search for truth, respect themselves and others, have the power of insight supported by accurate knowledge and rich sensitivity, and participate actively in society.

THE THREE PILLARS OF OJC EDUCATION

The first pillar is Christian Education.

Our education's goal is to build up students' character. Since we established our college we have tried to build character based on a Christian spirit. The goal is not for all students to become Christians, but for each student to realize the value of her existence, to respect others as humans, to grow up as a human who can work with and for others, and to become a member of society.

During students' two years at OJC they can participate in various Christian programs and these programs will give students a chance to realize their purpose in life. Students' experiences at OJC will surely feed their hearts in the future.

OJC's Christian programs include: 1) Christianity Class, 2) Chapel Hour, 3) Special Programs such as religious retreat, special worship services in the spring and fall, candlelight service, graduation worship service, and 4) Club Activities like bible study and gospel choir.

The second pillar is Human Rights Education.

In Japan we have human rights education in junior high and senior high school so most people already know the importance to studying human rights. But in our college we want our students to learn how to communicate with people from various countries. To have real communication it is very important to understand the problems that people have with each other. And the most basic problem people have concerns human rights.

If we ignore the human rights problems in the world, we can't have real communication with people from other countries. Recently, Japan's thinking about human rights is of concern to other countries. To meet with someone from another country in a meaningful way, we must address their concerns. One way that OJC is doing so is by holding human rights education. In 1973, the fifth year of our college, we had a workshop on Burakumin's rights (Burakumin refers to people who slaughtered animals and were traditionally discriminated against in Japanese history). Since then we have added topics, and in 2002 we had 12 subjects.

The third pillar is English Education.

Our goal of education is to build character and to build human beings. So learning English is not the only purpose of our education, it is only a part of our education. By studying English, a student can gain knowledge, learn about culture, realize who she is, realize what is of value to herself, and learn how to communicate with other people.

Communication needs both a sender and a receiver and what is to be communicated is not just information but the essence of herself; in other words, our aim is not to learn how to do daily conversation like in an English conversation school, but to have English education which can lead to a substantive dialogue. Accordingly, our goals are as follows:

- to challenge students to strive and continue to strive for an ever higher level of excellence in their studies.
- to encourage students to broaden and deepen their understanding of the world, learning to make autonomous decisions as they relate to it.
- to develop in each student a clear sense of her worth as a person—a unique individual of immeasurable worth in God's creation.

One of the characteristics of our English education is integrating the skills of reading, writing, listening and speaking. We give the students the opportunity to work on these skills in an integrated manner. Another characteristic is students have to be active in their English education; if they are passive, it is not our style of education. Our education is not one where teachers give information to students in a one-way fashion from teachers to students. Instead, students must share their ideas with each other and their teachers in discussions, essays, research papers, and presentations.

We think OJC is the place where students can study many things in English not only study "English." We are providing students with a two-year English curriculum that it is not only skill training. It is language education, which includes the expansion of knowledge and the building of thinking skills at the tertiary level.

Appendix B: Sample Reading, Discussion, and Writing Materials

The following activities for reading, discussion, and writing come from Unit 1, which has the theme of Peace Studies. The materials illustrate how similar topics are covered in the three courses.

SAMPLE READING ACTIVITY

Nobel Peace Prize Winners

Pre-reading Questions

1. What does "to pursue peace" mean?

2. Name three people in the world who pursued peace.

3. What are things you can do to pursue positive peace?

Those Who Pursued Peace

1There are many people and organizations who have made valuable contributions in the area of peace. 2Martin Luther King Jr., Mother Teresa, Aung San Suu Kyi, and Amnesty International are familiar to us. 3They are all Nobel Peace Prize winners. 4Other winners have also made a difference in the world we live in. 5For example, Ralph Bunche, the first black to win, won the award for his work as a U.N. mediator in Palestine. 6Andrei Sakharov was awarded the prize in 1975 for his work in the promoting of peace and opposing violence and brutality. 7Jody Williams and her organization, the International Campaign to Ban Landmines (ICBL), won the 1997 prize for their work in getting countries to abolish landmines. 8When Jody first began her work, she did not realize that in only six years they would succeed in getting 100 countries to sign a treaty outlawing landmines. 9More recently, Médecins Sans Frontières won the 1999 prize for their pioneering humanitarian work to help people by providing medical services in conflicts and natural disasters. 10People who pursue peace come from many different countries, but they all have one common goal—making the world a better place to live in.

Enter these names in an Internet search to learn more about how these people and groups pursued peace:

Martin Luther King, Jr.
Amnesty International
Jody Williams
Mother Teresa
Ralph Bunche

ICBL (Ban Landmines)
Aung San Suu Kyi
Andrei Sakharov
Médecins Sans Frontières

Comprehension Questions

1. Who are the people or organizations who pursued peace? Name all that appear in the paragraph.

2. What did Ralph Bunche do to be awarded the prize?

3. What did Andrei Sakharov do to be the prize winner?

4. What did ICBL achieve?

5. What does Médecins Sans Frontierès do to help people in the world?

Organization Questions
Directions: Write the sentence number(s) in the parentheses.

1. (   ): sentence(s) in the introduction

2. (   ): sentence(s) in the discussion

3. (   ): sentence(s) in the conclusion

4. (   ): topic sentence

Discussion Questions
Directions: Make notes of your ideas, but don't write every word you want to say.

1. How could you help peace organizations such as Amnesty International, the International Campaign to Ban Land Mines, and the U.N.?

2. Would you like to be a part of any of the peace organizations? Give reasons.

3. What can you do to "pursue peace"?

SAMPLE DISCUSSION ACTIVITY

Nobel Peace Prize information-gap activity (teacher key)

What country is _____ from?

When did _____ win the Nobel Peace Prize?

Who won the Prize in 19_____?

Who won the Prize for (reason) _____?

Why did _____ win the prize?

Person/Organization	Country	Date	Reason for Winning
Yasir Arafat Shimon Peres Yitzhak Rabin	Palestine Israel Israel	1994	For efforts to create peace in the Middle East
Rigoberta Menchu	Guatemala	1992	For work to gain respect for the rights of Guatemala's Indian people
Nelson Mandela Frederik de Klerk	South Africa South Africa	1993	For working to end apartheid in South Africa
Albert Schweitzer	German-born	1952	For his humanitarian work in Africa
Mikhail Gorbachev	Soviet Union	1990	For his efforts to promote world peace and reduce tension
Dalai Lama	Tibet	1989	For his nonviolent struggle to end China's rule of Tibet
Office of the UN High Commissioner for Refugees	United Nations	1981* 1954	For protecting millions of Vietnamese and other refugees
Elie Wiesel	America	1986	For his efforts to help victims of oppression and racial discrimination
Desmond Tutu	South Africa	1984	For leading a nonviolent campaign against racial segregation in South Africa
Oscar Arias Sanchez	Costa Rican	1987	For writing a plan to stop civil wars in Central America
Aung San Suu Kyi	Burma	1991	For her nonviolent struggle for democracy and human rights in Burma
Lech Walesa	Poland	1983	For his efforts to prevent violence while trying to gain workers' rights

SAMPLE WRITING ACTIVITY

Illustration Paragraph—The Pursuit of Peace

You will write an illustration paragraph about peace in this part of Unit 1. Here are some possible topics.

Illustration Paper Topic Ideas

1. One place that promotes peace

2. One group that aids refugees

3. One well-known person who has worked for peace

4. One international organization that promotes peace

5. One Japanese group that works for peace

6. Difficulties refugees face

7. Difficulties people face after a war

8. The benefits of Japan's peaceful constitution

9. (Your topic) _____

You are free to select a topic not on this list, but check with your teacher first.

Due Dates

Pre-writing is due on _____.

The rough draft is due on _____.

The final draft is due on _____.

Reminders

During this part of unit 1, you will learn how to:

- write a clear, specific topic sentence
- provide supporting details with examples and facts
- use appropriate transitions between ideas and examples
- write a concluding sentence that lets the reader know you have finished discussing your topic

We will study how to do these. Be sure to include them in the paragraph you write.

Appendix C: Student Evaluation Form (English Version) for Unit 1—Peace Studies

Class _____

	Strongly Agree			Strongly Disagree

Overall

1. My knowledge and understanding of the topic increased.

   4   3   2   1

2. My understanding of the Illustration pattern used in reading and writing improved.

   4   3   2   1

3. My understanding of the Process pattern used in reading and writing improved.

   4   3   2   1

4. My ability to participate in discussions improved.

   4   3   2   1

5. In writing, the amount of homework was appropriate.

   4   3   2   1

6. In reading, the amount of homework was appropriate.

   4   3   2   1

7. In discussion, the amount of homework was appropriate.

   4   3   2   1

Materials

8. The common course books were appropriate for my level.

   4   3   2   1

9. The common course books were interesting.

   4   3   2   1

10. Books I was assigned to read were appropriate for my level.

    4   3   2   1

11. Books I was assigned to read were interesting and informative.

    4   3   2   1

12. The content of the audio-visual materials was interesting and informative.

                                            4   3   2   1

13. The audio-visual materials were appropriate for my level.

    4   3   2   1

Class work

14. In discussion, there were sufficient opportunities for me to express my ideas.

    4   3   2   1

15. My ability to use speaking strategies (Speaking Keys) improved.

    4   3   2   1

16. In reading classes there were sufficient opportunities for me to discuss the readings.

    4   3   2   1

17. In reading classes there were sufficient opportunities for me to ask questions about the readings.

    4   3   2   1

18. In writing classes there were sufficient opportunities for me to understand the Illustration pattern.

    4   3   2   1

19. In writing classes there were sufficient opportunities for me to understand the Process pattern.

    4   3   2   1

20. In writing classes there were sufficient opportunities for me to work on improving my writing.

    4   3   2   1

Building Out and Building Within: The Development of a Communicative English Program

7

JUANITA HEIGHAM

Some of life's greatest opportunities appear suddenly and when least expected. For me, building the Communicative English Program (CEP) at Sugiyama Jogakuen University in Nagoya, Japan, has been one of those great opportunities—one I was neither expecting nor prepared for, but one that has been among the most rewarding of my career. It had a simple beginning in 2001, when I was offered the directorship of the Freshman English Program (FEP), the main developmental English component of the Department of English housed within the School of Literature. The faculty was looking for someone to revitalize a stagnant program with the hope that this revitalization would attract more students and rebuild withering enrollment caused by a steadily declining university-aged population in Japan. The directorship would be my first position that held such broad administrative duties, and I was excited about the possibilities of reworking a small program. However, after I accepted the position, what was to be a revitalization quickly became the creation of a completely new program.

In this chapter I discuss the context of the program, the development of the new program's proposal, how the curriculum evolved, and the connections that have been made during the program's 3 years. I also address methods of evaluating the program and the challenges that I experienced while working on this project.

The Curricular Context

Sugiyama Jogakuen University is a women's university that is well known in central Japan for its English language education. In 1986, when most universities throughout the country had not yet embraced the communicative approach, Sugiyama began the FEP, a semi-intensive program for English majors that applied this approach. Whereas it was, and still is, not uncommon for Japanese university students, both English majors and non-English majors, to have a single 90-minute English class each week, Sugiyama's program consisted of five. The program lasted for the duration of students' first year. The FEP had approximately 125 students who were randomly divided into six groups, and they stayed in these groups for all of their English classes. The program employed a mixture of full- and part-time teachers, but the majority of classes were taught by part-time teachers who were each assigned two classes a week.

After this 1-year program, the Department of English offered no more developmental English classes aside from an elective writing course. Beginning with the second year, students' classes focused on literature, British and U.S. culture, or linguistics and were mostly taught by Japanese instructors in Japanese. The School of Literature had a language lab, but it was not used in any capacity for the FEP or any English class. This curricular setup continued until 2000 when, in response to student complaints about having too few opportunities for developmental English, the faculty set up the fully elective Advanced English Program for sophomores and juniors. This primarily business-focused program provided courses for certificate preparation in the Test of English as a Foreign Language (TOEFL), the Test of English for International Communication (TOEIC), and Eiken, a multilevel standardized test written for Japanese students of English and recommended by the Japanese Ministry of Education. Business English, Writing and Presentation, and Listening Strategies courses were offered along with test preparation courses, all of which were generally expected to be teacher centered. There was no coordination among them.

The Motivation for the Program

In my first year as director of the FEP, I set out to collect information about the existing program, the students it served, and the teachers who taught in it. Specifically, I wanted to find out the attitudes, expectations, and goals of all the program's stakeholders. I began 2001 by giving out questionnaires to the Department of English faculty and the part-time teachers in the FEP and conducting informal interviews with students. Knowing that the teachers had heavy workloads and would not appreciate additional duties requested of them, I was reluctant to demand too much of their time, so I asked them to give written responses to simple questions or statements (described in more detail later in the chapter), which gave them the opportunity to share as much or as little as they wished.

Although only 3 of the 10 full-time faculty members taught in the FEP (all 3 were native English speakers), all faculty members were asked to answer the following question: "What is your vision for the FEP, and what do you see as its role in the department?" Two of the teachers, appearing to show little interest in the program, could not find time to respond. The completed questionnaires revealed that, due to the threats to enrollment, the department's ability to maintain its existence was the main concern for most of the faculty. In fact, one teacher wrote that the goal of the program was "to survive."

Twelve part-time teachers instructed the bulk of the developmental classes in the department, so I was particularly interested in their opinions. In general, part-time teachers in Japan are allotted two classes at a university, so they typically teach at numerous universities in their area and rarely have a voice in the design of programs in which they teach. In fact, there are few coordinated programs in which to work, and the programs that are coordinated are generally developed and maintained in a strictly top-down mode of management. Our part-time teachers were asked to describe the ideal teaching situation. I had hoped to collect some information about their philosophy of education in general as well as the kind of physical environment and equipment that would best support their teaching. All the part-time teachers submitted responses. One of them began by writing that he wanted to focus on the "ideal *learning* situation, not the ideal *teaching* situation," a comment that reflected the general attitude of the part-time teachers. Other significant comments, repeatedly seen in one form or another, include the following:

- Students should be grouped with same-level students.
- A lot of learning should take place outside of class.
- Goals for the program and courses should be set.
- Curriculum should address *five* skills—the traditional four and the skill of "critical thinking."
- The program should produce competent *users* of English.
- Students ought to know and understand where they are in their development.
- There should be more interfaculty discussion and sharing of ideas.
- Instructors from different courses should work together for special projects.
- The different classes should be integrated.

- Minimal furniture should be in the rooms; desks should be easy to arrange for group work and teacher circulation.
- Rooms should have TVs, video/DVD players, tape players, and so on.
- The language lab should be stocked and *used* for independent work.

In short, the teachers wanted students to be streamed and to develop more responsibility for their learning, and they wanted the program to be more coordinated so that students' needs could be more comprehensively met. As for facilities, they wanted audiovisual equipment in their classrooms, and they wanted desks to be arranged in a more learner-friendly configuration instead of in tight rows, as they were at that time.

When asked, most of the full- and part-time teachers were surprisingly willing to share their views in detail. In retrospect, I realize I could have collected more information without overburdening them if I had used a short series of well-focused questions instead of employing the format I used. The amount of information I received at this initial stage was smaller than it would have been had I not been hesitant to ask the teachers for their help; nevertheless, what I did receive was useful.

The questions I asked students were more extensive. They included questions about their goals, attitudes toward English, expectations of their university English education, study methods they thought were effective, and the ways they actually studied. One fourth-year student reported, "I will graduate this year but I can't speak English, so I am disappointed." Even though this was a good student who wanted to improve her English, when asked if she had ever been to the language lab to work on her English, she said she had not and even seemed surprised by the question. After reviewing the information I collected from students, two things became particularly clear. First, they were dissatisfied with their university English education; specifically, they wanted their developmental English courses to continue after their freshman year. And, second, few students felt confident learning independently.

CHANGE IN PLANS

During this first year of information gathering, the university administration decided to restructure the School of Literature, which housed the Department of English. In an attempt to improve its appeal to the growing number of internationally curious young women, the university decided to change the School of Literature into the School of Cross-Cultural Communication. As discussions and debates about this change got underway, it became apparent that the FEP, which the initial investigation had shown to be ineffective, and the Advanced English Program, which was newer but did not reflect new trends in language teaching and learning, could both be abandoned and an entirely new program could be introduced. With the encouragement of most of the Department of English faculty, I set out to propose a new program.

THE PROPOSAL

In drafting the proposal for the basic framework of the program, I was most conscious of the information gathered from students. They clearly wanted developmental English to extend beyond their freshman year, and they clearly needed learner training and independent learning opportunities. It seemed logical to assume that if students were more satisfied, they would attract others to the university and thus improve the declining enrollment that was such a dire concern of the faculty and the university administration. To address these key issues, the structure of the new program would allow developmental English classes to continue through the students' third year and would include a self-access component. The new program would consist of ten 90-minute classes: five in the first year, three in the second, and two in the third (see Table 1).

The School of Literature had an antiquated listening lab with audiotape listening stations primarily designed to be controlled by the teacher, but as mentioned earlier, it was not used by English language students. In fact, the FEP offered no training or encouragement for students to use the lab or do any independent work to help them develop learner autonomy. As Benson (2001) states, "the primary goal of all approaches to [language] learning development is to help learners become 'better' language learners. Current approaches also tend to view the development of autonomy as an integral part of this goal" (p. 144). So with a view toward updating the university's approach to language education and fostering student autonomy, one of the program proposal's recommendations was that a self-access center be built.

The proposal also stated that students would take a standardized test at the beginning of their freshman year, at the end of that year, and at the end of their remaining years at the university; based on the test results, students would be streamed. The General Tests of English Language Proficiency (G-TELP; n.d.) was selected because of its relatively low cost and the speed

Table 1. Communicative English Program Class Division

Year	Schedule				
1	Class	Class	Class	Class	Self-Access
2	Class	Class	Self-Access		
3	Class	Class			

with which its results could be returned to us. The G-TELP is an objective test that assesses general English language proficiency, as opposed to English for business or academic purposes, in language learners age 16 and older. It is designed for environments where English is not the primary language and has five levels, the top four of which are available in Japan. (Although we began using this test, we have since switched to the TOEIC Bridge for incoming freshmen and the TOEIC IP for all other students because of the wider application of these test scores for our students.)

Students entering the new program would be divided into six groups. They would stay in these groups for four of their five classes, but the Self-Access class would be a mixture of all levels. This mixture for Self-Access was necessary because if a group of similar-level students used the center together, the demand for that particular level of materials would be great and students would therefore have a narrow selection from which to choose. The grouping of students through the second year of the program would be the same, with Self-Access always being a mixed-level class. This testing and basic streaming procedure would satisfy the part-time teachers' desire for the students to be grouped according to ability level.

The finished proposal was submitted first to the Department of English (where it was approved) and then to the school restructuring committee, which included three representatives from the School of Literature and the acting chair of the university's board of trustees. The structure of the proposed program met with no resistance from the committee members, but they felt that not all students should matriculate through the 3 years of the program. They held this belief for several reasons. First, there was cost. Students at Sugiyama pay a flat rate for their classes regardless of the number they take. The university could not afford to have all students take so many additional classes without cutting others—something it did not want to do. Second, some faculty members believed that allowing all English majors to participate in the full 3-year program put too much emphasis on developmental English, detracting from the other English-focused disciplines in the department: literature, culture, and linguistics. Finally, the new Department of Foreign Studies, which was to replace the Department of English, was going to include other foreign languages, and it was felt that the proposed comprehensive program put too much focus on English, thereby diminishing the importance of other languages offered.

Thus, the committee recommended that the program be competitive, allowing only a set number of students to advance. I was opposed to this idea because I disliked the opportunity loss for late bloomers. There was considerable debate over the issue, but because there had to be a strict limit on the number of developmental English courses we could offer and the courses had historically been extremely popular, there was no way to keep the class size down if all students could elect to participate in the program throughout its 3 years.

In the end, I modified the proposal to make the program competitive, with the number of available seats decreasing every year within each cycle of the program; in the first year, 126 seats were divided into six groups; in the second year, 66 divided into three; in the third year, 44 divided into two. It was then decided that students would be invited to continue in the program, which would be elective after the first year, based on a combined score from teacher recommendations and students' year-end test results. I was not enthusiastic about this competitive change, but I understood its necessity, and with the compromise, the proposal was accepted.

The last step in the proposal process was performed outside the university. Because the program was to be part of the new School of Cross-Cultural Communication, the restructuring committee had to submit the plan to the Japanese Ministry of Education. The ministry approved it, and by July 2002 the basic foundation of the Sugiyama Jogakuen University CEP had been laid.

The Process of Designing the Curriculum

Once the skeleton of the program had been finalized, the real work began: curriculum design. The new program would begin with incoming freshmen, so although the groundwork needed to be laid for the full 3 years of the program, only the curriculum for the first year needed to be fully fleshed out right away. In my experience, what makes or breaks a semi-intensive language program is how well integrated the classes are. The pre-existing program had addressed all the major skill areas, but they were presented in detached courses, not as part of a program; there was no connection between classes, no participation from teachers in the planning of the courses (they had been assigned specific textbooks, which they had had no voice in selecting), and there was no organized communication between teachers. I wanted to create an integrated program that held excitement for teachers and students and in which different courses supported each other. I knew I could not do it alone, so I again approached the teachers in the existing program and asked them to contribute recommendations and ideas for the new curriculum. Most responded with enthusiasm. We quickly agreed that we wanted to create as learner-centered a curriculum as we could—one that covered the four skills, emphasized students' development of independence, and was integrated wherever possible, but one that would not take too much of the teachers' time to create.

Focusing on the freshman year of the program, we first agreed that each day of the week would represent a skill. For example, everyone teaching on

Monday would teach the same course. That way, teachers could collaborate on the course development more easily. Then we discussed which types of classes we would offer. At Sugiyama, the academic year is semester based, so we could offer semester or full-year courses. After numerous informal discussions at the lunch table and at social gatherings—we held no formal meetings, in part because there was no money to pay the part-time teachers for their time—we decided on the type of courses we would offer throughout the 3-year program. Table 2 shows these courses and compares them with the FEP.

COURSES

After the goals for each course were collaboratively set, teachers began to focus on materials that would facilitate reaching those goals. The teachers who decided to teach the Communicative Grammar and Reading and Writing strands of the program agreed that their courses should be text based, and they set out to choose texts and design supplementary activities. These two groups came to this decision because they felt that published materials met their needs, so they did not need to create original texts. However, teachers from other strands felt that they needed to design their own materials because of the particular nature of their courses. The teachers also devised ways to share the labor of simultaneously creating support materials and standardizing the curriculum. For example, the Communicative

Table 2. Course Comparison: The FEP and the CEP

FEP				
Listening and Speaking	Reading	Speaking and Drama	Reading and Writing	Speaking
Semester	**CEP First Year**			
1st	Communicative Grammar	Reading and Writing 1	Learner Training	Project-Based Speaking 1	Self-Access 1
2nd	Communicative Grammar	Reading and Writing 1	Drama	Project-Based Speaking 1	Self-Access 1
Semester	**CEP Second Year**			
1st and 2nd	Reading and Writing 2	Project-Based Speaking 2	Self-Access 2	
Semester	**CEP Third Year**			
1st	Reading and Writing 3	Debate		
2nd	Reading and Writing 3	Independent Projects		

Grammar teachers decided on a text with answers in the back of the book so that students could do exercises at home and check them independently. In class, the students would do communicative activities that required them to use the structures they studied. The teachers divided the weeks of the two semesters among themselves, and each teacher developed a set of activities for the relevant grammar structures covered during the weeks for which he or she was responsible. Once the activities were completed, the teachers had a partner check them. After the activities had been checked and revised, they were copied and distributed to the rest of the grammar teachers. This system allowed the teachers to focus on a relatively small design task; thus they produced high-quality work, and all of the teachers had the opportunity to creatively contribute to the standardized curriculum without being overburdened.

After we had decided to include a Learner Training course and a Drama course, each a semester long, I talked with the teachers to see who was most interested in teaching them. One teacher was quite interested because she had recently completed her master's degree and had many ideas she thought would be useful for Learner Training and because she had begun her career teaching children and had enjoyed using drama-based activities with them. It was decided that these two courses would be scheduled on the day that she already taught at Sugiyama and that she and I would plan the courses together.

As Dickinson (1992) states, "learner training . . . aims to make everyone more capable of independent learning" (p. 13), and because fostering independence was one of the program's primary goals, we believed that having a class dedicated to learner training was important. To create this course, we began by e-mailing all the teachers in the program to ask them about the most common problems their students were having in class and what learning skills they seemed to lack. We received a substantial list from teachers, and from this list we began to develop the Learner Training course. We created a wide variety of activities and consulted the teachers about the order in which the activities should be presented so that they would support, as best as possible, what was going on in other classes. Finally, we put the activities together and had them printed in book form by a local printing company. The teachers believed our in-house materials should be printed in this manner for two reasons: They felt that students should not be inconvenienced by numerous handouts and that materials should look as professional as possible so that our students, who are quite image conscious, would accept them as serious instruction.

The Drama course had a special role in the program. Sugiyama had had an English Festival since the FEP was first established. (There had been an FEP Drama course, but drama was not taught; it was called Drama because it was during this class that students prepared their plays for the festival.) The festival had been an afternoon of short student-written plays on a given theme that were performed in English. It was because of this festival that we decided to have a true Drama course. It could take advantage of the benefits that acting techniques have in improving intonation, expressiveness, and confidence, and it would provide a clear goal for students to work toward: their performance at the English Festival. We decided that this course would be content based and would teach acting techniques and principles. After reading a variety of authentic acting and drama course books, we created a group of activities, based mainly on activities found in *Acting One* (Cohen, 1984), to introduce students to acting. The Drama teachers coordinated with the Reading and Writing teachers and planned for students to write their plays in the Reading and Writing class at the beginning of the second semester, with support from the Drama teachers. Once the plays were completed, in the middle of the semester, students would apply the performance techniques they had learned and begin rehearsing their plays in Drama class; then they would perform them at the festival, which would be held at the end of the semester. All the activities and exercises created for the Drama course were compiled and again printed in book form.

The work behind Learner Training and Drama was quite collaborative, but this was somewhat less the case for the Speaking course. Several years before I was hired by Sugiyama, I had been introduced to project work, that is, "a theme and task-centered mode of teaching and learning which results from a joint scope of self-determined action for both the individual and the small group of learners within a general framework of a plan which defines goals and procedures" (Legutke & Thomas, 1991, p. 160). Within the teaching contexts I had experienced in Japan, project work had been tremendously successful and had become my method of choice for speaking classes. Because students choose the topics for their projects, the work motivates them by allowing them to use the target language to talk about topics that interest them. It also provides them with opportunities for genuine communication because each student has information that no other student has; thus students have a real reason to communicate with each other. Additionally, I wanted to use project work in the new program because I saw it as a tool to help build learner autonomy. Friend-Booth (as cited in C. Brown, 2001a) remarks that, "by its very nature, project work places the responsibility on the students, both as individuals and as members of a co-operative learning group. Autonomy becomes a fact of life" (p. 91). I asked if any other teachers had used it in their classes, and although none had, because I described the basic philosophy behind it and reported the success that I had had with it in my classes, many teachers were interested in learning more about it.

I knew of someone who could present the basics of project work and provide a good foundation for the teachers to build on, so I asked the department if I could invite him, and pay him, to give a workshop for the teachers in the program. The department had a budget for speakers, but this was the first time someone would be invited to speak primarily to part-time teachers. The faculty recognized the importance of program innovation and of demonstrating loyalty to our teachers, so they agreed. I announced the workshop to the teachers and told them that they were all welcome but not required to attend—the only people who needed to attend were the four teachers who would actually be teaching the project-based course. Nearly all the teachers attended, which showed me how eager they were to participate in the program development and, when given an opportunity, to learn in general. After the workshop, we decided that I would provide materials for the first semester so that the teachers would have a chance to gain some experience with designing projects and applying them in the classroom; then during the second semester, they would create their own.

One of the participating teachers suggested that each teacher create a single short project, present it to his or her class, and then go to another class and repeat it. Everyone agreed with this idea because they knew that their first attempt at project design would probably require considerable revision and that repeating projects in quick succession would allow for optimum refinement. When they carried out this idea, the teachers were very pleased with the results. They did not have the pressure of creating one lengthy project or several shorter projects on their own, so they were able to focus their energy on creating one quality project. Repeating the project allowed them to work out problems while the weaknesses were still fresh in their minds. In addition, having a different teacher helped diminish students' usual second-semester lethargy. I should point out that this exchange could be done because all the teachers teaching this course do so on the same day—one benefit of a small, tightly coordinated program.

While these activities were taking place, I was also working on the Self-Access Center. One of the first things I had done after coming to Sugiyama in 2001 was to begin plans for student self-access work. Not knowing that I would have the opportunity to build an entire center around this concept, I had begun work in the existing language laboratory. The lab had been allocated a small budget, and I had been able to use part of it to buy listening materials that students could use independently. Based on advice from directors of several self-access centers in Japan as well as other countries, I had selected published texts from a variety of levels that had clear instructions for students and user-friendly answer keys. Because our materials selection was quite limited, I had also asked all the teachers in the program to donate any listening texts and recordings they had but no longer needed. These two sets of materials combined totaled approximately 45 audio selections that I had separated into four levels and placed in the lab.

I had wanted students to have the chance to do extensive reading with books of their own choosing; however, there were no reading materials available in the lab and no remaining funds to purchase any. Not wanting to give up this opportunity for the students, I had begun investigating alternatives. I had found that I could use a portion of our department library budget for the main campus library, so I had purchased approximately 300 graded readers and placed them in the library. When the proposal opportunity arrived in early 2002, students were already at work in the lab in a required Self-Access course. They were able to choose level-appropriate listening materials and had extensive reading and conversation taping, recording a 20-minute English conversation with a partner each week for homework. The setup of the language lab was far from ideal; nevertheless, students responded well to the course, the first course any of the students had taken that allowed them to make choices about what they learned. From what we learned during this 1-year pilot course in the lab, we were much better prepared to make good decisions for the CEP's Self-Access Center, which was essential because the budget allotted for the setup of the new center and its future maintenance was small—there were no funds for trial and error.

During the 2002 academic year, plans for the new Self-Access Center got underway. I wanted to have a broad selection of electronic equipment, reading materials, reference resources, and conversation areas for students, but the space designated for our center was far too small for everything. This was disappointing, but having any center at all was such an improvement over the previous situation that the disappointment was short-lived. And I found that we could get an additional 300 graded readers for the library, so although the readers would not be in our center, at least students would have a wider variety of books from which to choose. We are now very happy that our readers are in the library; students have easy access to books, and we are not responsible for them. Because our program is run in many respects by "volunteers" (i.e., part-time teachers who contribute their time without compensation for nonteaching activities), that is a positive thing.

CURRICULAR CONNECTIONS

One of the primary aims in the development of the new program was to connect courses throughout each year as well as from year to year, so a considerable amount of time was spent devising ways to create this integration. One of the first steps was to provide a simple way for teachers who never saw each other to communicate. This was achieved through the addition of a teacher communication board: a whiteboard in the teachers' room where teachers leave messages for each other. It goes without saying that we regularly communicate via e-mail, but we have found that this board allows for easy communication from one group of teachers to another, and it offers greater assurance that each message is received by everyone to whom it is addressed.

Next to this board is a detailed schedule of all the courses in the program as well as a list of who teaches them. For example, Table 3 shows that the six groups of freshman are grouped in pairs, and teachers on each day teach one set of the pairs. At a glance, teachers can see who is teaching particular groups of students; if they want, for example, to have something returned to the students or to have a message relayed to them, they know which teacher to talk to. This type of exchange is encouraged in the program because it helps students see that their teachers work together, share responsibilities, and know what is going on even in classes that they do not teach. We also decided to invite teachers to teach on more than 1 day (in Table 3, the names in italics represent these teachers). Having part-time teachers teach multiple classes is not common at universities in Japan, and we had to ask the administration for special permission to make this change. Now we have part-time teachers teaching as many as eight courses spanning the 3 years of the program. This staffing change has had a positive affect on the program because the teachers who teach on different days can easily make links between classes.

First Year

As for connections within the curriculum, the most important step we took was to create a freshman student handbook. Written mostly in English but allowing difficult concepts to be explained in Japanese, the handbook includes program policies, all the first-year course syllabi, a variety of guidelines, and so on (see Appendixes A and B for excerpts from the handbook). It is used by all teachers, and students are required to bring it to every class. In a sense, it is a tangible symbol for the students that they are enrolled in a program, not simply a group of unrelated classes focused around the same subject. It is useful for teachers as well because all the basic classroom information about the five classes that students are taking is in one easy-to-access place.

Table 3. First-Year Group and Teacher Schedule

	Monday	Tuesday	Thursday	Friday	Self-Access
Groups 1 and 3	*Mary*	Steve	*Tony*	*Avril*	N/A
Groups 2 and 5	Jon	*Avril*	Lori	*Sara*	N/A
Groups 4 and 6	*Avril*	Sara	*Mary*	*Tony*	N/A

Another way that we have linked the first-year classes is through the design of the Learner Training course. After collecting information from teachers about what areas or skills the course should focus on, we built activities to address them. Learner Training includes topics such as becoming comfortable asking questions (not feeling comfortable asking questions is a serious problem among Japanese students), learning study planning and time management, learning how to use an English-English dictionary, learning how to type, understanding parts of speech, using context to understand vocabulary while reading, and learning basic note-taking skills. Many of the skills taught in this class are used in all other classes, and the rest are used in most, so this course makes immediate links throughout the program.

In addition to these connections, there are a number of smaller ways that we have integrated the classes in the first year of the program:

- All teachers are given a Grammar Study Schedule from the Communicative Grammar class so that they know what grammar structures students can be expected to use in conversation or in their writing at any given time during the year.
- Students are given vocabulary words related to classroom work in each of their classes (other than Self-Access) and are required to keep them in a vocabulary notebook. (Whenever possible, we keep the words for freshmen to those found in Waring's [2006] *Word Frequency Lists* for the 1,000 most frequent words in English and the sophomore and junior words to the 2,000 most frequent words so that the words the students learn directly build their daily communicative competence.)
- Each week students are given a short comprehensive vocabulary quiz that tests words program-wide.
- All teachers in the program use the same writing correction codes when marking students' written work.
- Writing correction/editing materials created by the Reading and Writing teachers focus on the grammar structures students have recently studied and provide a light review of structures studied earlier in the year.
- Students are taught how to type in their Learner Training class, after which all papers for the program must be typed.
- Students must follow a clear set of typing guidelines and format requirements when writing papers for any course in the program.
- The topics students choose for project presentations are used for papers and/or journal entries in their Writing class.
- Each week in Self-Access class, students are required to give a short written reflection on a different aspect of the program.
- Students write a full-page reflection on a different aspect of the program as extensive writing in their journal for Reading and Writing.

Second Year

Many of the links established during the first year are continued during the second. In fact, all guidelines and policies remain unchanged throughout the program. In addition to these preexisting connections, we tried to make the second-year curriculum grow directly out of the first.

As mentioned before, we decided early on in the program development that the Reading and Writing course would be text based. Because this course would be taught throughout the program's 3 years, we decided that it was important to use a textbook series so that students would not unnecessarily repeat things that they had learned before or miss out on things altogether by using a new, unrelated text at the start of a new year. Thus, as students progress from 1 year to the next, they move to the next book in a familiar series. Additionally, for both their first and second years, students are required to produce two pages of extensive writing—one page about a topic of their choice and the second page a reflection on some aspect of the program designated by the teachers. This reflection provides us with one means of program evaluation and is discussed in more detail later in the chapter. Other aspects of the second-year Reading and Writing course are different, but these two elements remain the same and thus link the first and second years.

In the second-year Speaking class, students continue with project work, but the projects become more learner centered and much longer. The incoming students at Sugiyama generally have high-beginning English skills, and lengthy projects with many self-directed tasks are too difficult for them. As a result, the projects used in students' first year are tightly structured and relatively short, typically only 3 weeks long, culminating in an individual presentation given at least twice to small groups. The first-year projects were created in-house and modeled after those found in *Projects From the University Classroom* (Ford & McCafferty, 2001); the second-year projects were selected from this book, so the same basic style used in the first year is continued in the second. In the second year, however, teachers play the role of guide more than leader because there is a greater opportunity for independent work among the higher level students and a single project lasts an entire semester. Even with these differences, the path of the first year flows smoothly into the second.

Self-Access, the third course taken by second-year students, is identical in in-class structure to the first year, but the homework component changes. In the first year, students do extensive reading and conversation taping for homework. In the second year, they do these assignments as well as weekly partner e-mailing and independent grammar work. The e-mailing is a completely new activity for students, but the grammar work is a continuation of sorts from their first-year Communicative Grammar course because, as already discussed, students use a grammar text that has answers in the back so that they can check their work as they move along. The familiar structure of the in-class Self-Access work and the continuation of grammar study help fulfill our aim of connecting the program across the years.

Third Year

For students' third and final year in the program, they continue with Reading and Writing and a projects course, but they no longer have a required Self-Access class. The Reading and Writing course is quite similar in design to the second year's course, with the only major change being that the length of their essays increases. On the other hand, the projects course changes significantly. In the first semester, the project theme is *debate*, and the project is similar in design to previous projects in which students have participated. However, a new homework assignment is added to projects: attendance in the Self-Access Center. Students must spend 18 hours there in their free time over the course of the semester. This is seen as a step toward greater autonomy. Students begin the program taking required classes in the center; then they must attend but in their own time; and finally, there is no requirement to attend, but they are free to use it whenever they wish.

In the second semester, students are introduced to Independent Projects. Modeled after the University of Helsinki's Autonomous Language Learning Modules (ALMS; n.d.) program, Independent Projects exercises students' language development and growing independence. Carver (as quoted in C. Brown, 2001b) points out that "just teaching new strategies to students will accomplish very little unless students want greater responsibility for their own learning" (p. 7). This course is designed to give students the opportunity to use what they have already learned and to develop confidence in directing their own learning with the hope that they will want to take control of their learning (and enjoy doing so). During Independent Projects, students work independently but must meet several basic requirements for the course:

- plan and carry out three or more learning activities designed to help them reach predetermined goals: one activity working with others, one working alone, and the third in whatever way they choose
- design some method of assessment for each activity
- keep well-organized reflections and assessment records
- account for 44 hours of study

The semester begins with two 3-hour class meetings in which students individually plan relevant and realistic course goals for themselves. This first step is done with classmates' support as well as teacher guidance, and once it is complete, the teacher collects the students' goals and groups students with similar goals so that they can work together if they choose.

Once students' goals are clearly set, they make plans for how to reach those goals both with their groups and alone. Here they can draw on their own creativity and all of the skills and methods they have practiced over the previous two and a half years in the program. During this second semester, students are no longer required to visit the Self-Access Center, but with their previous training, students know how to use the center and have the opportunity to see the benefits that can be derived from using it. The program is just beginning its fourth year, so we have only offered Independent Projects once, but during the first run of the course, nearly all the students used the center in some capacity while working on their projects.

The Independent Projects teachers meet with students individually three times during the semester, but regular classes are not held; students work completely independently. During the first meeting, students' goals and plans are examined and modified, if necessary. The purpose of the second meeting is to review what students have been doing to be sure that they are completing their plan and working steadily toward their goals. It is also an opportunity for students to revise their plans if they desire. The final meeting is a time of overall review and reflection. At any time during the semester, students are welcome to visit their teacher for advice or to modify their goals and plans. Although this course is entirely new to students, it draws on previous experiences and learning from the program, so even here there are important connections at work.

Challenges

Overall, the design and implementation of the program has been relatively smooth, but there have been a few troubles along the way. One has to do with the full-time faculty members. The department requires full-time native-English-speaking teachers to participate in the program. As a result, they are not free agents; they must teach the curricula on which the CEP team of teachers decides. Because the program has expanded to 3 years, more of their classes are now under the CEP umbrella. Whereas many of the part-time teachers have put considerable time and effort into their work for the program, the full-time teachers have been less enthusiastic. Periodically their lack of interest has had a negative affect on the program; from time to time a full-time teacher has been known to quietly go against group-decided policies, which has caused frustration for the part-time teachers, who see corners being cut by people getting paid for more than just the hours spent in the classroom. This has not been a serious problem because, in general, everyone gets along quite well, but it is one worth mentioning, and we hope it will improve as we continue our collaborative efforts.

Another problem that we have experienced in the program is different philosophies on the teaching of reading. Along with the CEP, freshmen may take introductory courses in literature, linguistics, and British and U.S. culture. Although most of these courses are taught by Japanese teachers in Japanese, many of the teachers use authentic English texts. (It is common in Japan for authentic texts to be used in many subjects related to English—regardless of students' English level.) Thus, most, if not all, of the English reading assigned to students by Japanese instructors in our department is intensive in nature. It is not uncommon for students to look up one quarter of the words on a single page of reading for these classes. In the CEP, we promote extensive reading, and students have been confused by these different approaches—especially because, as a rule, they have only done intensive reading prior to entering our program. Students tend to want to read above their level because they feel that reading at their level is not a proper challenge. We have tried to clearly explain to students the difference between the two reading styles and why we have them read extensively. We hope that this explanation will help them understand that there are different ways to approach reading and that each method can be appropriate given the right context, but that to increase the efficiency of their learning, they should read at their own level whenever possible.

Creating this innovative program at a conservative Japanese university has been challenging. Whereas the administration understands that teachers today need video equipment in their classrooms and willingly allocated funds from the budget to purchase TVs, video recorders, and DVD players for each of the five classrooms used by the CEP, it had significant trouble allowing us to move desks. The traditional classroom in Japan is tightly packed with rows of desks. Luckily for us, those desks were not bolted to the floor—unlike at many universities in Japan. We wanted to arrange the 60 desks in the five classrooms in a horseshoe shape so that students could group themselves easily and teachers could still address them conveniently. When I asked the administration if we could do this, they said we could do whatever we wanted while we were in the classroom. They meant that we could move the desks before each class began and return them when it was over. The administration's recommendation was not realistic because even the most dedicated teachers and students would tire of such a task, and in the end, the desks would stay in the teacher-centered row configuration. The administrators' concern was that teachers not teaching in the CEP but using the same rooms might not like the new arrangement of the desks. This was a valid concern, but when we looked at the schedule, we saw that these rooms were used by only a few teachers who were not part of the program. With the support of the department chair, we addressed each of the non-CEP teachers who were scheduled in our rooms and asked if they would mind the change in desk arrangement. Of those who did, we asked if they would be willing to be rescheduled in a different room. Everyone agreed, and now the desks are set in the horseshoe shape and our teachers and students are much happier.

Evaluation

The CEP is evaluated in several ways. We have university-wide, computer-tabulated evaluations; a program-designed evaluation system called Share Your Comments Week; student-teacher conferences once a month with first- and second-year students in Self-Access class; and students' written journal reflections on different aspects of the program.

The university-wide evaluations are the least useful; because they serve the entire campus, they must be quite general. To gain more germane information from students during each semester, we established Share Your Comments Week, during which students can voluntarily put comments or suggestions in a box just after midterm. Collecting information from students at this time allows us to make recoveries during the term if there are significant problems, instead of learning about troubles after a course has ended. When a change is needed, the group or groups of teachers who will be affected by it are consulted, and they make a decision together about how to make the change. Doing so maintains administrative transparency and enables teachers to participate in the continued evolution of the program. An example of a change we made based on student comments relates to the Self-Access class. Students complained that the TVs at the workstations were too close, and watching them hurt their eyes. The teachers decided to purchase large clipboards so that students could move out from their desks but still have a writing surface. Problem solved.

Another means of evaluation is the student-teacher conferences held once a month in Self-Access class. During these conferences, teachers meet with each of their students and discuss the student's progress and problems. The teachers make note of points that they think are important and share them with the other teachers in the program either on the communication board, directly with the teachers, or with me.

Finally, our best means of evaluation is the reflections that students write for extensive writing practice in their Reading and Writing classes. Each week the students are given a different aspect of the program to reflect on. The teachers collect these reflections and pass them on to the relevant teacher, who reads them, comments on them, and then returns them to the students. The result is that each month, every teacher gets a set of reflections about his or her class and has the opportunity to address student concerns promptly. We have found this process to be extremely beneficial for students' and teachers' development as well as for the ongoing improvement of the program.

Conclusion

The creation of the Sugiyama Communicative English Program has been hard work, but it has been, and continues to be, an amazing journey for me. With the help of many dedicated teachers, the program is now running strong at the start of its fourth year. Through various channels, we are regularly getting useful—and, I am pleased to note, often very positive—feedback about it. For example, one third-year student commented, "Through Independent Project I could find out not only my English's weak points but also the one of myself, so that I could improve both, which I really appreciate." Another student remarked, "To tell the truth, I had NOT studied too hard when I was a high school student. . . . However, I could change. After I entered Sugiyama, I changed to be a real English learner." Additionally, as a result of the comprehensive training in the program, students are developing a critical eye toward their education, and many provide us with candid and often perceptive suggestions on ways to improve the program to better meet their needs. Moreover, many are making perceptive observations about their own learning. A particularly insightful comment came from a third-year student reflecting on her experience in the Independent Projects class: "After I chose materials to use for the project, I could keep studying by myself, however I felt the Independent Project was homework for me. It's not real self study, is it?"

Technically, she was right—it was homework. Nevertheless, we hope that participating in our program laid a solid foundation for her, and for all our students, so that in the future they will be able to practice "real" self-study with the tools we have helped them develop.

The success and satisfaction displayed by CEP students has been encouraging; it has given both the faculty of the Department of Foreign Studies and the university administration a new sense of hope during a time of extreme, and for some universities lethal, competition. This means that the ongoing building and refinement of the program is likely to receive their continued support. At present, the future of the Sugiyama Communicative English Program is brimming with provocative opportunities for students and teachers alike.

Appendix A: How to Build Your Vocabulary Notebook

[Note: This information is presented to students in Japanese.]

This explanation is to help you use your vocabulary notebook more effectively. When you find a word that you don't know, you should follow these steps:

1. Look up the new word in your English-English dictionary. If you understand the definition well, write it in your vocabulary notebook *in English*. If you don't understand the definition, DON'T WRITE IT. Instead, you should . . .

2. Look it up in your English-Japanese dictionary. After you understand the meaning . . .

3. Try to write one of the following:

    a. a simple English definition IN YOUR OWN WORDS
        fireworks—<n> fire designs in the sky, usually in summer

    b. some examples in English that help you understand it
        author—<n> Natsume Soseki, Mark Twain

    c. a sentence in English that will help you understand it
        fabulous—<adj> My mother is a fabulous cook.

    If you can't think of any English to help you understand the meaning of the new word, then . . .

4. Write the meaning in Japanese.

Note:

Most of your definitions should be in English.

All the meanings should be on the **right side** of your book (not immediately beside the word on the left).

You should add the part of speech in the space provided < >.

n = noun	adj = adjective
v = verb	adv = adverb

You should study your vocabulary a little bit most **EVERY DAY** because studying vocabulary for small amounts of time frequently is better than studying once or twice a week for a long time. Also, you should practice using the words—vocabulary that you know but can't *use* has no value.

If you have any questions about this explanation, please **ask your teacher**. From now on, you will be expected to build your vocabulary notebook in this style and you will be graded on it.

Appendix B: Learning Plan

Organized and active learners are the most successful. To help yourself learn English better, you are going to make a Learning Plan. You will make goals about how much and how often you will study. You need to divide your time among different skills, and remember, studying several times a week for short times is MUCH BETTER than studying once a week for a long time. On this sheet you will make a plan to help you become an organized and active learner. Look at the example below and then design a plan for yourself. *Important note: **be realistic**.*

Area	*Goal!* How much will I study each week?	How many times will I study this? When will I study? For how long each time?	Did you keep your goals?				
Extensive Reading	*1 hour & 30 min*	*1. Mon 3rd period – 45 min* *2. Sat morning – 45 min*	Y N	Y N	Y N	Y N	Y N

Area	*Goal!* How much will I study each week?	How many times will I study this? When will I study? For how long each time?	Did you keep your goals?				
Grammar Study			Y N	Y N	Y N	Y N	Y N
Reading & Writing			Y N	Y N	Y N	Y N	Y N
Journal Writing			Y N	Y N	Y N	Y N	Y N
Extensive Reading			Y N	Y N	Y N	Y N	Y N
Vocabulary Study			Y N	Y N	Y N	Y N	Y N
Projects		*regular week:* *presentation week:*	Y N	Y N	Y N	Y N	Y N
Other:			Y N	Y N	Y N	Y N	Y N

If you don't keep your goals, ask yourself the following question. Which should change: my goals or my study habits?

Curriculum Design: Furniture for a College EFL Program

8

GREGORY STRONG

Fourteen years ago, a coworker and I started the Integrated English Program (IEP) in the English Department at Aoyama Gakuin University, a well-known private institution in Tokyo with some 20,000 students. At a university whose origins stretch back to several Methodist-Episcopalian missionary schools started in 1874, the English Department wanted to uphold its reputation for language teaching expertise. It hoped to improve the language skills of approximately 650 freshmen and sophomores in the English Department who would be taking courses in British literature, U.S. literature, and linguistics.

Until our arrival, the 36-member department had organized language teaching along fairly typical lines for Japan. Each of the four skill areas had a freshman and sophomore year. Native English speakers, mostly part-time or adjunct faculty, taught Oral English I and II and were given a brief outline of the courses and a list of suggested textbooks by a faculty coordinator. Native English speakers also taught Composition II, a course that might or might not include essay writing and the use of sources. Japanese teachers were responsible for Reading I and II, Listening Comprehension I and II (which were delivered in a language lab), and Composition I (teaching writing through the grammar-translation method). In these classes, Japanese was the language of instruction. On the positive side, the department had already recognized that Oral English and Composition classes should be limited in size to 25 students instead of the 50–75 students often found in similar classes at other universities.

Before we could do anything, our first problem was communications. The language courses were taught by 5 faculty members and 45 part-time teachers on two campuses, 5 days a week, in the mornings and afternoons. How would we share ideas and, in those days before widespread access to e-mail, even circulate notices? Recalling *pigeonholes*, or teachers' mailboxes that I had seen elsewhere, I suggested buying a plastic mailbox with a drawer for each instructor and placing it alongside a bulletin board outside the department office. Resistance came from every direction. No one would use it. Student papers left there would be stolen. A mailbox in the hall would become a fire hazard. Finally, when the cleaning staff complained that the mailbox would get in the way of their vacuum cleaner, I told my coworker, "If we can't get this done, we won't be able to change anything." So we pressed even harder for the mailbox, and finally the department chairman approved it.

One day, two movers carted in a large, custom-built, wooden mailbox that stood more than a meter high and two meters across. This grand piece of furniture held 60 mail slots and had been artfully assembled without the aid of finishing nails. I turned to the secretary in some alarm. She whispered, "Don't ask the price." We put teachers' names on it and sent out notices, the students left assignments, and within days, everyone used it and forgot all their complaints. Then we understood: We had some ambitious curricular innovations planned, and we would know when we succeeded. Everyone would find them as useful and as effective as the new office furniture.

Drawing upon our experience, this chapter describes the evolution of that EFL program. Important components in the development process of the IEP include (a) the institutional context, (b) the scheduling and placement of our students, (c) the articulation of IEP goals and learning outcomes, (d) program evaluation and development, and (e) IEP administration and teacher support.

The Institutional Context

Our situation at Aoyama Gakuin University was an unusual one because curriculum change on this scale is infrequent in Japan. And in charge of it were two young, very junior, newly hired faculty members. In addition, it was not like language teaching at Canadian or U.S. universities, where we would be relegated to a university-affiliated language institute or a continuing education department. We were *sennin koushi,* or full-time lecturers, with a tenure track to the rank of professor, full members of an academic department with all the rights and privileges of university professors. This was because English has such a prominent position in Japanese education.

According to Takanashi (2004), 90% of Japanese students begin studying English in junior high school, and the national curriculum stipulates a minimum of 3 hours of classroom study per week. At the tertiary level, English is an examinable subject on most college and university entrance exams, and it is taught in many university faculties.

In our department, the impetus for change came from the chairman, a number of senior Japanese professors, several U.S. professors, and some of the younger Japanese faculty, particularly one professor who had completed his PhD in the United States, taught Japanese there, and thus been exposed to communicative language teaching. My coworker, a Canadian who had previously taught in a Japanese university and had excellent communication skills, was brought to the department as the IEP coordinator. Then I followed—another Canadian with cross-cultural university teaching experience—to assist in program management and to write course materials. We both had a full teaching load as well. Initially, to provide limited assistance as well as to keep an eye on us, an IEP Committee was formed, and it was headed by a senior professor and four associate professors. We had to convince the committee of the merit of an idea, then advocate it to the department, and in some cases, even take it to the university administration.

Designing the New Curriculum

SCHEDULING AND PLACEMENT OF STUDENTS

We wanted to provide students with semester-length courses in their freshman and sophomore years that would integrate the four skills into a single 90-minute language class with the same teacher for 4 days a week. That was the origin of the *Integrated English* name for our program. Language teaching in the department was to become more like an immersion course with frequent exposure to English as the sole language of classroom instruction. It was the intuitive way to teach a language and would be closer to the circumstances in which language is acquired. Peregoy and Boyle (2005) make the case for an integrated skills curriculum: "The relationships among listening, speaking, reading and writing are mutually supporting and contribute to the reservoir of second language knowledge which is then available for other acts of listening, speaking, reading or writing" (p. 121).

But the plan proved impractical for a couple reasons. First, most of the teachers in the program, both native English speakers and native Japanese speakers, were adjunct faculty, and the Japanese teachers were not comfortable teaching in English. If we had hired more native English speakers, there would have been a large disparity between their numbers and the Japanese teachers, some of whom were graduates of the English Department. Second, because most of our teaching personnel were part-time, they would have had to commute as much as 2 hours per day, four times a week, just to teach one 90-minute class. They also would have had to quit some of their part-time classes at other universities to have the time to commute to our university. With our part-time teachers carrying 14 to 20 classes per week at four or five different universities, none would have agreed to this loss of income. We compromised by creating a schedule with a double-period IE Core class of 180 minutes on one day, taught by a native-English-speaking teacher and integrating all four language skills; an IE Listening class on a second day, taught by a Japanese instructor; and an IE Writing class on a third day, taught by a Japanese teacher or a native English speaker. Each course was taught over the course of a 14-week semester.

The second innovation we sought was to stream our students into different levels of language ability in the IEP. The mixed levels in the existing Oral English courses frustrated the students and the teachers alike. Up to this time, all students had taken Oral English I no matter how well they spoke English; each of the 2 years of the department's language courses was a credit requirement from which a student could not be excused. However, the idea of streaming students immediately encountered some legitimate cultural objections. In Japan, elementary and high school students are almost always taught in large classes of mixed ability, so streamed or leveled classes appeared elitist, even seeming like a disincentive to students with weaker skills. It took all our persuasiveness to win over the IEP Committee, the English Department, and the university administration to the idea that streamed classes challenged the strongest students, protected the weaker ones from embarrassment, and made it easier for teachers to plan and to provide effective instruction.

Ultimately, the university agreed to establish three different levels of the IE Core, IE Writing, and IE Listening courses. The IE I level would serve advanced beginners who were often graduates of high schools where they had rarely spoken or listened to English at all. IE II would be for students with low-intermediate ability. The top level, IE III, would accommodate the strongest students, including returnees (i.e., Japanese students who had returned to Japan after studying in high schools in other countries where the language of instruction had been English). The students at the IE I level would progress to IE II, then to IE III, improving their language skills along the way. Once students completed the IE III level, they would be allowed to choose a semester-length seminar from a variety of topics in literature, linguistics, or communications.

Next, we had to choose a test to stream students into the three levels of the program. Unfortunately, we never convinced our colleagues to give us the time and support we needed to write, pilot, and administer a placement test that would have fit with the learning objectives we were developing for the program. Instead, we purchased an off-the-shelf placement test, the McGraw-Hill Comprehensive English Language Test for Learners of English (CELT; see D. Harris & Palmer, 1986). Some years later, pressure for a test with greater face validity led the department to adopt the norm-referenced Test of English as a Foreign Language (TOEFL) Institutional Testing Program (ITP; Educational Testing Service, 1998), with its multiple-choice items on listening, grammatical structure, and reading. An inexpensive version of the TOEFL for low-intermediate to advanced students of ESL, the ITP provided results within 3 to 5 days of students taking it and could be administered by student aides. Because it had the features of the TOEFL, the ITP grew popular with students in our program, who viewed it as practice for a test that many of them planned to take later in their university education.

However, some students with good speaking abilities or who failed to complete the test were inappropriately placed in lower classes. More important, the test items never reflected our program goals, including improving students' speaking and essay-writing abilities. And every now and then, one of our Japanese colleagues argues for testing students with the ITP at the end of our 2-year program to rate their progress and to evaluate the efficacy of the IEP. This would be the ultimate irony: that a placement test chosen for convenience ended up evaluating our program.

ARTICULATION OF IEP GOALS AND LEARNING OUTCOMES

Now that we had a schedule and three courses, we had to create program goals for the IEP and learning outcomes and course materials for IE Core, IE Listening, and IE Writing. Good program design should begin with a thorough needs assessment and an orderly development process (J. D. Brown, 1995; Richards, 2001). However, Brown concedes that "it's often the case that needs analysis, the formation of goals and objectives, the articulation of tests, and the delivery of instruction are all going on at the same time" (p. 217). That is exactly what happened to us. After our protracted negotiations over the schedule and placement test, we had only 6 months left in the academic year to do everything else.

We raced to articulate the IEP goals—the philosophical and pedagogical framework of the program. The overall goals we set were to increase students' understanding and appreciation of English literature and linguistics and to improve their English skills in order to enhance their employment prospects. We aimed for an affective dimension, trying to foster a positive attitude among students toward language learning and greater confidence in using English. In IE Core, we hoped to provide them with the tools to become better readers and critics of literature, opportunities for self-expression and greater self-awareness, and a measure of linguistic fluency in discussions of contemporary issues and in journals of personal writing shared with their peers. In IE Listening, we wanted to sensitize students to the distinctions between different genres of listening and to encourage them to become more active listeners who are prepared to make predictions and to construct meanings. In IE Writing, we wished to impart knowledge of academic writing in paragraphs and essays in such genres as classification, compare-contrast, and persuasion, and to enable students to research and write an academic essay.

A THEME-BASED APPROACH

The new schedule left us with the problem of unifying three different courses and the efforts of three different teachers. We found a way to connect them through content-based instruction, linking the three courses through common themes that would also help integrate the skills of speaking, reading, listening, and writing in our IE Core classes (Brinton, Snow, & Wesche, 1989). Furthermore, a theme-based curriculum promised to be interesting to our students, who had already had several years of instruction in English in high school, mainly in grammar, and in reading. We selected four different themes for each level of the IEP: in IE I, memories, urban life, food, and travel; in IE II, changing times, the workplace, geography, and biography; and in IE III, relationships, cross-cultural values, the environment, and the media. We did this to knit together language skills and to motivate students more than they would be in traditional learning contexts, in which each skill is studied through exercises and activities (see Figure 1).

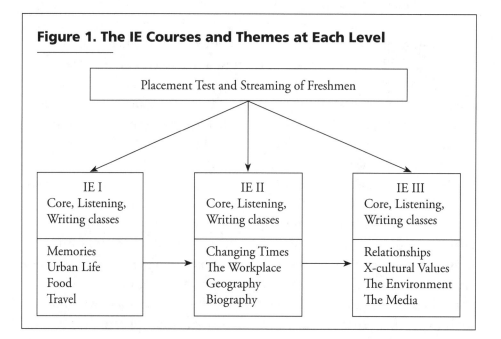

Figure 1. The IE Courses and Themes at Each Level

In IE Core, the use of themes helped pull together the variety of different skill-related activities taking place in a 180-minute class. For example, we employed the themes to link the four skills in the IE Core I course in the following way. A teacher distributed magazine photographs of different types of food to each student. Students worked individually at first and then in groups, speaking and listening, to name the food in the photographs and classify it in terms of color, texture, cost, or healthiness. Later, the teacher assisted the class in listing the names of different foods and the food categories on the blackboard. Afterward, small groups of students were asked to prepare questions such as "What kind of food is it?" or "What color is it?" Then students worked in pairs, using these questions to guess the food depicted in one another's photographs. The gamelike nature of the activity motivated students and helped them remember the vocabulary. The teacher also used additional listening work, such as encouraging students to anticipate the directions for a recipe by making predictions and then, after hearing the teacher or a recording provide the recipe, trying to list the verbs in the explanation and trying to reconstruct it. To consolidate the vocabulary introduced in class, the teacher gave a homework assignment in which students had to write a paragraph about the food in their photographs or the recipe that they had heard.

For the next part of the unit on the food theme, the IE Core teacher employed a reading activity, using a cartoon to pique students' interest and then giving them an article about healthy diets. The teacher encouraged them to make predictions about the article and to write these down. As part of this prereading activity, students checked their predictions by scanning the article for names of foods and statistics related to different diets; then they skimmed the article for its main ideas. After each process, they worked with a partner to compare their results, and for homework the teacher prompted students to reread the article and summarize it. For an additional speaking and listening activity, they were asked to prepare a role play in class about a doctor and a patient with a bad diet. In so doing, they further consolidated the vocabulary, linguistic, and content-area knowledge they had gained from this IE Core I unit (see Table 1 on p. 160).

Besides linking the activities in the IE Core class, the themes also connected the three IE courses to one another (see Figure 2 on p. 160). The IE Core I class provided students with vocabulary and content knowledge about food, which was recycled into their IE Listening and IE Writing courses. This knowledge contributed to the background knowledge that is so helpful in listening comprehension, according to researchers such as Chamot and O'Malley (1994). For example, in the prelistening phase of a food unit in IE Listening I, the listening teacher showed a video sequence of two customers ordering food in a restaurant, without sound, and asked the

Table 1. IE Core I: Integrating the Four Skills
With the Food Theme

Skills	Activities
Writing	1. Prewriting: classifying photos, listing categories, brainstorming vocabulary 2. Paragraph writing
Speaking	3. Brainstorming questions (e.g., What colour is it? What kind of food is it?) 4. Information-gap speaking activity
Listening	5. Selective listening for question words and key phrases 6. Listening for names and classifying terms such as size, texture, and cost
Reading	7. Prereading: making predictions about content, scanning, and skimming 8. Reading, answering comprehension questions, and summarizing the article

students to guess the situation from the context, identify the types of food, describe them with adjectives, and determine the characters' reactions to the meal. Pairs of students compared their analyses of the video, and then the teacher replayed the video with sound so that the students could check their answers. On a second viewing with sound, the teacher asked students to predict information such as the names of dishes at the restaurant, particularly

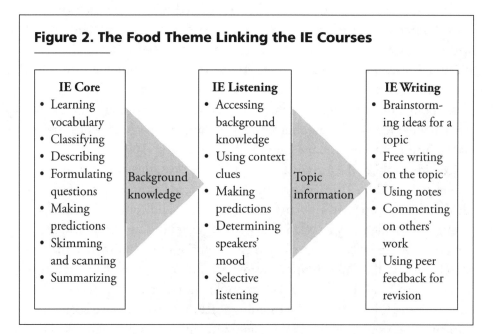

Figure 2. The Food Theme Linking the IE Courses

IE Core
- Learning vocabulary
- Classifying
- Describing
- Formulating questions
- Making predictions
- Skimming and scanning
- Summarizing

Background knowledge

IE Listening
- Accessing background knowledge
- Using context clues
- Making predictions
- Determining speakers' mood
- Selective listening

Topic information

IE Writing
- Brainstorming ideas for a topic
- Free writing on the topic
- Using notes
- Commenting on others' work
- Using peer feedback for revision

the dishes ordered, their price, and the customers' reactions to the food. Then students listened to the tape for the answers to these questions. Afterward, they compared answers with one another and listened to the scene again, discussing their answers with the teacher. Finally, the teacher showed them a transcript of the conversation.

The food theme was then introduced into the IE Writing I course as a writing topic. According to Tedick (1990), topic knowledge is an important factor in the writing performance of ESL students. There was also carryover of vocabulary from the other two courses, so the names of foods and their descriptions that were introduced in IE Core and recycled in IE Listening were included in the students' preparations for writing a compare-contrast paragraph. The teacher explained the process of brainstorming and successive drafts in terms of the process approach to writing. In small groups, students brainstormed different types of foods and the adjectives, verbs, and categories used to describe them. They engaged in freewriting to develop their own ideas about the contrasts between two different types of food. Then they retrieved the notes they had written earlier and the summaries of their reading, and they introduced parts of these into long descriptive paragraphs. Then they took their paragraphs home to complete them. In the following class, they read, rated, and discussed one another's paragraphs, and then revised them.

USING COMMERCIAL AND AUTHENTIC LEARNING MATERIALS

Given the fact that we had to create a new program in such a short period of time, plus meet our own teaching demands, we only had time to create teacher syllabi with program goals and some learning outcomes in those early years, and we could not produce many of the teacher materials we needed for the new program. Brinton, Snow, and Wesche (1989) suggest that, if chosen carefully, textbooks and other commercially produced language teaching materials can augment course syllabi and other materials specially prepared for a language program. The authors describe how this is especially true if the following criteria are used:

- Does the language curriculum focus on skill attainment (e.g., grammatical accuracy) which might be best served by the use of commercial materials?
- Would the use of a commercial textbook as a supplement to photocopied materials give the course more face validity for students?
- Would the use of a commercial textbook as a supplement help to alleviate the materials development burden faced by teachers?
- Are commercially-produced textbooks available which contain passages

(e.g., readings or exercises based on a specific text) from the content area of the course?

- Alternately, are commercial content-based materials available in the discipline of choice which could be supplemented by additional authentic materials? (p. 92)

For the IE Core courses, we selected two commercially produced textbooks that met these criteria. One of them combined writing, listening, speaking, and reading activities and included audio recordings of conversations and minilectures as well as a videotape of short dramatic sketches based on the units in the textbook. The other textbook, a reader, consisted of a variety of short passages: timed readings, poems, captioned cartoons, charts and diagrams, newspaper and magazine articles, essays, and short stories. Altogether, there was enough material for all three levels of the IE Core course. The textbooks also made it easy for teachers to assign homework, which was essential in such a short course in which students only had 20 contact hours throughout the entire semester.

For IE Writing and IE Listening, we used a combination of authentic materials and a textbook. For each of the three levels of IE Listening, we purchased 10 documentaries and dramas to match the themes at each level, and we prepared questions and activities to be completed before, during, and after listening to the video. For IE Writing, we gave the teachers the option of using a text that contained sample paragraphs and essays or using their own materials.

During the next few years, we expanded these learning materials. To our course syllabi, we added a scope and sequence, worksheets, and a list of resources, and we published contributions from teachers in the program as well as many samples of students' work in a student resource book. We also incorporated an extensive reading component in the IE Core class. Each semester, students choose two books from several thousand high-interest readers from a variety of commercial publishers. The readers are abridged versions of classic novels or books based on contemporary films and TV and are graded for difficulty by vocabulary and length. We placed them in a specific area of the library where they could be easily accessed by students. Finally, we established a resource centre with Internet access in the English Department office and stocked it with a collection of authentic listening materials such as songs, TV programs, feature movies, magazines, and newspapers. Extra copies of individual teacher syllabi and additional reference materials were left in the resource center as well.

A TASK-BASED FRAMEWORK

Despite these improvements, we identified two major problems with the IEP. First, we lacked any objective measures to assess student progress in the IE Core courses. This was not a problem in the other two courses because IE Listening incorporated a midterm and a final exam, and in IE Writing, students had to produce paragraphs and essays that were graded. Second, the activities seemed too similar at all three levels of the IE Core and IE Listening courses. Once again, the IE Writing course was not a problem because students learned different genres of writing at the various levels. For the IE Core and IE Listening courses, however, we needed to identify activities at each of the levels that were distinct from one another.

In 1998, after suggestions from a colleague who was active in research on second language acquisition, we began to formulate a task-based approach to language teaching. There was considerable variation in the literature about the definition of a *task*, but for our purposes, we employed the terms *pedagogical* and *real-world*. Richards (2001, p. 162) suggests the same breakdown of tasks. Pedagogical tasks are those that deal with information gaps, problem solving, decision making, exchange of opinions, jigsaw listening, and jigsaw reading, which were already used in our program. Real-world tasks, on the other hand, as the name implies, are those that are useful in the real world outside class; they might be part of an assignment in another course or be important to students who are planning to pursue an advanced degree. We identified these tasks and tried to establish specific standards of measurement so that we could assess whether or not students had achieved mastery of them. In our educational context, one of the most important real-world tasks was the ability to participate in a discussion. Students had to acquire sufficient English and enough confidence in using it to express their ideas and opinions in a small group.

DEVELOPING A REAL-WORLD DISCUSSION TASK

We had introduced small-group discussion in the first few years of the program because students had expressed their dissatisfaction with the speaking component of the IE Core course. They had found the discussion exercises in their textbooks to be uninteresting, and they had wanted to talk about things that were more meaningful to them. However, they had lacked the content knowledge in English to participate in or lead a free discussion on most topics, so several teachers in the program started assigning topics to students in advance so that they could prepare for a small-group discussion beforehand by reading and making notes on the topic.

Before we formulated the discussion activity as a task, we reviewed the research on student discussion in EFL/ESL classes. That review revealed that very little had been written in this area, although there was consensus about its importance in postsecondary education in the United States. In a large English for academic purposes (EAP) survey at four tertiary institutions in California, Ferris and Tagg (1996) found high levels of concern among 234 content-area instructors about ESL students' lack of interaction with others and their unwillingness to participate in class discussions or respond to questions. A subsequent study by Ferris (1998) disclosed similar apprehension among 476 ESL students at three tertiary institutions; these students reported that they found it difficult to answer questions in class and to take part in small-group discussions.

Many textbooks professed to teach students how to participate in a discussion, but there was no research evidence that any specific approach or methodology was more effective than another. We decided to develop one of our own, to teach small-group discussion and then evaluate it. We started working on the problem by videotaping students engaging in a discussion, viewing their discussions, and categorizing their discussion behaviours. We found four main aspects (gestures, eye contact, speech actions, discussion content), and we created a 3-point performance scale for IE I and IE II to evaluate these discussion behaviours; higher scores indicated better discussion behaviours (see Table 2).

To determine whether or not the discussion task was improving students' discussion abilities, Robinson, Strong, Whittle, and Nobe (2001) operationalized two methods of teaching students how to participate in small-group discussions over the course of 10 hours of instruction. The first method was derived from Willis's (1996) cycle of task-based teaching, which includes pretask, task, and posttask phases. Two classes of students reviewed notes on a topic, took part in a small-group discussion that was recorded,

Table 2. Performance Scale for IE 1 and IE II Discussions

Score	Discussion Behaviours			
	Gestures	Eye Contact	Speech Actions	Discussion Content
3	Both arms and head used to communicate	Frequent eye contact with other speakers	Turn taking, agreement, and disagreement	Examples used to support a position
2	Pointing, nodding, and turning	Most eye contact with one speaker	A few phrases used to initiate or end turns	One or two unsupported points made
1	Little body language	Limited eye contact	Almost no turn-taking language	Very little said

and then analyzed their performance by listening to comments from peers and their teacher and reviewing the recording themselves. They repeated that cycle several times. The second method was a traditional skill-based one in which two classes of students worked mostly in pairs as their teachers taught them discussion skills such as agreeing, disagreeing, exemplifying points, and turn taking. There were no small-group discussions. There was also a control group for this study, which included two classes that used the speech activities in a conversation textbook. The pretask and posttask phases for the groups consisted of participating in a discussion that was videotaped and then being given blind ratings by IE Core teachers who had been trained to use the performance scale.

We found that both the task-based and skill-based groups showed significant increases in student eye contact and use of gestures, in contrast to the group that used the textbook conversation exercises. Given the opportunity to engage in small-group discussion activities, students improved their abilities, perhaps due to their increased confidence and frequent participation in discussions or, in the second group, to activities similar to discussion. There was no improvement for the control group. There were also significant increases in student language production in the two experimental groups.

The experiment validated the use of a task-based methodology in the IE Core course. Afterward, we combined elements of the skill-based and task-cycle approaches into a methodology that could be introduced into all three levels of IE Core. We established differences between the levels in two ways. First, there was the source of the discussion topics. In IE Core I, students brainstormed topics in class and prepared notes for them at home. In IE Core II, students were required to listen to the news on TV or the radio in English or in Japanese, or to read a newspaper article in either language, and to provide a summary as background for their discussion. For IE Core III, students read and summarized an article from an English-language newspaper and then discussed it. Second, we employed an expanded 4-point performance scale for IE III small-group discussions to reflect the higher student abilities at this level. The fourth point was awarded for gestures, eye contact, speech actions, and discussion content that was more like the performance of native English speakers.

The following semester, we introduced the small-group discussion task into the IE Core I, II, and III syllabi and provided teachers with a number of workshops about using the task in class and rating students on the performance scales. We copied the videotapes we had used in the experiment for teachers to show to their classes.

We also defined two other tasks for all three levels of IE Core: writing a book review and writing a journal. Writing a book review was a real-world task because some students aimed to become English teachers and professors. For the review, they analyzed a book with regard to plot, setting, viewpoint, conflict, climax, symbolism, irony, and theme, and they prepared written reports. To turn this activity into a task, we collected sample book reports, had teachers rate them, and created a performance scale for each level of the IE Core course. We differentiated among the three levels in terms of not only the length of the book students were required to read but also their written reports on the books, so that the higher the level, the more detail, analysis, and use of literary terms we expected to see from students. The second real-world task was to maintain a journal of personal writing to communicate with a partner. Here, we differentiated between the levels of the course based on the length and sophistication of the students' journals; at the higher levels, they responded to movies, expressed opinions about literature, and generally moved beyond the lower level task of simply creating a diary of weekly activities. Again, we organized workshops for IE teachers to review and rate the journals using performance scales.

Ultimately, we found that there were limitations to language learning tasks as an organizing principal in our curriculum. So we decided on themes to help link the IE Core, IE Listening, and IE Writing courses. By doing so, we basically employed a hybrid curriculum with both themes and tasks (see Figure 3). This was not as unusual as it might seem. Both content-based and task-based curricula provide a learning environment in which students use language for genuine communicative purposes (Eskey, 1997). However, content by itself is not as important for students in an academic setting as is learning various academic tasks. Carson, Taylor, and Fredella (1997) support this idea: "Task-based EAP also requires mastery of content, but it is the task that focuses the way that language learners will read/write/listen/speak about content" (p. 367).

Unfortunately, we were not successful in introducing tasks into the IE Listening course. For one thing, listening is a receptive skill, unlike speaking or writing. Aside from performance on a paper test, we could not find a way to measure it. It was also hard to see much progress in a single semester. In contrast, in IE Writing, students could learn the form of an essay, if not produce relatively error-free prose. And in IE Core, as students learned how to participate more effectively in small-group discussions, at least part of their improvement could be attributed to their familiarisation and growing confidence with the task. Furthermore, the other problem in IE Listening was to try to create meaningful differences between the three levels of the course. How would listening to the news at Level I be different than listening to the news at the other two levels, especially when listening to news items was so difficult for the students in any case? There were classroom issues, too, regarding the physical environment of the language lab as well as teacher practise. Most of the listening classes had 35–40 students, so they

Figure 3. Themes and Tasks at Level I

Themes

Memories
Urban Life
Food
Travel

Core Course Tasks

Speaking and Listening

a. Use gestures and eye contact in a discussion
b. Express agreement and disagreement
c. Use turn-taking language in a discussion
d. Use examples to support an argument

Writing

e. Maintain and exchange a personal journal

Reading

f. Identify a text by genre
g. Skim an article for the main ideas
h. Scan an article for details
i. Understand and use charts and graphs
j. Use context clues to learn new vocabulary
k. Use prefixes and suffixes in word meanings
l. Read two books, summarize and evaluate them, analyzing their setting, point of view, conflict, climax, symbol, irony, and theme

Writing Course Tasks

a. Identify and employ such features of paragraph writing as topic sentences and transitions within a sentence and paragraph
b. Identify and employ the paragraph genres of description, classification, and compare-contrast
c. Use examples, specific details, names, and numbers

Listening Course Tasks

Drama

a. Identify and employ idiomatic phrases
b. Use context clues to identify character, setting, mood, and conflict

Documentary

c. Listen to and note main ideas and details
d. Use context clues to identify place, subject, and perspectives

Music

e. Identify and employ poetic devices such as rhyme and alliteration

News

f. Identify key elements of a news broadcast such as *who, where, when, what, why,* and *how*
g. Summarize a news item in oral/written form
h. Use context clues to understand new vocabulary

were much larger than the IE Core and IE Writing classes, and because they were held in a language lab with fixed desks, the students had little chance to move around the room and work in pairs or small groups. In addition, the Japanese teachers delivering the course were accustomed to teaching it by showing a video sequence to students, giving them multiple-choice questions, and then correcting their answers orally. The teachers were uncomfortable with small-group work and some of the other activities that we had tried to introduce into the course. As a result, students complained that the IE Listening course was dull and uninteresting.

Program Evaluation and Development

There had never been any formal evaluation of the IEP. That changed with a program review by an English Department committee in 1998. The committee members collated student and teacher comments, which revealed the same Listening-related complaints that we had noticed earlier. Also, they observed an overlap of IE Writing III and Academic Writing, a year-length course for sophomores that the department had offered for many years. Students took them simultaneously and were frustrated by learning about essays in two different courses and with two different teachers. As a result, the department dropped the Academic Writing course and created two new semester-length courses that became part of the IEP: New Academic Writing, in which students acquired research skills and wrote a 2,000-word research paper, and Academic Skills, in which they learned how to listen effectively to lectures, take notes, and participate in a seminar discussion. In the development of these new courses, we tried to apply what we had learned from our experiences in creating the IEP.

For New Academic Writing, we consulted with the part-time instructors who taught this course and IE Writing III to determine the tasks to assign to each course. Through trial and error over the next few semesters, we made changes to both courses. For example, we started teaching the use of quotations and sources in IE Writing III because Academic Writing teachers found it too difficult to teach this in addition to teaching the process of writing a major paper.

In 1999, we enlisted the help of an external reviewer from the Ontario Institute for Studies in Education. He conducted a number of workshops on second language writing and educational research with our part-time teachers, observed IE classes, and met with us, the program coordinators, to review the IEP (Strong, 1999). He reported the achievements of the program, the enthusiasm of the students and instructors, and the general effectiveness of the program. Then he made three important proposals: that we develop a rationale for the program and create clearer goals and learning objectives, use a task-based framework to organize the curriculum, and establish criteria for formative and summative student evaluation. He also suggested that we establish performance scales for the tasks. Coming when they did, his suggestions on goals and learning objectives were gradually incorporated into the hybrid course framework of themes and tasks described earlier. The following year, we published performance scales for the new tasks and samples of student performance in a new and expanded teacher guidebook.

However, the reviewer's strongest critique, about the inappropriateness of the IE Listening course, proved more difficult to address. In addition to offering criticisms similar to those we had received before, he thought the listening theme units that we had written were more suitable to student self-access materials than to classroom materials. They relied too heavily on multiple-choice questions instead of introducing other listening tasks. The materials did not seem to help students acquire either listening strategies or microskills such as identifying contractions and reductions in speech. His comments called for major changes.

The external reviewer also suggested that we connect student assessment more closely to the successful performance of tasks in the curriculum and to both their initial course placement and their assessment at the end of the three levels of the program. We recognized the value of this suggestion, but once again, we faced the issue of the placement test and of our failure to build support within the department to properly develop and implement one. On the positive side, the impetus from this substantial review led us to initiate two major research projects on listening courses, and the results of these projects focused our subsequent curriculum development efforts.

THE ACTION RESEARCH TOOL

Our first research project associated with the new courses was action research focused on the Academic Skills course. Our learning outcomes for the course included teaching students to listen for discourse markers, to access past knowledge, and to use note taking for organizing and encoding information and acquiring vocabulary. We were developing six 20-minute videotaped lectures in literature, linguistics, and communication, and we prepared a draft of a course booklet with six units of instruction and pedagogical tasks. The course introduced listening strategies and encouraged students to engage in listening more actively through predicting, guessing, and inferring meaning. In each unit, students progressed from easier pedagogical tasks to more difficult ones that required them to listen to longer portions of a lecture. In addition, each unit had three phases. In the prelistening phase, students made predictions, checked their work with partners and in small groups, and read a passage about the lecture content to gain background knowledge. During the listening phase, students watched a video to identify the vocabulary and concepts they had read and discussed earlier. They also transferred the information they saw on the video to written form (e.g., noting numbers and dates, filling in an information table) or edited a transcript to eliminate repetitions. Then in the postlistening phase, the students compared and discussed their work, after which the teacher discussed the answers with the class and replayed the relevant sections of the video.

We used the action research model to assess the Academic Skills course, provide ongoing feedback for its revision, and assist in implementing it. Beginning in 1999, and continuing until the fall semester of 2001, several Academic Skills teachers piloted the course materials and tested students with a pretest and a posttest. We revised the course several times and retested students. The last time we collected data on pretest and posttest scores, it showed significant improvement in students' listening and note-taking skills (Strong, 2004).

As is typical of many action research projects, our experiment consisted of intact classes and lacked a control group, so our study was an exploratory one with limited generalisability to other educational contexts. However, the course developers and the teachers involved in the project agreed about the benefits of an action research approach to curriculum development, implementation, and evaluation. The teachers who were part of the experiment also provided great assistance in implementing the new course. They knew more about it than the other Academic Skills teachers, and they had a personal stake in its success. Through workshops and meetings throughout each semester, they mentored other instructors in effective methods of teaching the course. They also provided timely and detailed feedback on the course.

THE IE COURSE AND STUDENT SURVEYS

As described earlier, we had known about the weaknesses in the IE Listening course for a number of years, but we had no idea how to improve it. Fortunately, at this time, an English Department graduate studying in the United States contacted us about access to students for his master's degree research. We suggested an analysis of our listening courses, and when he accepted, we helped him gather data. Kikuchi (2001) conducted a needs analysis of the IE Listening course by triangulating interviews with 15 students, 9 teachers, and the 2 IEP coordinators and two versions of a questionnaire administered to 585 students and 9 teachers. The questionnaires asked about the learners' target tasks, priorities, abilities, attitudes, problems, and solutions. The statistical results are summarized in Table 3.

The findings indicated that students saw their future use of English primarily in terms of recreation. Their identification of vocabulary, colloquial expressions, and rapid speech as their chief problems in IE Listening helped

Table 3. The Survey Questions and a Summary of Responses

(Kikuchi, 2001, pp. 39–45)

Question	Summarized response
1. *Target tasks*: What kinds of things would you like to do in the future using English?	Many students wanted to learn English to watch movies, travel, or study abroad.
2. *Problems*: What kinds of things would you have difficulty with in listening?	Many students had a hard time with unknown vocabulary, colloquial expressions, and rapid speech.
3. *Priorities*: What kinds of things would you prefer to listen to in English?	Most students would prefer to watch movies and TV dramas and listen to pop songs.
4. *Abilities*: What kinds of things can you do using English now?	Most students felt that they could give directions; many felt that they could hold a conversation with a foreigner.
5. *Complaints*: Do you have any problems in the IE Listening class?	Some students complained that there was less focus on daily conversation, little variety in the video materials, and not enough class time.
6. *Attitudes*: How do you like your IE Listening class?	Many students liked it somewhat or had no strong feelings about it.
7. *Solutions*: Do you feel that your IE Listening class helps you to be a better listener? If not, do you have any ideas about certain things that need to be changed in the IE Listening courses?	Many students felt the course helped them become better learners. Most students felt the course should focus more on daily conversation and use more varieties of videos and popular songs, and they felt that teachers should show listening transcripts and provide students with a tape to review after class.

us see that future materials would have to include more vocabulary work and strategies to help students with learning new words and using contextual clues. The problem with teaching colloquial expressions, however, was that many of these had to be memorized. Also, most of them came from movies or TV dramas, the very materials that students most liked to watch. The students' responses also demonstrated their wish for more diversified listening materials, movies, TV dramas, and pop songs to introduce more variety into the course. Students felt that they could handle conversation and directions in speaking to a foreigner, and for the most part, they liked the course or were neutral in their feelings about it.

One of the most useful questions in the study asked students for their suggestions to improve the IE Listening course (see Table 4 on p. 172). More than 80% agreed or strongly agreed with focusing more on daily conversation skills, and approximately 68% agreed or strongly agreed with the need for more variety in the selection of videos. Some 63% wanted popular English songs to be used, and slightly more than 63% wanted to see the transcripts after viewing a video. And 55% wished to have a copy of the recording to view after class.

Afterward, we embarked on a substantial revision of our learning materials for IE Listening. We tried to enhance their variety and length and to teach more vocabulary and colloquial expressions. It had been our practice to provide students with transcripts of most of the units, so we made certain that we provided any missing transcripts. Copies of the videos shown in class were left for student use in the student-access area of the library and in a specially designated part of the English Department office that had been equipped with a DVD/video player.

Table 4. Solutions to Problems in the IE Listening Class

(Kikuchi, 2001, p. 45)

Solution	M	SD	Strongly disagree	Disagree	Neutral	Agree	Strongly agree
Focusing more on daily conversational skills	4.20	0.92	1.63%	3.80%	13.86%	34.51%	46.20%
Using more varieties of videos	3.98	1.00	2.17%	4.08%	25.54%	30.43%	37.77%
Using popular English songs in class	3.85	1.15	3.26%	10.60%	23.10%	24.18%	38.86%
Showing the scripts after watching the video in class	3.81	1.16	4.89%	8.70%	22.83%	27.99%	35.60%
Giving students a chance to review the class by listening to a tape of it	3.46	1.21	7.14%	14.56%	28.30%	25.00%	25.00%
Using English for all the instruction	2.81	1.27	15.53%	30.52%	26.16%	13.35%	14.44%
Giving some listening homework assignments	2.64	1.22	22.28%	23.10%	30.98%	15.49%	8.15%

A literature review on listening comprehension pinpointed the weaknesses in the methodology of our previous IE Listening units. Although we had incorporated prelistening and postlistening activities into these units, the activities that students engaged in while listening were largely confined to discrete-point exercises of true-false, multiple-choice, and matching items that failed to impart strategic listening skills. Mendelsohn (1995) proposes that listening courses provide strategy training and extension tasks in speaking and writing that replicate how people listen naturally. Consequently, we worked on creating a template for a listening unit that would incorporate the new methodology, encourage pair and small-group work in class, and serve as a model for the revision of our existing units.

We based one of our new listening units on the first scene in *Guess Who's Coming to Dinner?* (Kramer, 1967), a movie dealing with an interracial engagement, which fit the relationship theme of IE Listening III. During the prelistening phase of the unit, we included prediction tasks such as one that required students to use their prior knowledge of typical romantic courtships to guess the events in the young couple's courtship. Listening tasks while viewing the video included the use of visual and linguistic clues to determine personality types and interrelationships between characters. Finally, during the postlistening phase, we integrated listening with discussion and writing tasks. Students wrote letters from the point of view of one of the characters, then sought and gave advice orally while role-playing a character from the film.

In addition to new units on popular film, we tried to introduce more variety as well. We purchased music videos and compilations of news items. We wrote units on the music videos that included cloze dictations and cohesion tasks that required students to reorder scrambled stanzas from songs. Furthermore, students had to identify sound devices, such as rhyme and alliteration in songs, as well as the poetic devices of allusion and metaphor. In listening to news, we emphasized the use of key words and finding the main idea. These changes in the IE Listening course meant that we now had to assess students differently for grading. Previously, they were graded based on class participation and scores on midterm and final exams. As we tried to implement a more active class through more diverse classroom activities and pair and small-group work, we sought to compel the Listening teachers to grade their students differently. Class participation and small homework assignments took their place alongside paper-and-pencil tests. We began explaining these changes and demonstrating different listening techniques in workshops throughout the year, but progress was slow and remains so, because the IE Listening teachers must adopt new classroom practices and the coordinators must take a more active role in observing listening classes.

IEP Administration and Teacher Support

Over the years, teacher support has been essential in the IEP, especially because of the large number of adjunct faculty in the program and the high turnover rate among native-English-speaking teachers as well as Japanese teachers. Of the former group, as many as 20% leave the IEP every year, either for new positions or to return to their countries of origin. As for the Japanese adjunct staff, more of them are leaving the program, too, as they struggle to find full-time positions in a time of declining university enrollment.

Today, we provide extensive teacher support. We have a preservice orientation for new teachers and a complete learning-materials package consisting of teacher syllabi, teacher copies of textbooks, and student workbooks for each course, which include sample book reports, paragraphs, and essays. These materials make teaching in the IEP easier and are particularly helpful for new teachers. The English Department provides access to clerical support, copiers, computer accounts and Web hosting, library borrowing privileges, and storage lockers. We maintain an e-list of program updates and job postings that have been passed on to us. As described earlier, we have set aside a teacher resource area with professional journals, authentic listening and reading materials, and other teacher references. We try to grant part-time teachers some of the privileges that full-time staff enjoy, including the right to publish in the department's academic journal. On each day that the part-time teachers have classes, a full-time teacher who is a member of the IE Committee is on campus to offer assistance. We use our annual teacher orientation to explain any course changes, to identify problems with the program or with the materials, and to provide teachers with a professional forum to share new materials and techniques that they may have developed. In the past, this orientation has also helped teachers refine presentations that they give later at national and international conferences.

We give feedback to teachers in the form of end-of-semester student evaluations of each course. We began using course evaluation forms in the second year of the IEP after developing the forms with the participation and input of part-time teachers. Ever since then, we have collected them at the end of each semester, reviewed them, and then returned them to teachers. In terms of assessing individual teachers and the program in general, these remain our primary resource, a situation common to many universities. Peer assessment and teacher self-reflection would certainly effectively augment our efforts, but with such a large adjunct faculty and our limited resources of time and full-time personnel, we will not use them. However, student evaluations can offer a reasonable degree of accuracy (Aleamoni, 1987, p. 28).

Our procedure is to distribute the evaluation forms to students in class at the end of the course. The teacher leaves the room to allow students to complete the forms. One of the students sends the forms to the English Department office, and they are reviewed by the course coordinators. The forms are returned to the teachers after they have assigned student grades. The coordinators usually respond with a short note; sometimes this note is congratulatory, and sometimes it is a carefully worded suggestion that a teacher might try a different approach to a problem. In a few cases, the coordinators schedule a meeting with a teacher, or even arrange a classroom observation, and try to work with the teacher to develop solutions. We have found from experience that it helps to get the teacher to try to identify the problem, rather than to seek explanations or excuses. Sometimes, we invite new teachers or teachers who may be having difficulties to sit in on classes taught by our strongest teachers. Seldom is a teacher found to be unsuitable for a teaching position, but on those few occasions, we inform the Personnel Committee of the English Department, which holds a meeting with the teacher to discuss the situation.

On a personal level, we try to promote a relationship between the part-time teachers and the IEP coordinators based upon mutual respect so that a teacher in the IEP has a clear idea of the department's expectations. Yet we also try to put teachers at ease so that they feel comfortable enough to make suggestions to improve the program. To remain relevant and effective, an EFL program such as ours needs to incorporate contemporary teaching methodology, introduce new educational technologies, and include teachers' contributions. As J. D. Brown (1995) suggests, "involve all the participants in the process of curriculum development . . . [and] remember that much more can be accomplished through discussion and compromise than through dictated policy decisions and inflexibility" (p. 190).

Building consensus among teachers and introducing new ways that instructors can teach their courses requires leadership. Parry (1996, p. 220) describes leadership as a role that encourages and guides collaborative plan-ning efforts, mentors the development of others, and seeks to expand their capabilities by building mutually supportive networks and relationships that reinforce positive efforts to grow and learn. In that sense, a curriculum coor-dinator has to be an effective leader who is articulate in his or her vision of the program and able to suggest directions for change. We need to encour-age our teachers to do their best, to set goals for themselves while drawing upon our experience teaching in Japan, and we need to provide mentorship, especially to those who are relatively new to the profession. Many potential criteria can be used to evaluate the successes and shortcomings of a program such as ours, but my list would be a modest one: Are the students more satisfied with the courses than in the past? Do they feel that the program is helping them learn a language? Do teachers joining the program have a clear idea of our expectations of them? Are the supporting documents, curriculum guides, and other teacher resources adequate for the needs of the students and teachers?

Conclusion

Not many EFL teachers who undertake program design will enjoy the same measure of departmental support that we have had. On the other hand, the evolution of the IEP was the result of long hours of labour, strategic planning, and a number of difficult decisions and compromises. Developing an effective EFL program requires sensitivity to the context, decisions about the scheduling and placement of students, the articulation of goals and learning outcomes, ongoing program evaluation, and effective administration and teacher support. To conclude by revisiting the metaphor of curriculum design as the furniture in a room, furniture directs our use of the space just as good curriculum design provides a framework for teachers to plan and shape their students' educational experience.

Acknowledgments

I would like to acknowledge the efforts of past IEP co-coordinators James Ellis and Jennifer Whittle, as well as Joseph Dias, who currently coordinates the program with me, and longstanding IEP Committee members Hiroshi Yoshiba, Peter Robinson, and Teruo Yokotani. I would also like to acknowledge my colleagues in the English Department and among the adjunct faculty in the program who have made many contributions.

Teacher Preparation

Focusing on Teaching From the Get-Go: An Experience From Brazil

9

DENISE M. DE ABREU-E-LIMA, LUCIANA C. DE OLIVEIRA,
AND ELIANE H. AUGUSTO-NAVARRO

It is widely recognized in Brazil that the elementary and secondary schools (especially the public ones) are not considered, even by English language teachers themselves, as places where EFL instruction has satisfactory results. It has been argued that the main reason for the failure in these contexts is the poor education of preservice English teachers in undergraduate programs in languages and literatures (Almeida Filho, 1997; Basso, 2001; Maza, 1999; Paiva, 1997; Vieira Abrahão, 1992, 2004; Vieira Abrahão & Barcelos, 2006).

The educational context described in this chapter is the undergraduate Languages and Literatures Program at the Federal University of São Carlos (UFSCar) in Brazil. As the chapter title suggests, focusing on teaching from the get-go is a major component of our program. Discussing future professional practice with undergraduate students in EFL programs from the very beginning of their studies is vital to educating preservice teachers; otherwise anyone proficient in English would qualify as an EFL teacher. It is essential to not only give these students opportunities for language development, but also prepare them to reflect on this development process. The experience that we report in this chapter draws on just such an idea. Students enrolled in the Languages and Literatures Program at UFSCar are highly motivated about their preparation as preservice teachers due to their systematic reflection on the program content and its relation to the needs of EFL teachers.

Basso (2001) and Maza (1999) conducted studies involving preservice teachers from programs of leading universities in the field of TEFL. These universities are located in states that are considered to be excellent centers of teacher education, but Basso concluded that in the EFL education program where she got her data, the content was inconsistent with its goals. Teachers undergoing training in such programs not only are unmotivated and limited as professionals but also do not see their professors as being attuned to their needs. Maza had similar results; after analyzing preservice teachers in a teacher education program and later in their professional practice, she reported that these EFL elementary and secondary teachers were not able to detach their actions from outdated values and beliefs transmitted by the university. For these teachers, EFL teaching and learning meant speaking the native language in class and keeping classroom order with authority. Teaching and learning was, for them, a mechanical process based on grammar exercises and text translation. Maza claimed that these teachers simply reproduced schematic structures and models learned at the university. The conclusion, then, is that there are two main limitations in these teachers' education and performance: lack of comprehensive knowledge of the content to be taught and lack of pedagogical education.

As professors and researchers in the area of TEFL teaching and learning in Brazil, we have seen the drawbacks of a system that has long taught English in TEFL undergraduate programs the same way one would teach it to students who want to learn the language for any other purpose, such as for tourism, business, or general communication. The UFSCar program described in this chapter was designed to address this issue, and because of its innovative approach, it has received special attention from several researchers in Brazil. According to several research studies (Claus, 2005; Höfling, 2006; Margonari, 2001, 2006; Silva, 2005), teachers who graduate from this program reveal that their preparation is appropriate for classroom practice in terms of classroom management, teaching methods, and materials development. These teachers also express a greater awareness of their teaching contexts, showing that in spite of being new to the profession, they are prepared to deal with different target groups, including children, adolescents, and adults. The studies found that these teachers are also reflective of their practice, aware of their strengths and weaknesses as new teachers, and know how to overcome hurdles that they may encounter (Claus, 2005; Margonari, 2001, 2006; Silva, 2005). Other recent studies (some of which are still underway) are investigating different aspects of the UFSCar program, including the evaluation of preservice teachers (Donadio, 2007), changes in preservice teachers' expectations about their first year in a teacher education program (Emidio, 2007), the use of technology in EFL teacher education (Nunes, 2007), and the role of Multiple Intelligences theory in EFL teacher education (Abreu-e-Lima, 2006). Data collected from recent graduates have shown that the program enables them to either find jobs right after they finish the program or get admitted into master's programs in major Brazilian universities.

We believe that part of our program's success comes from the collaborative teamwork developed by its EFL teacher educators. But our experience has also shown that another crucial requirement for satisfactory results in educating EFL teachers is the appropriateness of the program content. In this chapter we, the curriculum designers, describe how we selected content and developed the program. We also discuss our successes and setbacks since the program was founded in 1996.

The Brazilian Higher Education System

Before we describe the program itself, it is important to discuss some major characteristics of the Brazilian higher education system. Students take entrance exams to be admitted to undergraduate programs, and as soon as they register for these exams, they must indicate the major for which they are applying. Different universities give different entrance exams, and public universities receive the highest number of candidates because they are known for offering free, high-quality education. For some majors, such as medicine, dentistry, physical therapy, and psychology, competition is extremely high (sometimes with 80 applicants per student position).

In the UFSCar program, which certifies Portuguese and EFL teachers, there are about 15 applicants per student position, and students take classes in their specific major starting with their first day at the university. They know that they are going to be prepared to be teachers, and most of them, despite the common perception that it is a less popular program, want to be teachers. Of all students admitted to the program, about 15% would rather study law or journalism, but they end up changing their plans because of the high competition for those courses. These students want to get a degree from a well-recognized public university, even if it means pursuing a career path that they did not originally intend to follow. Some fall in love with teaching and go on to seek a career in education, whereas others do not embrace the program's objectives as fully and end up working in an area other than teaching in which language knowledge is also important.

The Program of Languages and Literatures at UFSCar

UFSCar is a public university in the central part of the state of São Paulo. It has 5,700 undergraduate students and 1,600 graduate students distributed among 27 undergraduate programs (e.g., Engineering, Biology, Physical Education, Physical Therapy, Social Sciences, Psychology, Languages and

Literatures, Librarianship) and 32 graduate programs. The university is recognized as an excellent higher education center and receives students from all over the country, but mostly from the state of São Paulo.

In 1995, a survey[1] carried out in the public and private schools of São Carlos to determine the percentage of teachers who were certified to teach demonstrated the importance of a program in languages and literatures. The survey showed that almost 50% of the English teachers had never attended a university and did not have a degree in English. Most of them had taken independent courses at private schools that offered English instruction or had lived in other countries for a while and, therefore, had some knowledge of the English language. The underlying problem of this situation was that none of them had attended a teacher education program, which has contributed to a decrease in the quality of education as a whole, not to mention the teaching of EFL. Other issues, such as the low income of teachers and poor working conditions, have also contributed to the decrease, but these are not within the scope of this chapter.

The goal of the undergraduate Languages and Literatures Program is to prepare students to be teachers of languages as well as literature. The program certifies teachers to teach Portuguese and a foreign language: English or Spanish. Students who are on the English language track earn a degree that will certify them to teach Brazilian Portuguese as a first language (L1), EFL, Portuguese/Brazilian literatures, and English/North American literatures. Students on the Spanish track have the same curriculum to follow, except that English is replaced by Spanish language and Latin American and Spanish literatures. Some students in our program are preservice teachers who have never taught, and others are in-service teachers. One goal of the English program is to develop students' proficiency so that they can work as English teachers. More important, though, professors in this program are aware that they are preparing future teachers of the language, and as a consequence, pedagogical issues are a major concern. Because we take into consideration not only the foreign language learning itself, but also discussion and reflection about teachers' actions, both groups of students (pre- and in-service teachers) find it helpful to learn more about language pedagogy, in addition to simply learning the language.

Challenges Faced by the Curriculum Designers

Supported by the survey cited earlier, the Department of Languages and Literatures, which is composed of most of the professors from the Program

---

[1] This survey was carried out by a program committee and published for the Ministry of Education only as an internal document.

of Languages and Literatures, decided to create a 5-year program that would be offered in the evenings to cater to people who work during the day and are thus unable to attend most federal universities because they offer classes during the day. An evening program would also enable current practicing teachers who lacked a teaching certificate to get their degree. Luckily, at the time, the Brazilian government was encouraging universities to start new programs, so the idea of creating a new program was not a challenge in itself.

One of us (Abreu-e-Lima) was asked to design an EFL curriculum for the new program. After it was created, another EFL professor joined the program, and later two other members got involved, de Oliveira as a consultant and Augusto-Navarro a professor. We faced the challenge of creating a new, different program that would minimize difficulties that were present in other programs. Some of these difficulties are described in the following sections.

A HETEROGENEOUS GROUP OF STUDENTS

Most of the students admitted to the university to get a degree in English are not proficient in English. They have some knowledge of the language (e.g., they can identify some basic English nouns or adjectives and some verbs), but they are unable to read a text or engage in a conversation in the target language. Other students come to the university having taken several years of English courses in private schools of English and are able to read, write, and carry on conversations with others in the target language; some of these students already teach, most often in private language schools, and are considered in-service teachers.

THE DIFFERENCE BETWEEN A BACHELOR'S DEGREE AND A TEACHING CREDENTIAL

Most of the time, Brazilian programs of languages and literatures offer students two tracks: a bachelor's degree and a teaching credential. Traditionally, both groups started off by attending the same 3-year series of content courses, which focused on content development. Those who wanted only the bachelor's degree were finished with their schooling at the end of these 3 years (or 4 years in the case of evening programs).

Those who wanted the teaching credential, however, had to complete 1 more year of educational courses, which focused on pedagogy, methodology, and other teaching issues. These subjects were taught mostly by professors from the Department of Education and were held during the fourth and final year of the undergraduate program. The idea was that 1 year would be enough to prepare them for their teaching practice. Therefore, there was no intersection between the content and pedagogical courses.

LACK OF CONNECTION BETWEEN CONTENT AND EDUCATIONAL COURSES

Because both groups of students (those who would be certified to teach and those who would not) took the same content courses, no reference to educational issues was made during these courses. The focus on the language and the lack of focus on educational issues led to a lack of critical reflection on established teaching patterns such as teaching grammatical structures using the native language, working with the textbooks usually adopted by language schools, and working with translation.

In 1995, when the new program was being developed at UFSCar, these were some of the issues facing almost all Brazilian undergraduate programs in languages and literatures that certified teachers of a foreign language. In fact, even most of the professors at UFSCar had faced these constraints in their own undergraduate courses when they were getting certified to teach. The challenge was to think about a different curriculum that could enhance students' language knowledge as well as their teaching skills.

Of the three challenges presented earlier (heterogeneous student population, bachelor's degree versus teaching certificate, lack of connection between courses), the second and the third could be addressed while creating the new program. The first step was to determine if the program would only certify teachers or would grant bachelor's degrees as well. We were convinced that different forms of education were needed for each group because the students' professional situations after graduation would be different. As a result, we chose to focus on teacher certification.

The second step involved dealing with some professors' teaching beliefs. These professors, from the Department of Languages and Literatures, still believed that the traditional undergraduate education (i.e., content courses that were unrelated to education courses) was a good way of preparing preservice teachers. They did not see the need to modify the curriculum at all and would have preferred to continue relying on the old models and patterns of teaching, which they had experienced. This is described as the *craft model* (Wallace, 1991) or sometimes as an *apprenticeship of observation* (Grossman, 1990; Lortie, 1975). However, the group who wanted to modify the curriculum thought it was essential that the preservice teachers become innovative in order to effect change in the country's educational situation.

One of the solutions that we proposed was to concentrate our efforts on how to teach the same content in a different way, that is, by focusing on pedagogical issues. For example, to teach a grammar point, an author, or a literary period, we could teach the previewed content and then discuss how to apply this content, whenever possible, in different teaching situations to different target groups. That was our first attempt at persuading the group of professors to design a curriculum that would enable preservice teachers to discuss the teaching reality as early as their first year in college. To demonstrate the urgency of the need for such a change, we had to show a rationale for developing a new curriculum.

Rationale for Developing a New Curriculum

Studies investigating the education of preservice teachers in Brazil have shown that the strategies used to teach English to these learners have been ineffective (Almeida Filho, 1997; Paiva, 1997; Vieira Abrahão, 1992, 2004). New, more effective, ways of teaching were needed for various reasons. First, preservice EFL teachers had different proficiency levels when they were admitted to college; in the same class, some students could understand and communicate effectively in English, whereas others could barely understand or speak the language at all. This meant that there was a need for English communication courses that would cater to both advanced- and beginning-level students. Second, many university programs designed for preservice teachers designed English language courses in terms of general English only. Instructors of such courses generally did not discuss contexts for teaching, except during the teaching practicum. Programs that prepare EFL teachers should integrate the learning of teaching skills with the learning of language skills and knowledge about language. Both Paiva (1997) and Vieira Abrahão (1992) recognize that the lack of instruction in specific language teaching skills has negative consequences in the careers of Brazilian EFL teachers.

Furthermore, Almeida Filho (1997) discusses the complexity of the process of educating an English teacher. He calls attention to the importance of increasing EFL teachers' awareness of the fact that the end of the undergraduate course is only the beginning of teacher education. According to Almeida Filho, only through what he calls *progressive education* (i.e., continuing education throughout a teacher's professional life, including critical self-analysis of teaching events and analysis from outsider specialists) can a teacher surmount the everyday challenge of his or her job.

Language proficiency is one of the requirements for a good language teacher. However, it is just as important to be able to critically analyze one's teaching options regarding approaches, materials, methods, and procedures. The main way to provide prospective EFL teachers with this capacity for self-reflection is to discuss with them the processes of learning and teaching EFL as they develop English proficiency throughout their undergraduate studies.

After we explained our rationale to the department, our proposal was accepted and we were ready to go.

Beginning the Process of Curriculum Development

The main challenge of adopting the idea of focusing on teaching from the get-go in our program was to develop appropriate educational materials. Excerpts from theoretical texts aimed at EFL professionals were chosen as the basis for the preparation of lessons. To complement these texts, scenes from movies, advertisements, and other authentic sources were selected because they presented rich contexts with which to analyze language use and to discuss why language is used in certain ways.

By observing language in use, teachers are able to discuss pragmatics, grammar choices, and a wide range of other factors with students. Students can then reflect on the difference between, for example, studying grammar from a textbook and analyzing how and why it is used in a given situation. These discussions are especially significant for preservice teachers because they can experience a different way of learning and reflect on its effects on the learning process. As a consequence, students become more aware of the importance of selecting and/or developing appropriate teaching materials when they become EFL teachers.

The practical classes, based on language in context, prepare students for the theoretical classes. The practical classes are mostly content based and use various subjects such as psychology, linguistics, education, and literature to focus on language. The first step in a practical class is for the professor to select spoken and written texts that focus on a content area that is in some way related to teaching and learning. After students read or listen to these texts, they discuss them based on a series of questions that guide the discussion. This discussion can involve aspects of language as well as content. The goal is to help preservice teachers deduce the way language operates in a particular subject area. Then the professor leads a discussion about the reasons for adopting this teaching process instead of presenting language inductively, thereby relating its approach to EFL teaching and learning theories. When preservice teachers experience this kind of approach, at first they often feel uncomfortable because, instead of having all of the information presented by the professor, they have to analyze the texts to find patterns of language use. This is an important step in our program because, as Freeman (2002) points out, preparing teachers implies dealing with, and sometimes challenging, common beliefs about teaching. We deal with many preconceived and often misleading ideas about EFL teaching and learning. Students enter UFSCar with a wide range of (mis)conceptions about how teaching and learning processes work. As a result, our job as teacher educators is to deconstruct these preconceived notions so that students can be more open to understanding the language learning process as a subject for study, analysis, and discussion, not as something intuitive that one already possesses.

Whenever we read texts that discuss teaching languages communicatively (e.g., Batstone, 1994; Fotos, 2001; Larsen-Freeman, 2001; Widdowson, 1978), we notice that the heart of the communicative approach is to use language with real meaning, that is, to convey and receive information that is relevant to those involved in a given speech act. In the 1970s, language started to be understood as a system for expressing meanings. As Nunan (1999) explains,

> if language is a system for expressing meanings, and if different learners have different communicative ends in view, then surely these different communicative ends should be reflected in the things that learners are taught. In other words, there ought to be different syllabuses for different learners. (p. 10)

We used this premise when we began thinking about designing a program for future language teachers. By teaching the language itself through the discussion and analysis of content that deals with TESOL matters, we initiate our students in the discourse community of TESOL from the very beginning of their time in the program.

The Results of the New Program

Our 5-year program consists of courses in the L1 (e.g., Linguistics, Brazilian and Portuguese Literature, Latin, Portuguese Language Studies) and foreign language courses. The program is divided into semesters, and each course involves 60 hours of instruction. In addition to required courses, electives are offered throughout the program, but we suggest that students take some before others. The structure of the English program is displayed in Table 1 (on p. 188).

The Department of Education teaches both Practicum courses, Structure and Functions of Basic Education, Pedagogical Strategies, and Education and Society. And the Department of Psychology teaches Educational Psychology and Adolescence and Psychosocial Problems. These courses are part of the program of Languages and Literatures from the second through the fifth year.

AN INTERDISCIPLINARY FOCUS

Even though Practicum courses are offered by the Department of Education, they are listed with the courses offered by the Department of

Table 1. Courses Offered by the English Program

Year	Course
1	Topics in English Study 1 Topics in English Study 2
2	Oral Ability: Development and Teaching Practice 1 Oral Ability: Development and Teaching Practice 2
3	Written Ability: Development and Teaching Practice 1 Teaching and Learning a Foreign Language: Projects *Electives*—English Grammar Studies: Context and Teaching Practice; Oral Ability Development
4	Production and Evaluation of Teaching Material English Literature 1 American Literature 1 Applied Linguistics *Electives*—ESP Methodology: Teaching Practice Pronunciation; Teaching English to Adolescents
5	English Literature 2 American Literature 2 Practicum 1 Practicum 2 *Electives*—Teaching English to Children; Oral Proficiency; Literature Through Movies

Languages and Literatures because the Practicum professor and the English-track professors plan the Practicum curriculum collaboratively. The Practicum professor negotiates the curriculum with the applied linguistics professors from the Department of Languages and Literature to ensure that both courses are congruent yet not repetitive. Preservice teachers are able to use the materials they design throughout the English track in the Practicum courses.

The Practicum usually occurs in the last 2 years of the program and is divided into two phases: a theoretical one, when preservice teachers read theories, discuss ideas, and develop lesson plans, and a practical one, when they go out into elementary and secondary schools to teach these lessons. Practicum supervisors observe these lessons and provide feedback to the preservice teachers on several aspects of teaching.

First, the preservice teachers visit public schools to observe English classes. They also interview in-service teachers and students. During Practicum classes, they discuss and review their class observation reports and interviews with the other preservice teachers, facilitated by the Practicum professor. Then they design a class plan to be used with the same target group that they observed. After they teach their lessons, they write a final report in which they describe and discuss the entire process, from observing and interviewing teachers and students to teaching a lesson on their own.

DIFFICULTIES FACED BY PROGRAM DESIGNERS DURING THE FIRST 3 YEARS

Program Constraints

The interdisciplinary coordination was not an easy task at first. The program faced many challenges before striking a balance between what was desired and what was necessary. One of the most significant difficulties was that just one professor was responsible for the entire English track within the Languages and Literatures Program for the first, second, and part of the third year of the Program. For various reasons three professors had left the university, leaving just one full-time professor (the first author of this chapter) in charge of curriculum development. At that time, political changes affected the way these vacancies would be filled, and the Brazilian government decided to hire short-term, part-time lecturers to support programs.

In 1998 and again in 2002, however, two other professors joined the department (one of whom is the third author of this chapter). They shared with the original professor a background in applied linguistics and similar teaching philosophies. These three were eager to promote a scaffolded learning process, which enabled the development of courses with congruent goals, which would in turn enable students to understand the goals of the program.

Class Materials

Another important issue that had to be resolved was related to the choice of class materials. The problem was not related to the textbook itself, but to the target group: preservice teachers at the basic level. It is difficult to find basic-level language textbooks that use topics related to teaching and learning. There are few, if any, specific materials for this population; most materials aimed at preservice teachers are at an intermediate level or higher. Therefore, the group of English professors decided to design their own materials and select some others that would be appropriate for each course. An added benefit was that this would enable the choice of current texts that would put students in contact with recent research. Therefore, we were able to select texts and write some others about teaching and learning theory as well as about practical situations and to establish goals to be achieved in each course (see the appendix). All of these things would help students reflect on their future practice.

The selection of texts proved to be a difficult task. The most important aspect was to choose appropriate materials that would expose preservice teachers to different models than they were used to as learners of EFL.

In every course, students were asked to prepare various kinds of practical materials. However, it was not easy to explain to students the importance of such focus. Many did not believe that a new approach would work because they lacked confidence in it as a means of improving their English abilities. For example, in response to questions such as "How much did you develop your English?" a couple of typical answers were "How can I say that? I don't know if I developed my English. I think I have a lot mistakes of grammar" (Cristine) and "This is a problem! I'm not sure I developed my English during this semester. I probably learnt some new things by doing the project and during the classes, but I don't know how to measure it, and so I can't measure the things I forgot" (Rodrigo).

From what some students reported, we noticed that their idea of language development was related to grammar points or to narrowly measurable items. This is easy to understand, considering that they had been exposed to traditional grammar and audiolingual ways of teaching and learning the language. So we had to reinforce and prepare activities that would increase students' awareness of the fact that a language can be learned in different ways and for specific reasons.

Division of Abilities

To begin with, two professors would work with each class; one would be in charge of listening and speaking, and the other, in charge of reading, writing, and grammar. The reason for this setup was to guarantee that all abilities would be given the same emphasis in the curriculum development. After some years of using this system, however, we realized that we were overwhelming students with too much work. As a result, we decided to keep one professor for each course, varying the amount of emphasis on either spoken or written language throughout the entire program, although still encompassing the range of skills within any one semester. As a result of this change, in the first 2 years of the program, students would be able to develop their oral abilities (listening and speaking) more than the written ones, mainly to ensure their participation in class discussions. After the second year, more emphasis would be placed on written abilities, mainly on written production.

Textbook or No Textbook?

Another difficulty was gaining acceptance for a course with no textbooks; students kept questioning this choice. As teacher educators, we had a responsibility to broaden students' perspectives so that they could evaluate their needs more effectively. We had to prepare units that would increase students' awareness of their needs instead of ones that would simply give in to their wants. Students often reported feeling insecure about not having a textbook. One reason was that they used textbooks to measure their learning according to how many units had been covered in a semester. We wanted to encourage a more reflective kind of self-evaluation based on their developing abilities to do things with the language. At the end of every course, students were asked to evaluate the process that they had gone through and, especially, how much they thought their English had improved. Gauging improvement in students' language skills was easy for the professors, but when students evaluated themselves, they did not notice the same things that professors did. Many times even students who had started the program with almost no English, just knowing *yes* or *no*, did not recognize how much they had learned. These students were able to give 40–50 minute presentations in English after 4 years in the undergraduate program and still thought that they were not able to say how much they had improved.

After 4 years of no textbooks and continuing pressure from students to have one, the group of English professors decided to adopt a textbook for the first 2 years of the undergraduate program. The idea was to do so as an experiment to investigate whether students would develop proficiency more effectively if they first focused more on language than on teaching and learning. The student population was heterogeneous, representing many language levels, so students in the first year thought that they were disadvantaged in comparison with other colleagues who were more proficient. Therefore, the textbook would serve as a homogenizing tool; everyone would be more or less at the same level, and there would be less discrepancy. Students thought they would be more confident with the textbook.

After the fourth semester (second year), students were given a test to assess their language proficiency. The results showed no differences from previous students, who had not used textbooks. However, the textbook group had missed opportunities for professional discussions and practice, which the other group had benefited from by preparing miniclasses, giving presentations, receiving feedback from students, and taking part in other activities related to teaching practice. Even though the professors tried to discuss ideas related to language teaching and learning in every activity of the textbook, the focus was on the language itself: There was not enough time for students to use what had been discussed because their main goal was to cover the textbook.

At the same time, students were calling for more practice. They felt that they had not been offered the same opportunities as other groups of students and that they lacked knowledge about how to teach and how to prepare activities. These students came to realize that having a textbook did not address their needs, and professors were able to show, through the students' own experiences, why the textbook was not effective in achieving their goals. Thus we were able to come back to the idea that the best course of action was to design our own materials focusing on developing linguistic competence through professional competence.

New Curriculum

English classes from the first through the fourth semesters (first and second years) use content-based texts, listening materials, and movie excerpts to teach the English language. These materials are selected based on topics that might be of interest to students who are preparing to become EFL teachers. Students have the opportunity to learn the four language skills, with rather more emphasis on speaking; increase their awareness about the processes of teaching and learning a foreign language; and discover introductory concepts of phonetics and phonology.

Students give oral presentations, which are videotaped throughout the program. These presentations allow professors and preservice teachers to assess the linguistic and professional competences of each teacher, and they are part of a personal archive that preservice teachers have access to throughout the program. At the end of the program, these teachers can look back at all of their presentations and assess what they have learned and how much they have improved, both linguistically and professionally.

Texts concerning the teaching and learning of a foreign language are used as the basis for reading comprehension, work with vocabulary and grammar, and teaching of reading strategies. Students write short summaries about what they have read and develop a plan for a class discussion on the topic. At the end of each month, preservice teachers provide their professors with feedback through their reflections. The following is an excerpt from the reflections of one preservice teacher, Rosana, who entered the university in 2004 after completing her studies in public schools. She had been studying for 1 year in a private language school but was still at a basic level:

> *At the beginning I couldn't understand a word, but I'm studying hard and now I can get some meaning. I didn't like when you [the teacher] talked in English, but I have noticed that the more you spoke the better my listening got. (translated by the authors)*

Our program has also been useful for in-service teachers because they take into consideration not only the foreign language learning but also the discussions and reflections about teachers' actions. Bernardo, a 23-year-old student, was an in-service teacher at a private language school and had been learning English for 10 years. He discussed what he had learned after the second month of the UFSCar program: "This month I learned minimal pairs. I have always told my students that they should put their tongue between their teeth to teach 'th' sounds, but now I consider that this explanation is too simple and maybe too superficial."

In-service teachers also increase their confidence about their roles in a heterogeneous class and begin to reflect on their own attitudes toward the preservice teachers who do not have the same level of proficiency: "Several times I interrupt what someone is saying and don't give chances to others [to] express their ideas. In fact, sometimes I monopolize the class. I confess that I ought to avoid it. I promise to take care" (Bernardo).

In the fifth semester more attention is given to writing. The courses discuss writing as a process and introduce genre analysis. Many texts are written and edited, sometimes by the whole group. Genre characteristics of fables, fairy tales, novel summary, academic text summary, and conference abstracts are discussed. This study of genre is mostly based on Swales (1990) and Swales and Feak (1994, 2001).

In the sixth semester students learn to prepare classes based on multiple intelligences theory (Gardner, 1983); they learn how to use the view of people's multiple intelligences to create activities to teach English to students in public elementary and high schools. They also learn how to integrate these activities in interdisciplinary projects.

The seventh and eighth semesters are explained in more detail below. During the last 2 years of our program, English language classes are offered as electives, and students take Literature (English and American) and Applied Linguistics—with a focus on EFL.

TEACHING ENGLISH TO ADOLESCENTS

The Teaching English to Adolescents course is given in the seventh semester (fourth year) of the program. This course focuses on how preservice teachers can use fairy tales as a metaphor for talking about transversal subjects (e.g., ethics, sexual guidance, work and consumerism, the environment, health, cultural diversity) because in 1997 the Ministry of Education established a requirement that these themes be addressed by all courses at public schools in the country. The purpose of using such guidelines in our program is to prepare preservice teachers to use projects in a real educational context and to design interdisciplinary activities.

For the final project of the course, preservice teachers are required to design a unit that promotes the teaching and learning of different skills by using a fairy tale to explain a transversal subject. One of our most critical students, Laura, had never imagined herself teaching English but was amazed by the results obtained with her final project, designed for sixth graders, in which she used J. K. Rowling's Harry Potter series as a fairy tale. In her comments, we notice criticism of some textbooks that contain seemingly arbitrary dialogues:

I have learned how to create interesting activities to adolescents, and how to organize these activities in a class plan. In my work I tried to run away from all that boring things I had do face while learning English at school, like vocabulary lists, completing phrases that have nothing to do with anything, saying those terrible dialogues, like: "What kind of sport do you like? I like soccer." "Is Diane Korean? No, Diane is Japanese." And so on.

Many people have been exposed to fairy-tale messages and morals since they were toddlers. But these messages are not often discussed or analyzed from a critical point of view. Many of people's misconceptions may come from beliefs that were true in an ancient past, but not anymore. These beliefs (e.g., the perfect prince, the devoted maiden, the treasure at the end of the rainbow, magic saviors) remain in the subconscious mind, creating an unsatisfactory environment for adolescents who may want what they do not have and hope that happy endings are made with magic. Many people might keep these beliefs without looking at them more critically or evaluating them more consciously. In our opinion, fairy tales are a great resource to bring these beliefs to the surface to help students reflect on them.

One of our goals is to develop preservice teachers' awareness of their target group in order to motivate their future students to learn and participate in foreign language classes. Adolescence is a critical period for students; they face physical and psychological challenges. Yet most of the time teachers do not feel confident enough to help them and can feel unprepared to challenge students the way they should be challenged. These reasons motivated us to create a course that would help preservice teachers design projects using transversal subjects, with adolescents as their target group.

EVALUATION AND PRODUCTION OF TEACHING MATERIALS

A course on the evaluation and production of materials is given in the eighth semester (fourth year) of the program. This required course consists of 60 hours divided into 36 classes. It teaches preservice teachers to analyze teaching materials and requires them to write a project with a research question based on their EFL teaching and/or learning. An important component of the course is the combination of the analysis of teaching materials and their relevance to a particular target group of students. Because many preservice teachers are already teaching when they are in the fourth year of the program, their teaching experience can inform their analysis and project writing.

As suggested by several researchers in the area of second language teaching, in this course we provide several theoretical texts on teaching and discuss them with preservice teachers, based on their experience and the information needed to better prepare them for their future practice. Several researchers (e.g., Almeida Filho, 1997; Vieira Abrahão, 2004) suggest that discussing theoretical texts about teaching is an effective strategy in preservice training. We ask students to read and discuss concepts presented by, for example, Larsen Freeman (2001), Celce-Murcia (2002), Nunan (1999), Swales and Feak (1994), and Gardner (1999) to relate them to their own experience and to consider the implications for their future practice. An important aspect of this course is that preservice teachers, in anticipation of future practice, select specific topics that they feel they need more information about. Students first read theoretical texts about EFL teaching/learning and come up with questions to discuss in class. Then, in class, students present their point of view about the text, and others raise questions and express their opinions. The professor is the mediator of the discussion. After students begin to develop a theoretical background in this way, they select an EFL textbook and choose one of its units for detailed analysis, taking into consideration the theory previously studied, the book's target population, and the teaching context (e.g., school-aged children in a public school in São Carlos).

Each preservice teacher presents his or her analysis in writing and in an oral presentation. The teachers receive feedback on their oral presentations from their peers and on their writing from the professor. The professor then initiates a discussion about how theories are generated and how research is developed. This is followed by classes about how to design and implement a study about EFL teaching/learning, and students outline a project with research questions and a hypothesis based on their own EFL teaching and/or learning experience.

This class has proved quite satisfactory, as evidenced by Miriam's comments:

> We have always heard that classes should be communicative and that research is very important, but nobody had told us what it really means to be communicative or how to develop research. Professors from LP 8 [a course on L1] praised us for already knowing how to write a research project.

Many preservice teachers say that this class helps them make sense of the process of developing educational materials. They report becoming more critical of textbooks and other teaching resources.

Conclusion

Teaching English to preservice EFL teachers provides a rich opportunity to teach meaningfully and communicatively, as has been widely recommended by several researchers in the area of TESOL (e.g., H. D. Brown, 2001; Ellis, 1994; Lightbown & Spada, 1993; Widdowson, 1978). It is a unique opportunity to teach the language by using EFL teaching and learning processes as the foundation of the lessons.

There are four advantages to teaching the course this way. First, the students learn language through a communicative and meaningful approach. Second, the content is EFL learning and teaching processes, so students are not only learning language but learning about how to teach language. Third, they learn the content in active and meaningful ways. As a consequence, they are able to reflect on their experiences as both learners of English and teachers of English.

The fourth advantage is that students with high levels of proficiency as well as those with lower levels can benefit from our classes. The more proficient ones can still be motivated as they learn about TESOL through studying the language; even when they already know vocabulary and structure, for instance, they will still learn something new and relevant for their career. And the less proficient ones can develop language skills while taking part in professional development as teachers. This context simultaneously provides students with an opportunity to reflect on their own learning processes and enables them to think about their future professional practice.

We have noticed that several factors contributed to the success of our program: a communicative approach to language teaching as the foundation of the program, an interdisciplinary approach to program content, a focus on preservice teachers' future educational contexts using guidelines proposed by the Brazilian Ministry of Education, and a strong belief that the time to begin preparing teachers to face their future challenges is while they are in a teacher education program. Teachers should have opportunities to express their feelings, their creativity, and their thoughts in the language they are learning.

In 2002 the Brazilian Ministry of Education developed educational parameters for teacher education that have to be followed by all universities. According to these parameters, programs must change and adapt their curricula to prepare teachers for their practice, combining content and professional development. The program described in this chapter already combines these two components, enabling students to become more aware of their practice from the start. The experience reported in this chapter shows a continuing process of curriculum and professional development—for preservice teachers as well as teacher educators. We try to show the importance of this continuing process of development to students, emphasizing the need for continual professional participation and growth. This process has to start with us, within the academic boundaries, by providing preservice teachers with meaningful experiences and models to be followed. These models show that constant reflection and search for improvement are the main ingredients of professional development. Teacher educators must be coherent about what they teach and must practice what they preach by focusing on teaching from the get-go.

Appendix: Course Goals

Teaching English to Adolescents
The aim of this course is to prepare the pre-service teachers to recognize the genre Fairy Tales as a possible way of teaching English to adolescents. These students will be taught how to design, adapt or create EFL teaching activities organized in projects. Each project will be conceived taking into consideration transversal subjects that could promote interdisciplinary work. Pre-service teachers will be supposed to create the projects, design activities and present them to their colleagues who will play the role of students in each project. The pre-service teachers will also be required to evaluate their peer presentations, that is, the way they have evaluated and (re)designed EFL teaching activities as well as how they present their projects. In this way, they have to reflect about the theory they studied during the term in the presence of practical tasks. By analyzing their peers' performance they will have a chance to reflect critically about their future professional practice.

Evaluation and Production of Teaching Materials
The aim of this course is to prepare the pre-service teachers to recognize theories on which teaching materials, such as textbooks, are based. These students will be taught how to redesign, adapt or create EFL teaching activities, by respecting the profile of each target group of learners and the teaching materials adopted by different kinds of institutions where they may have to teach. Throughout their evaluation students will be required to present the analysis they have made in teaching materials, both orally and through written texts. The students will also be required to evaluate their peer presentations, that is, the way they have evaluated and (re)designed EFL teaching activities as well as how they present their analysis. In this way, they have to reflect about the theory they studied during the term in the presence of practical tasks. By analyzing their peers' performance they will have a chance to reflect critically about their future professional practice.

Building Teacher Preparation Programs for TESL/TEFL

10

KLAUS GOMMLICH, SARAH RILLING, AND KARL UHRIG

Teacher development is an exciting process to facilitate. The goals and motivations of future language teachers are many, and students come to higher education programs with rich backgrounds and interests in cross-cultural exchange, linguistic learning and analysis, and teaching of learners in the United States and around the globe. Potential language teachers have varied career interests, which provides teacher educators with exciting opportunities to meet and expand on student interests and workplace needs.

In this chapter, we outline curricular innovations in the language teacher education programs at Kent State University, in the United States, at the undergraduate level. We highlight institutional strengths and connections as well as integration of the *TESOL/NCATE Standards for the Accreditation of Initial Programs in P–12 ESL Teacher Education* (TESOL, 2003b), and we incorporate information from five professional domains (language; culture; planning, implementing, and managing instruction; assessment; and professionalism).

In our curriculum development process, we have made extensive use of TESOL's Web site through simple searches for standards documents, position statements, and links to program models, enabling us to found our programs on the following core values:

- professionalism in language education
- individual language rights
- accessible, high-quality education

- collaboration in a global community
- interaction of research and reflective practice for educational improvement
- respect for diversity and multiculturalism (TESOL, 1996–2007, ¶ 2)

The strengths of our university include a successful MA TESL program; collective faculty and administrative international exchange and language learning/teaching experiences; and institutional connections with, among others, northeastern Ohio schools and Technische Universität Dresden (TU Dresden), a public university in Saxony, Germany, which, like Kent, hosts programs in applied linguistics and language teaching.

Motivation for the Programs

In addition to global calls for teachers of ESL/EFL, three recent changes prompted us to develop and expand our programs: (a) increased levels of student interest in foreign/second language teaching, especially at the undergraduate level; (b) regional need for licensed language and literacy teachers; and (c) increased cooperation with TU Dresden.

In addition to the MA in TESL, English faculty oversee and teach undergraduate linguistics courses (Grammar, History of the Language, and Introductory Linguistics) that are required in majors such as English, education, journalism, and speech pathology. Many undergraduates express interest in ESL/EFL teaching, and some are interested in eventually pursuing advanced degrees in TESL/TEFL or related areas. Our programs receive requests for further coursework, degrees, and certificates to expand professional preparation in applied linguistics, and potential students want practical (and perhaps international) teaching experience along the way.

The state of Ohio has recently allowed, and is beginning to require, licensure in ESL for public school teachers who are engaged in teaching ESOL. Previously, ESL had been treated as an add-on endorsement, but with the recent change in state law, teachers can now be licensed directly in ESL without another specialty subject. Many of the requests for program information that we receive from potential students include queries about licensure, and schools in northeastern Ohio have requested our assistance in locating, training, and providing professional ESL teachers.

As we contemplated expanding our undergraduate offerings, TU Dresden contacted us to intensify our cooperation by developing joint initiatives in applied linguistics. The idea of creating a TEFL certificate program through this institutional link presented itself as a major potential milestone in our curricular planning because it changed our focus from a U.S. program to a truly integrative, international program that could provide numerous practical teaching and cooperative opportunities, including the development of new courses and content modules benefiting students at both Kent and TU Dresden.

The Curricular Context

PROPOSALS AND PROCESSES

We have recently passed three new undergraduate programs designed to prepare TESL/TEFL professionals through Kent and Ohio's curriculum proposal process: the TEFL Certificate, the BA in TESL, and the education minor. Each program builds on existing offerings and faculty expertise. Curriculum review and revision are ongoing as knowledge and theories develop, pedagogical tools and insights refine, and collaborative partnerships create cooperative opportunities.

Kent certificates are an add-on to an undergraduate major course of study and are so noted on the student's transcript. This TEFL Certificate, with a required study-abroad component in Dresden, serves as an introduction to the field and comprises 18 credit hours, including the practicum courses in Dresden (see *Undergraduate Certificate*, 2006).

The BA in TESL, which prepares undergraduates to teach domestically and internationally, is a 36-credit major. It has core courses overlapping the TEFL Certificate and courses that add content understanding of language and culture, language and culture learning, and pedagogical theory and practice. In addition, students complete course-distribution requirements through various disciplines on campus as well as other university requirements (see *Bachelor of Arts in TESL*, n.d.).

The education minor, which is an option to accompany the BA in TESL, adds 30 credit hours to the major, expands on knowledge and practice, and prepares students to meet Ohio requirements for state licensure in ESL. Field experiences allow students to observe and participate in ESL classrooms in area schools early in the program, and student teaching and an electronic portfolio provide capstone experiences.

Any curricular innovation involving new degree programs in higher education is a lengthy and often tedious process involving prescribed documentation and review. Kent is no different, with each proposal moving through careful review by curriculum committees composed of faculty and administrators at various institutional levels. After university approval, proposals are circulated to other state institutions for review and then forwarded to the Ohio Board of Regents to ensure that programs meet regional and state needs. The curriculum proposal process for new degree and certificate programs takes 2 or more years. Making extensive use of the *TESOL/*

NCATE Standards (TESOL, 2003b) has supported our efforts to gain Kent's approval and receive positive reviews from other Ohio universities because the standards legitimate our proposals and provide a sound framework for development and review. The successful approval and implementation of the TEFL Certificate, including student satisfaction and continuing enrollment, and support from Kent (e.g., new faculty hires, increased library allocations) ensured that the BA and the minor in education were approved despite a climate of budget cuts in U.S. higher education.

CURRENT PROGRAMS AND COLLABORATIONS

Kent is a midsized public university in the midwestern United States that is known for preparing students in fields as varied as nursing and liquid crystal physics. The English Department has hosted our master's program in TESL/TEFL (see *Master of Arts: English*, n.d.) for well over a decade and prepares graduate students and area teachers for a variety of career contexts, from language programs in other countries to adult literacy and intensive English programs (IEPs) at various levels in the United States. ESL endorsement at the graduate level has also been a possibility at Kent, providing an add-on to a current Ohio teaching license. Connections with public schools in our region and with international partner institutes have provided Kent graduate students with many opportunities for practice and development, and graduates of the MA and/or endorsement programs have gone on to teach in and administer programs around the world. The English Department also manages an IEP that serves approximately 120 international students per year with language enrichment and academic preparation courses. And the ESL Center, in addition to providing quality English for academic purposes (EAP) instruction, serves as a laboratory school for our programs in TESL—teachers in training can observe ESL Center classes, collaborate on curricular and extracurricular activities for international students, practice materials/tasks experimentation and implementation, and so on.

The TESL graduate program shares a portion of its curriculum with the pedagogy unit of the Department of Modern and Classical Language Studies (MCLS, which administers foreign language programs). Applied linguistics courses in our respective graduate programs are taught by English or foreign language (FL) faculty and attended by graduate students from both programs. The interchange of perspectives of ESL/EFL and FL students and faculty provides rich opportunities for idea exchange on theory and practice in second/foreign language teaching and teacher education. MCLS also maintains undergraduate BA programs in foreign languages, literature, and translation studies, with the option of a minor in education, which served as a model for our minor in education.

English and FL faculty in applied linguistics have a history of connections with colleagues in the Department of Education because many students who take undergraduate linguistics courses are preparing to teach in public schools. Licensure programs are held to National Council for the Accreditation of Teacher Education (NCATE) accrediting procedures (last completed at Kent in 2001) and currently follow a 7-year cycle. Understanding and application of the *TESOL/NCATE Standards* (TESOL, 2003b) has been essential in developing the new education minor as we collaborated with Education faculty and gained approvals through their college curriculum review processes.

Students who pursue undergraduate degrees at Kent typically come from northeastern Ohio, whereas graduate students, especially those in the TESL program, come from the broader midwestern United States as well as such countries as Brazil, China, the Czech Republic, Germany, Japan, Palestine, Russia, Saudi Arabia, Serbia, Taiwan, and Turkey. TESL faculty hold doctorates (tenure track) or master's degrees (non–tenure track) in applied linguistics, have international teaching experience and multilingual skills, and are experienced applied linguistics researchers.

Program Design

In this section we describe the curriculum development processes involved in proposing and piloting our programs, and we discuss how the *TESOL/ NCATE Standards* (TESOL, 2003b) provided a framework for the content development of our new courses as well as other professional development opportunities in TESL/TEFL.

THREE NEW PROPOSALS AT KENT STATE UNIVERSITY

TEFL Certificate

Previously, undergraduates had few opportunities to pursue applied linguistics interests at Kent. So we studied existing certificate programs at U.S. universities and considered TESOL's (2003a) *Position Statement on Independent TESL/TEFL Certificate Programs* to determine the minimum requirements needed and which courses to offer. Our comparison of U.S.-based certificates revealed a breadth of program options; it seems that a TEFL certificate can be earned in as few as 4 weeks or as many as several months, making compatibility of programs almost impossible. Furthermore, there appear to be three options for location of training: (a) the entire program takes place in the United States, (b) the entire program takes place in a non-English-speaking country, or (c) domestic and international study are combined. Our certificate combined coursework completed at Kent with the practicum components offered only in Dresden, which ensured authenticity in EFL teaching/learning environments.

We contemplated short-term intensive workshops, but this ran counter to TESOL's (2003a) advice to "serve as a gateway to the field and profession" and "provide a balance of theory and practice" with a minimum of "100 instructional hours plus a supervised practice teaching component" (p. 1). We decided to keep the semester-long course structure, far exceeding 100 instructional hours, knowing that doing so would result in a program requiring more time and resources than short-term workshops. There were two additional reasons for offering semester-long courses: Students in other majors, such as English or education, could also take TEFL Certificate courses, and semester-long courses lay the foundation for a BA in TESL.

Existing courses at Kent and TU Dresden were examined to determine which would be suitable in meeting our goals. Beyond existing undergraduate linguistics courses, three courses (TESL/TEFL Pedagogy, TESL/TEFL Practicum, and Computers in Second Language Teaching) existed only at the graduate level, so new undergraduate versions of these courses needed to be developed. At TU Dresden, equivalents of all courses existed in applied linguistics degree programs, although most were at the graduate level. Overlap in course offerings encouraged us in the first year of the program to allow students to enroll in courses at either Kent or TU Dresden, but the Practicum was instituted as a study-abroad requirement to take place in Dresden under Kent faculty supervision. However, early in the first year, we encountered a problem in trying to establish a common philosophy for a certificate program—a concept unknown in Germany, where all teachers receive specialized training for a period of 5 or more years in a rather lock-step manner. Because of this, the TEFL Certificate curriculum was redesigned to require Kent courses only. These courses can be taken in Dresden from Kent faculty or at Kent with only the Practicum being completed in Dresden. Courses in Dresden are supplemented with content support in the form of modules presented by TU Dresden or Kent faculty.

The development of the TEFL Certificate was enabled by generous support from TU Dresden, which has provided observation facilities as well as office and classroom space. Practicum opportunities in Dresden include public school classrooms, English for specific purposes (ESP) and EAP courses at TU Dresden, and community education courses offered to the public through two companies in the Dresden area. Kent students spend 1–3 months in Dresden studying, observing classes, and preparing lessons, all while living in student apartments near TU Dresden, riding public transportation to schools and teaching sites, and experiencing Germany and German student life in an historically significant city rich in cultural and political history. Recent graduates of the TEFL Certificate program have gone on to teach in China, Japan, Korea, Germany, and Turkey, and many have entered an MA TESL program at Kent or another university.

The BA in TESL

The proposal for a new bachelor's degree in TESL capitalized on the TEFL Certificate, responded to student interest in professional development for teaching English in the United States and internationally, and met regional and global need in schools. We gained preapproval for the proposal from the Ohio Board of Regents, which is a preliminary step toward developing new degree programs in the state. Expanding the TEFL Certificate into a degree program required the addition of several new courses, an action welcomed by the English Department because it meant that English majors and minors, who are generally literature and writing students, would have additional elective opportunities. We expanded and enhanced the already approved certificate's focus on language, culture, pedagogy, and hands-on practice by further developing multicultural competence, writing skills, and assessment practices.

We generated several course proposals before deciding on core and ancillary requirements for the new BA. Existing courses in other departments on campus (such as Psychology and Speech Communication) and English courses leading to the TEFL Certificate were matched to the *TESOL/NCATE Standards* (TESOL, 2003b). We believe that experience as a second language learner is key to the development of language teaching professionals because individual insights into language learning processes with concomitant sociocultural stumbling blocks can more easily be gained through direct experience. Fortunately, the College of Arts and Sciences at Kent requires majors to complete 2 years of study in a modern or classical language (including American Sign Language) as part of liberal studies requirements; thus, our proposed major suited the college's existing language and culture learning goals. We incorporated existing university courses (including World Literature, Multicultural Psychology, Intercultural Communication, and Advanced Writing) into the degree program. We collaborated across campus to ensure that our proposal met university standards but did not duplicate content provided in other departments. Making use of available resources enhanced our proposal in the eyes of curriculum review committees at Kent. The university requires undergraduates to take one discipline-specific intensive writing course within each major, so we decided to make World Englishes and Sociolinguistics in Schooling writing-intensive courses that, in addition to expanding linguistic, cultural, and pedagogical content knowledge, train students to write as applied linguists.

The Minor in Education

As evidenced by the 2000 census, Ohio demographics are changing, and there are increased numbers of limited-English-speaking children and families in the public schools in both urban and rural areas. Kent has received numerous requests for qualified ESL professionals from local school administrators and has seen an increase in student interest in state licensure in ESL at both undergraduate and graduate levels. In response to the change in Ohio law allowing ESL licensure, we developed a proposal for a minor in education, which provides undergraduates with an option to work toward state licensure by continuing coursework in both TESL/TEFL and education. Development of the minor involved considerable collaborative effort with various committees in Kent's Department of Education. Most licensure candidates from Kent are education majors in programs of study focusing on different age groups (e.g., early childhood, middle childhood, secondary students) and different content (e.g., science, social science), and they have the equivalent of minors in disciplines across campus. Our proposal was different because of the BA is in the content area (TESL) and because we planned to prepare students to teach more broadly with a P–12 license. Fortunately, MCLS's minor in education, which accompanied a BA in foreign language, provided an ideal model for our proposal.

To meet P–12 standards for ESL and to address needs at different educational levels in local schools, our proposal allowed students to tailor a program to the age group they wished to eventually teach. Faculty in Education advise English faculty and students on current courses and state licensing requirements as well as provide timelines for completion of early field experiences, practicum, and student-teaching courses. Field experiences and placements are facilitated through Education and supervised by English faculty. We built in flexibility so that teacher candidates could work with various age levels in schools, select appropriate courses, tailor course projects to professional interests, and plan student teaching and portfolios to shape their own career paths.

INTEGRATING TESOL/NCATE STANDARDS

Although NCATE procedures for program review would normally be applied only in accrediting the minor in education, we integrated the *TESOL/NCATE Standards* (TESOL, 2003b) in designing each of the three new programs because the standards ensured quality and provided consistency across programs, even those that do not provide ESL licensure. These standards outline five domains (language; culture; planning, implementing, and managing instruction; assessment; and professionalism), each of which has two or more standards. The standards can be used "for professional preparation and employment, continuing education, and student programs" (p. 3), and their main purpose is to produce highly qualified English language teachers. Overall, they provided us with a framework for course and program development as well as ideas for assessment tools to use in ongoing evaluation of courses, programs, students, and alumni.

Language

The language standards ensure that teachers are able to foster ESL students' social and cognitive development through content and language learning and promote academic and interpersonal proficiency in urban and rural settings in the United States. The first standard in the language domain (describing language) is met through courses such as English Grammar, Linguistics, History of the English Language, and Lexicography/Lexicology, which interpret language as a social phenomenon used for communicative and cognitive purposes. Linguistics and language courses, including foreign language study, concentrate on developing a fundamental understanding of how human language develops and functions and how different linguistic structures are expressions of various communicative ends. Students learn how meaning is realized at syntactic, morphological, and phonological levels and learn that systematic diversity of spoken and written English creates social cohesion and/or distance. The Lexicography/Lexicology course includes in-depth study of words in use against a backdrop of continuous language change and expansion as well as study of the lexicographer's tools (e.g., electronic dictionaries, corpora, concordancers) and their use in language education. Students also take two writing courses: an advanced university course aimed at developing expository and argumentative skills and a writing-intensive applied linguistics course (whose content falls under the culture standards) in which students practice writing different discourse forms that are preferred in the field (e.g., essays, annotated bibliographies, research reports). Language standards support teacher candidates' academic learning and encourage development of core knowledge and professionalism in the field.

More than any other single course, our Child Second Language Acquisition course, with its focus on additional language acquisition, cuts across the standards and provides insights into language, culture, style and preferences, learning theory/practice, and professional research practices. In terms of language, linguistic tools of phonology, morphology, and syntax are used in analyzing child language patterns and pattern development. Cognitive science plays a central role, as do child development and social interaction in the analysis of language products and learning processes—concepts that make up the second language standard: language acquisition and development.

Culture

The culture standards support teacher understanding of home language and culture and their influence on students' prior and current school and other language learning experiences. The cultural domain includes two standards: understanding the nature and role of culture and understanding the role of cultural groups and identity in language teaching. A sociocultural perspective enhances teacher candidates' understanding of foreign cultures within which they might teach and of what it means to teach English in an English-speaking culture. Understanding the role of culture in human interaction highlights individual and societal effects and affect in language learning. Language forms realize social patterns, traditions, and norms (or vice versa), and courses emphasize the connection between society and language from varying epistemological standpoints.

Students take courses imbued with cultural learning, including foreign languages, literature, Child Second Language Acquisition, Multicultural Psychology, Intercultural Communication, World Englishes, and Sociolinguistics in Schooling. Cultural learning courses expose students to language variation and change within social/cultural contexts. Topics are varied and include language politics and policies with an emphasis on literacy and education within an electronic age, interaction between society and language with pedagogical implications, cultural practices that facilitate or cause breakdowns in communication, and cultural and age-related influences on education and learning. Students in the TEFL Certificate program are immersed in a foreign culture. Field and practical teaching experiences provide opportunities for intercultural exchange to students seeking the BA and the education minor; they experience firsthand the challenges faced by young English language learners and their families in the United States so that as teachers they can advocate for students while teaching and learning with them.

Planning, Implementing, and Managing Instruction

The standards related to planning, implementing, and managing instruction include a focus on content curriculum for a variety of teaching contexts (e.g., multilevel, multilingual) using appropriate materials and technological support. Managing instruction is practiced mainly in pedagogy and practicum courses in which students engage theory in practice. In pedagogy courses, we differentiate among approach, method, and techniques as they relate to language learning and teaching. We contextualize instruction in various social, historical, and educational contexts, and we establish a common basis for communicative teaching of language and literacy. Materials review; lesson, task, and assessment planning and implementation; and professional development (e.g., using applied linguistics databases and references) permeate instructional management courses, and a computer-assisted language learning (CALL) course introduces students to current tools and practices in teaching with computer-based technologies. Additionally, the CALL course provides opportunities to generate original teaching and assessment materials and to practice using technology in teaching.

Courses address the third standard in the domain of planning, implementing, and managing instruction (using resources effectively in instruction) and familiarize students with varied foreign/second language situations, giving them opportunities to explore ESL/EFL instruction in classes with

- learners of different ages, educational backgrounds, and proficiency levels (either homogeneous or not)
- large and small numbers of students (at times, perhaps tutoring one on one)
- groupings of culturally/linguistically homogeneous or heterogeneous students
- lessons and courses with varied goals (academic or social)

These opportunities are vital for addressing the first standard (planning for standards-based ESL and content instruction) as students gain hands-on experience teaching English under foreign and/or second language conditions. Lesson planning, preparation, implementation all serve to prepare students for teaching in a variety of professional contexts. Supervision of field experiences and reflective practices taught throughout the curriculum ensure adherence to the second standard in this domain: managing and implementing standards-based instruction. Students pursuing the minor in education are additionally expected to meet standards prescribed by the state of Ohio (Ohio Department of Education, 2006) and reflected in TESOL's (2006) *PreK–12 English Language Proficiency Standards in the Core Content Areas*.

Assessment

The assessment standards support teacher knowledge and use of effective measures for evaluating proficiency and achievement of students and programs. Teacher candidates must be able to develop and use assessment tools to facilitate student learning. Through pedagogy courses and throughout students' academic programs, they create, evaluate, reflect on, and participate in implementation of tasks, activities, materials, and content learning, with formal and informal assessment practices for both formative and summative purposes. Pedagogy and multicultural courses problematize culture as an influence on assessment processes and outcomes because dialect/language and social context affect language production, which addresses the first standard in this domain: understanding the issues inherent in assessment.

Students practice assessment by incorporating plans, procedures, and instruments into projects and teaching, especially in pedagogy and practicum courses, addressing the second and third standards (language proficiency assessment and classroom-based assessment), using a variety of standards- and performance-based instruments to inform instruction. In addition to being able to use appropriate assessments as teachers, students must be able to assess their own teaching. Incorporated into this assessment framework are multiple opportunities for self-reflection, and the culminating process of producing a professional portfolio to document development in the teaching profession serves as a capstone experience and prepares candidates for the job market.

Professionalism

The standards related to professionalism relate to teachers' knowledge of the field, partnerships with students and their families, and collaboration with school staff to serve as resources in improving learning for ESL/EFL learners. The professionalism domain ties together the standards in the other domains through an emphasis on the consistent application of professional principles. Throughout the curriculum, students use applied linguistics resources, explore and reflect on theory and practice, and develop skills and resources of their own. In doing so, they enhance their professional skills, all of which are important components of the first standard: demonstrating knowledge of ESL research and history.

The course module concept from collaborations with TU Dresden faculty has been an exciting addition to pedagogy, practicum, and child second language acquisition courses and specifically addresses the second and third standards: partnerships and advocacy, and professional development and collaboration. Modules of interest to TESL/TEFL professionals (e.g., locating and securing jobs, reviewing language learning textbooks or multimedia environments, creating a professional portfolio with products developed in courses) are infused into courses throughout the degree and certificate programs, allowing cross-institution faculty collaborations and cooperative teaching opportunities. For students pursuing the minor in education, issues of professionalism include Ohio state professional teaching standards.

Program Cohesion

Figure 1 illustrates how the TEFL Certificate provides the foundation for coursework in the BA in TESL. Our general objective for the TEFL Certificate program is to provide preliminary training for EFL teachers, including basic understanding of the role of language and culture in teaching and learning. TEFL Certificate courses reflect this goal and include two courses in language study (English Grammar and Linguistics), an ESL/EFL pedagogy course, and a course on technology in the second/foreign language classroom. The BA expands on this foundational coursework through additional language courses (History of the English Language, Lexicography, foreign languages, and writing), sociocultural/multicultural courses (World Englishes, Sociolinguistics in Schooling, Multicultural Psychology, and Intercultural Communication), and learning theory and practice courses (Child Second Language Acquisition and TESL Pedagogy). Courses in the minor in education prepare students for licensure exams and school practices and include courses in teaching language and literacy, managing classrooms, and multicultural/multilevel education, which examine in more depth the topics addressed in TESL Pedagogy that are related to English language learners in the U.S. educational system. In addition, the education minor requires field experiences and student teaching to round out the students' preparation for teaching ESL.

Practicum options in each new program, as opposed to the field experience and student teaching included in the education minor only, are represented in Figure 1 as overlapping possibilities, which students can tailor to their own career goals. The TEFL Certificate requires students to complete two practicum courses in Dresden, where they participate in teaching and support roles in a variety of school contexts, including providing assistance to classroom teachers, acting as language informants, analyzing and adapting

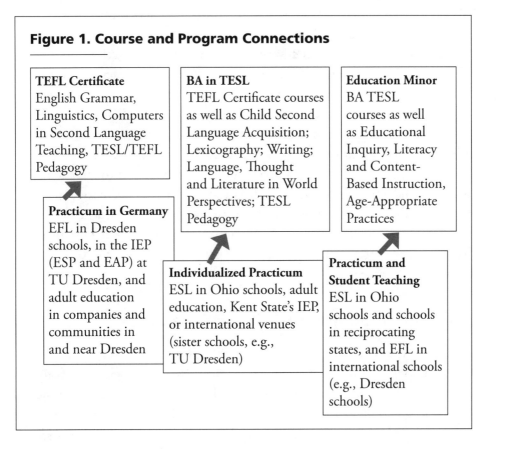

Figure 1. Course and Program Connections

TEFL Certificate
English Grammar, Linguistics, Computers in Second Language Teaching, TESL/TEFL Pedagogy

BA in TESL
TEFL Certificate courses as well as Child Second Language Acquisition; Lexicography; Writing; Language, Thought and Literature in World Perspectives; TESL Pedagogy

Education Minor
BA TESL courses as well as Educational Inquiry, Literacy and Content-Based Instruction, Age-Appropriate Practices

Practicum in Germany
EFL in Dresden schools, in the IEP (ESP and EAP) at TU Dresden, and adult education in companies and communities in and near Dresden

Individualized Practicum
ESL in Ohio schools, adult education, Kent State's IEP, or international venues (sister schools, e.g., TU Dresden)

Practicum and Student Teaching
ESL in Ohio schools and schools in reciprocating states, and EFL in international schools (e.g., Dresden schools)

course materials and tasks, and preparing and implementing lessons or portions of lessons. Students are partnered up for observation and participation in two or more of the following venues around Dresden, selected based on students' backgrounds and career interests:

- EFL classes in public schools: an elementary school (*Grundschule*) attended by all pupils 6–10 years old; a middle school (*Mittelschule*) with 11- to 16-year-old vocational preparation students; or a high school (*Gymnasium*) where 11- to 18-year-old students are preparing for university studies
- university-level EAP and ESP courses at TU Dresden serving a variety of academic disciplines such as law, mechanical engineering, computer science, and international relations
- community adult education classes with large numbers of local residents of various ages who are eager to improve their conversational English skills
- classes focusing on conversation and business interactions organized for small groups of mixed-level employees (in terms of both employee rank and language skills) for local companies (Currently we provide instruction at pharmaceutical and information technology companies.)

BA TESL majors can also optionally complete practicum work in Dresden. And they can gain experience in classroom observation and practice in schools and adult education centers in northeastern Ohio or at Kent's IEP, the ESL Center. Placement at an appropriate practicum site is planned through the advising process and takes into account student interest, background, and career goals. Students minoring in education are able to participate in practicum courses, field experience, and student teaching in schools in Dresden or Ohio. By giving students flexibility in practicum and student-teaching placements, individual goals can be met through careful planning and advising. We have been fortunate to have excellent cooperation with teachers and administrators at various practicum sites, and Kent faculty supervision in all venues throughout field experience requirements has proven essential in ensuring reflective practice, experimentation, and substantive feedback.

Program Implementation and Evaluation

Student reflection and evaluation of the TEFL Certificate program has been central in our curriculum development process because it helps us improve the program by responding to student and institutional needs. Sixty-nine students had completed the TEFL Certificate as of fall 2006. In the first few years of the program, evaluation was conducted informally through student-faculty discussions. We found that informal assessment was only the first step in systematically addressing student concerns and professional development needs, so we devised the following two tools: a reflective guide used in the practicum to develop student professionalism and an end-of-program evaluation based in part on H. D. Brown's (2001, see chapter 23) suggestions but tailored to meet program needs.

The TEFL Certificate Reflective Guide (see Appendix A) is a tool that encourages student introspection on the *TESOL/NCATE Standards* (TESOL, 2003b) and teaching dispositions. The guide is completed by students in practicum courses near the end of their stay in Dresden. By reflecting on professionalism, students are encouraged to reexamine what they have learned and what they still need to learn as professionals.

The TEFL Certificate End-of-Program Evaluation (see Appendix B) provides a means for students to address various aspects of the program, including predeparture activities, logistics on the ground in Dresden, facilities, and academic programming. This anonymous assessment provides us with ongoing input on all aspects of the program for continuing improvement.

Findings from informal and formal assessments of the TEFL Certificate program reveal that implementation has run smoothly for several reasons:

- We have enjoyed strong interest, collaboration, and participation among TU Dresden and Kent students, faculty, and institutions.
- Support from TU Dresden is ongoing in the form of an office and classrooms for our course meetings; ESP and EAP classes for participant observation; and student status for Kent students, which provides them with such benefits as TU Dresden services and Dresden-area discounts.
- Highly capable bilingual assistants hired by Kent have helped administer community courses by placing advertisements in local newspapers and providing information to potential learners. These assistants have also provided logistical and bilingual support (on such issues as housing, visas, local transportation, and medical emergencies) to Kent students and have acted in university liaison roles between Kent and TU Dresden.
- The Dresden-area residents, who experience our students firsthand in their classrooms and communities, have been generous and forthcoming in welcoming our students.

Faculty collaborations across applied language programs at Kent and TU Dresden have resulted in an especially notable international exchange. Kent faculty accompany students to Dresden in the spring and/or summer each year, where they teach certificate courses, supervise and oversee community classes, make essential contacts with school and community officials, and participate in academic activities at TU Dresden. In particular, instruction modules, which can be delivered to Kent and TU Dresden students independently or simultaneously, promote professionalism through knowledge sharing and are prepared and delivered by faculty from both universities. Other positive evaluations about the Dresden exchange can be summarized as follows:

- Whether students stay in Dresden for the 4-week practicum only or for an entire semester of coursework plus the practicum, most report that components of the program integrate well into a holistic experience.
- Language courses taught in Dresden (e.g., English Grammar, Linguistics) may have a more pedagogical focus than in similar courses taught on the Kent campus, contributing to a more positive impact on overall training.
- Pedagogical flexibility (e.g., varied school types, learning environments with different age groups and proficiency levels) throughout the EFL practicum give all participants broad hands-on experience in authentic EFL environments.
- With clear cultural integration, the program helps students gain knowledge and skills that go beyond their expectations. Only a few students arrive in Dresden with much (if any) knowledge of German language, culture, and history, yet all gain insights into surviving in another country.
- The program, a genuinely international one, requires participants to make adjustments in their study style, lifestyle, and contact with content area and teaching because living in another country means they lack or have limited linguistic, pedagogical, and interpersonal knowledge and skills.
- For most undergraduate participants, this program provides unique opportunities to focus on and pursue realistic career goals.

Complaints about and modifications to the program are inevitable. Previously, students complained about limited access to computer technologies. We recently invested in better computer facilities to include loaner laptops for students and a projection device for classrooms. We have also established wireless access to the Internet in student apartments and in our TU Dresden classroom and office, enabling more effective communications, materials resources access, and materials/assessment production capabilities. Some recent criticism has focused on factors outside our control (e.g., construction in student apartments, dirt and lack of elevators, long travel distances to practicum schools). Many of these complaints reflect cultural and logistical adjustment to living in an urban environment, but we do try to address them when we can. For example, by pairing or grouping students for practicum placements, we have minimized discontent about travel times.

Early in the program, non-German-speaking Kent students (the majority) had difficulties finding their way around Dresden. Lack of bilingual skills put many of them at a disadvantage, but we addressed these concerns through better preparation and orientation to survival in a foreign country prior to departure. We also ensured increased contact in schools, bilingual assistance from program assistants, better organization of materials (e.g., maps, train schedules), and a more formalized structure for disseminating other resources, such as those left by former participants (e.g., tips on grocery stores; restaurant and bookstore recommendations; directions to famous sites related to the arts, entertainment, and history).

The few Kent students who do speak German and understand something of German history, society, and educational systems bring a more informed view to the experience, and they enrich pedagogy and practicum class discussions. When students lack such experience, faculty and program assistants provide cultural insights into the international educational experience. As a European Union lingua franca, and as the preferred foreign language in schools since 1989 (Russ, 1994), English is generally adequate for communications around Dresden, especially when addressing younger people or people in the tourist industry. Kent faculty participating thus far in the TEFL Certificate program are all bilingual (English-German) and include graduates of Kent's MA TESL program, a Kent faculty member native to the Dresden area, and another who taught the spring/summer term recently at both TU Dresden and Universität Leipzig (another partner university with which Kent has had a productive and highly successful faculty exchange in linguistics and the sciences for more than three decades). As multilingual world citizens, TESL faculty model core values related to language learning and use in communities and classrooms.

Conclusion

The BA in TESL and the minor in education were approved in late 2006, and we will participate in our first NCATE review in ESL licensure in 2008. We anticipate that because we prepared our programs by applying the *TESOL/NCATE Standards* (TESOL, 2003b) as a framework, the preliminary accreditation process will be a smooth one. In addition, evaluative tools developed for the TEFL Certificate will provide models for preliminary program assessment. Beyond such formalized review processes, the *TESOL/NCATE Standards* will continue to serve as a guide in the preparation of professional applied linguistics teachers at Kent across our programs.

Appendix A: TEFL Certificate Reflective Guide

1. Thinking back on the objectives you set for yourself for the program during pre-departure meetings for the program, which did you achieve?

2. Which objectives didn't you achieve? Why not?

3. What is your most remarkable achievement in this program?

Language Teaching Dispositions

Please evaluate yourself as an EFL professional using the scale:
5 = excellent, 4 = above average, 3 = average, 2 = below average,
1 = unsatisfactory

	5	4	3	2	1
Linguistic Knowledge					
English phonology					
English grammar					
English textual patterns					
English vocabulary (word meanings and contexts)					
Understanding my own processes of foreign/second language learning					
Pedagogical Skills					
I understand and use a wide variety of techniques.					
I know how to design lessons.					
I know how to design a course.					
I can identify the linguistic needs of my students.					
I know how to stimulate interaction, cooperation, and teamwork.					
I know how to manage a class.					
I can creatively adapt textbook material and other teaching aids.					
I can create new teaching materials when needed.					
I know how to motivate learners in EFL situations.					
Interpersonal Skills					
I know how to handle cross-cultural differences.					
I know how to work with others to share thoughts, prepare and conduct classes, and provide feedback.					
I can cooperate with supervising teachers.					

Personal Qualities					
I know what it means to be flexible.					
I know how to be tolerant of ambiguity.					
I understand ethical and moral standards for teaching.					

Now, for each category, provide a narrative statement in which you reflect on your learning in, or outside of, the TEFL Certificate program that particularly addresses your strengths and weaknesses as a TEFL professional.

Linguistic Knowledge

Pedagogical Skills

Interpersonal Skills

Personal Qualities

Appendix B: TEFL Certificate End-of-Program Evaluation

Please take a few minutes to evaluate the program. Your opinion is very important for our future decisions, so feel free to elaborate on any of the following. Thanks for your time!

1. How did you hear about the program?
   a) In-class presentation
   b) Friend
   c) Internet
   d) Other (please name)

2. Why did you choose this program over other TEFL certificate programs? Choose all that apply.
   a) Needed the credit anyway
   b) Interested in Germany
   c) Interested in traveling
   d) Length
   e) Curriculum
   f) Value for money
   g) Reputation
   h) Other

3. After receiving the Certificate, do you think you'll:
   a) Work in TEFL sometime soon
   b) Continue your education in the field
   c) Continue education in another field
   d) Other (please name)

4. Tell us about your coursework. Which courses did you complete on the Kent campus and which on the TU Dresden campus?

   <u>Kent</u>   <u>TU Dresden</u>

5. Please provide us with a brief written evaluation of how the program contributed to your learning in the following areas:

   A. Linguistic Knowledge

   B. Pedagogical Skills

   C. Interpersonal Skills

   D. Cultural Understanding/Exchange

6. Please evaluate the following points using this scale. Write additional comments on any of these points at the end of the survey.

   5 = excellent, 4 = above average, 3 = average, 2 = below average, 1 = unsatisfactory

	5	4	3	2	1
Preparation					
Pre-departure information was provided.					
Pre-departure meetings were helpful.					
Pre-departure questions were answered.					
Arrival					
Support was provided when I arrived in Dresden.					
Expected personal attention was provided when I arrived.					
Academic Program					
The program offered a suitable introduction to German culture.					
The program kept what it promised in terms of intensity.					
The program respected the intellectual level of the students.					

The schedule was appropriate.					
The curriculum included all necessary components for a certificate.					
Practicum placements addressed my needs.					
The Practicum provided suitable training.					
Cooperating teachers in Dresden schools met my needs.					
Kent faculty met my needs.					
Modules taught by Kent faculty met my needs.					
Modules taught by TU Dresden faculty met my needs.					
Stay/Living Conditions					
Personal assistance was adequate during my stay in Dresden.					
My living situation was appropriate.					
Access to computers and the Internet was adequate.					
The city of Dresden was a suitable place of study.					
I participated in Dresden-area cultural and sight-seeing opportunities.					
I participated in TU Dresden cultural and social events.					
General					
The program met my needs.					
I would recommend this program to others.					
I advise Kent's English Department to continue the program.					

Students in this program may take courses in Kent and Dresden or in Dresden only. In either case, did you find courses provided appropriate preparation for the Practicum in Dresden?

Elaborate on any of the above, or provide other additional comments. Thanks! Your comments help in our curriculum development process!

References

Abreu-e-Lima, D. M. (2006). *Towards a macro organizational model of preservice language teacher education: The communicative approach through projects and the development of competences under the multiple intelligences theory perspective.* Unpublished doctoral dissertation, Universidade de Campinas, Campinas, Brazil.

Aleamoni, L. M. (1987). Typical faculty concerns about student ratings of teaching. In L. M. Aleamoni (Ed.), *Techniques of evaluating and improving instruction* (pp. 25–31). San Francisco: Jossey-Bass.

Almeida Filho, J. C. P. (1997). Tendências na formação continuada de professores de língua estrangeira [Tendencies in the continuous education of teachers of foreign languages]. *Ensino & Pesquisa, 1*, 29–41.

American Council on the Teaching of Foreign Languages. (1986). *ACTFL proficiency guidelines.* New York: Author.

American University of Sharjah catalog. (1998). Sharjah, United Arab Emirates: American University of Sharjah.

Autonomous Language Learning Modules (ALMS) at Helsinki University Language Centre, Finland. (n.d.). Retrieved April 7, 2007, from http://www.helsinki.fi/kksc/alms/

Bachelor of arts in TESL. (n.d.). Kent State University. Retrieved April 12, 2007, from http://dept.kent.edu/english/underg/batesl.htm

Barrett, P. (1982). *The administration of intensive English programs.* Washington, DC: National Association for Foreign Student Affairs.

Basso, E. A. A. (2001). *Construção social das competências necessárias ao professor de língua estrangeira: Entre o real e o ideal—um curso de letras em estudo* [Social construction of necessary competencies for the foreign language teacher: Between the real and the ideal—a course in languages studied]. Unpublished doctoral dissertation, Universidade de Campinas, Campinas, Brazil.

Batstone, R. (1994). *Grammar.* Oxford: Oxford University Press.

Benson, P. (2001). *Teaching and researching autonomy in language learning.* Harlow, England: Longman.

Black Hawk College. (2003). *Self study report summary: Prepared for the Higher Learning Commission North Central Association of Colleges and Schools.* Moline, IL: Author.

Brender, A. (2003). Japan's junior colleges face a grim future. *Chronicle of Higher Education, 50*(12), p. A39.

Brinton, D., Snow, M., & Wesche, M. (1989). *Content-based second language instruction.* New York: Newbury House.

Brown, C. (2001a). Project-based teaching promotes autonomy in L2 learning. In A. Mackenzie & E. McCafferty (Eds.), *Developing autonomy: Proceedings of the JALT CUE Conference 2001* (pp. 89–92). Tokyo: Japan Association for Language Teaching College and University Educators Special Interest Group.

Brown, C. (2001b). Promoting autonomy and/or self-direction in SL teaching. *On CUE, 9*(1), 6–8.

Brown, H. D. (2001). *Teaching by principles: An interactive approach to language pedagogy* (2nd ed.). White Plains, NY: Longman.

Brown, J. D. (1995). *The elements of a language curriculum.* Boston: Heinle & Heinle.

Brundage, D. H., & MacKeracher, D. (1980). *Adult learning principles and their application to program planning.* Toronto, Canada: Ontario Institute for Studies in Education.

Budd, R., & Wright, T. (1992). Putting a process syllabus into practice. In D. Nunan (Ed.), *Collaborative language learning and teaching.* Cambridge: Cambridge University Press.

Carson, J. G., Taylor, J. A., & Fredella, L. (1997). The role of content in task-based EAP instruction. In M. Snow & D. Brinton (Eds.), *The content-based classroom: Perspectives on integrating language and content* (pp. 367–370). White Plains, NY: Longman.

Celce-Murcia, M. (Ed.). (2002). *Teaching English as a second or foreign language.* Boston: Heinle & Heinle.

Chamot, A. U., & O'Malley, J. M. (1994). *The CALLA handbook: Implementing the cognitive academic language learning approach.* New York: Addison-Wesley.

Chen, J.-Q., & Dym, W. (2003). Using computer technology to bridge school and community. *Phi Delta Kappan, 85*(3), 232–234.

Chihara, T. (1998). Ko kara tougou e: Eigo kyoiku 30 nen no ayumi [From independent to integrated: 30 years of English education]. In Souritsu 30 Shuunen Kinen Iinkai (Ed.), *"Nani ga dekite, nani ga deki nai ka":*

Souritsu 30 shuunen kinen "jiko kensa hyou" (pp. 27–42). Osaka, Japan: Osaka Jogakuin Junior College.

Clair, N., & Adger, C. (2000). Sustainable strategies for professional development in educational reform. In K. E. Johnson (Ed.), *Teacher education* (pp. 29–49). Alexandria, VA: TESOL.

Claus, M. M. K. (2005). *A formação da competência teórica do professor de língua estrangeira: O que revelam os estágios* [The development of a theoretical competence of foreign language teachers: What the practicum reveals]. Unpublished master's thesis, Universidade de Campinas, Campinas, Brazil.

Cohen, R. (1984). *Acting one.* Mountain View, CA: Mayfield.

Coulson, E. (1972). *Confessions of a forward looking educational conservationist. Inaugural lecture 24th March 1972.* London: Chelsea College, University of London.

Coxhead, A. (2000). A new academic word list. *TESOL Quarterly, 34,* 213–238.

Dave's ESL cafe. (1995–2007). Retrieved April 4, 2007, from http://www.eslcafe.com/

Dickinson, L. (1992). *Learner autonomy 2: Learner training for language learning.* Dublin, Ireland: Authentik.

Donadio, L. F. P. S. (2007). *Content-based instruction para professores pré-serviço: Uma análise da problemática do processo de avaliação* [Content-based instruction for pre-service teachers: An analysis of questions concerning the evaluation process]. Unpublished master's thesis, Universidade Federal de São Carlos, São Carlos, Brazil.

Educational philosophy. (n.d.). Osaka Jogakuin College. Retrieved April 6, 2007, from http://www.wilmina.ac.jp/2yrs/english/curriculum_e.html

Educational Testing Service. (1980). *Secondary Level English Proficiency Test.* Princeton, NJ: Author.

Educational Testing Service. (1998). *TOEFL—Institutional Testing Placement.* Princeton, NJ: Author.

Ellis, R. (1994). *The study of second language acquisition.* Oxford: Oxford University Press.

Emidio, D. E. (2007). *Análise do processo de conscientização do licenciando em letras sobre as especificidades de se aprender inglês para ensinar* [Analysis of the awareness process of pre-service teachers about the specificities of learning English to teach it]. Unpublished master's thesis, Universidade Federal de São Carlos, São Carlos, Brazil.

Eskey, D. (1997). Syllabus design in content-based instruction. In M. Snow & D. Brinton (Eds.), *The content-based classroom: Perspectives on integrating language and content* (pp. 132–141). White Plains, NY: Longman.

Ferris, D. (1998). Students' view of academic aural/oral skills: A comparative needs analysis. *TESOL Quarterly, 32,* 289–318.

Ferris, D., & Tagg, T. (1996). Academic oral communication needs of EAP learners: What subject-matter instructors actually require. *TESOL Quarterly, 30,* 31–58.

Fiser, N. (2005). On the brink of the digital divide. *European Integration Studies, 4*(1): 115–123.

Ford, K., & McCafferty, E. (2001). *Projects from the university classroom.* Tokyo: Japan Association for Language Teaching College and University Educators Special Interest Group.

Fotos, S. (2001). Cognitive approaches to grammar instruction. In M. Celce-Murcia (Ed.), *Teaching English as a second or foreign language* (pp. 267–282). Boston: Heinle & Heinle.

Freeman, D. (2002). The hidden side of the work: Teacher knowledge and learning to teach. *Language Teaching, 35,* 1–13.

G-TELP. (n.d.). *Overview—G-TELP.* Retrieved April 7, 2007, from http://www.g-telp.jp/english/index.html

Gardner, H. (1983). *Frames of mind: The theory of multiple intelligences.* New York: Basic Books.

Gardner, H. (1999). *Intelligence reframed: Multiple intelligences for the 21st century.* New York: Basic Books.

Genesee, F., & Upshur, J. A. (1996). *Classroom-based evaluation in second language education.* Cambridge: Cambridge University Press.

Gibbons, J. (1982). The issue of the language of instruction in the lower forms of Hong Kong secondary schools. *Journal of Multilingual and Multicultural Development, 3*(2): 117–128.

Grossman, P. L. (1990). *The making of a teacher: Teacher knowledge and teacher education.* New York: Teachers College Press.

Hargreaves, A. (1997). From reform to renewal: A new deal for a new age. In A. Hargreaves & R. Evans (Eds.), *Beyond educational reform: Bringing teachers back in* (pp. 105–125). Buckingham, England: Open University Press.

Harris, D., & Palmer, L. (1986). *A comprehensive English language test for learners of English: Examiners' instructions and technical manual.* Singapore: McGraw-Hill.

Harris, J. (1998). *Design tools for the Internet-supported classroom.* Alexandria, VA: Association for Supervision and Curriculum Development.

Hecht, I. W. D., Higgerson, M. L., Gmelch, W. H., & Tucker, A. (1999). *The department chair as academic leader.* Phoenix, AZ: American Council on Education and Oryx Press.

Developing a New Curriculum for Adult Learners

Höfling, C. (2006). *Traçando um perfil de usuários de dicionários—estudantes de letras com habilitação em língua inglesa: Um novo olhar sobre dicionários para aprendizes e a formação de um usuário autônomo* [Delineating a profile of dictionary users—undergraduate students of languages with a specialization in English: A new look at dictionaries for learners and the formation of autonomous users]. Unpublished doctoral dissertation, Universidade Estadual Paulista, Araraquara, Brazil.

Hood, S. (1995). From curriculum to courses: Why do teachers do what they do? In A. Burns & S. Hood (Eds.), *Teacher's voices: Exploring course design in a changing curriculum* (pp. 21–33). Sydney, Australia: National Centre for English Teaching and Research.

Jordan, R. R. (1997). *English for academic purposes: A guide and resource book for teachers.* Cambridge: Cambridge University Press.

Kaneko, M. (1997). Efficiency and equity in Japanese higher education. *Higher Education, 34,* 165–181.

Kikuchi, K. (2001). *Analysis of listening needs for EFL learners in a Japanese college.* Unpublished master's thesis, University of Hawaii at Manoa, Honolulu.

Kohonen, V. (1992). Experiential language learning: Second language learning as cooperative learner education. In D. Nunan (Ed.), *Collaborative language learning and teaching.* Cambridge: Cambridge University Press.

Kokuritsu dai iki nokori "kouyaku": Houjin kanochi no shinkijiku tsugitsugi [National universities still have life "commitment": Boards following novel ideas one after another]. (2003, October 17). *Yomuri Shimbun* [Yomuri Newspaper; morning edition], p. 21.

Kramer, S. (Producer/Director). (1967). *Guess who's coming to dinner?* [Motion picture]. United States: Columbia Pictures.

Kumaravadivelu, B. (1991). Language learning tasks: Teacher intention and learner interpretation. *ELT Journal, 45,* 98–107.

Larsen-Freeman, D. (2001). Teaching grammar. In M. Celce-Murcia (Ed.), *Teaching English as a second or foreign Language* (pp. 251–266). Boston: Heinle & Heinle.

Legutke, M., & Thomas, H. (1991). *Process and experience in the language classroom.* Essex, England: Addison-Wesley Longman.

Lightbown, P. M., & Spada, N. (1993). *How languages are learned.* Oxford: Oxford University Press.

Long, M. H., & Crookes, G. (1992). Three approaches to task-based syllabus design. *TESOL Quarterly, 26,* 27–56.

Lortie, D. C. (1975). *Schoolteacher: A sociological study.* Chicago: University of Chicago Press.

Mackenzie, A. S. (2002). Changing contexts: Connecting teacher autonomy and institutional development. In A. S. Mackenzie & E. McCafferty (Eds.), *Developing autonomy: Proceedings of the JALT CUE conference 2001 held at the Miho Kenshukan of Tokai University* (pp. 223–332). Tokyo: Japan Association for Language Teaching.

Mackenzie, A. S., & McCafferty, E. (2002). *Developing autonomy: Proceedings of the JALT CUE conference 2001 held at the Miho Kenshukan of Tokai University.* Tokyo: Japan Association for Language Teaching.

Margonari, D. M. (2001). *O papel do humor no processo de ensino-aprendizagem de língua Inglesa* [The role of humor in the English language teaching/learning process]. Unpublished master's thesis, Universidade Estadual Paulista, Araraquara, Brazil.

Margonari, D. M. (2006). *A competência humorística e a criatividade no processo de formação de professores de língua inglesa* [Humoristic competence and creativity in the English language teaching/learning process]. Unpublished doctoral dissertation, Universidade Estadual Paulista, Araraquara, Brazil.

Markee, N. (1997). *Managing curricular innovation.* Cambridge: Cambridge University Press.

Master of arts: English: Teaching English as a second language. (n.d.). Kent State University. Retrieved April 12, 2007, from http://dept.kent.edu/english/graduate/masters.htm#TESL

Mavis Beacon Teaches Typing (Version 17) [Computer software]. (2006). San Francisco: Broderbund. http://www.broderbund.com/jump.jsp?itemID=1044&mainPID=1044&itemType=PRODUCT&path=1%2C2%2C8%2C64&iProductID=1044

Maza, F. T. (1999). *Pesquisa em formação de educadores: O professor de inglês e o ensino superior* [Research on teacher education: The English teacher and the undergraduate studies]. Unpublished master's thesis, Pontifícia Universidade Catolica, São Paulo, Brazil.

McVeigh, B. J. (2002). *Japanese higher education as myth.* Armonk, NY: M. E. Sharpe.

Mendelsohn, D. (1995). Applying learning strategies in the second/foreign language listening comprehension lesson. In D. Mendelsohn & J. Rubin (Eds.), *A guide for the teaching of second language listening* (pp. 132–150). San Diego, CA: Dominie Press.

Menges, R. J. (1997). Fostering faculty motivation to teach: Approaches to faculty development. In J. L. Bess (Ed.), *Teaching well and liking it: Motivating faculty to teach effectively* (pp. 407–423). Baltimore: Johns Hopkins University Press.

Messick, S. (1994). The interplay of evidence and consequences in the validation of performance assessments. *Educational Researcher, 23*(2), 13–23.

MicroType (Version 4) [Computer software]. (2006). Mason, OH: Thompson South-Western. http://www.microtype.swlearning.com/mt4/

Military Language Institute. (2001a). *Family, student's book 2.* Abu Dhabi, United Arab Emirates: Author.

Military Language Institute. (2001b). *Food, student's book 4.* Abu Dhabi, United Arab Emirates: Author.

Military Language Institute. (2001c). *Myself, student's book 1.* Abu Dhabi, United Arab Emirates: Author.

National Telecommunications and Information Administration. (2000, October). *Falling through the net: Toward digital inclusion: A report on Americans' access to technology tools.* Retrieved April 4, 2007, from http://www.ntia.doc.gov/ntiahome/fttn00/contents00.html

New Oxford Picture Dictionary [Computer software]. (1997). Oxford: Oxford University Press. http://www.us.oup.com/us/corporate/publishingprograms/esl/titles/picturedictionaries/nopd/

Norris, J., Brown, J., Hudson, T., & Yoshioka, J. (1998). *Designing second language performance assessments.* Honolulu: University of Hawaii Press.

Nunan, D. (1999). *Second language teaching and learning.* Boston: Heinle & Heinle.

Nunes, M. (2007). *Ensino semipresencial e formação de professores pré-serviço: Análise da junção do ambiente virtual ao presencial na formação de futuros professores* [Semi-presential teaching and preservice teacher education: Analysis of the combination of a virtual space and a presential mode in the education of future teachers]. Unpublished master's thesis, Universidade de Campinas, Campinas, Brazil.

Ohio Department of Education. (2006). *English language arts academic content standards.* Retrieved April 12, 2007, from http://www.ode.state.oh.us/GD/Templates/Pages/ODE/ODEDetail.aspx?page=3&TopicRelationID=330&Content=2416

OJJC Karikyuramu Iinkai. (1998). Sukiru toreiningu no genkai no kanta [Beyond skill training]. In Souritsu 30 Shunen Kinnen Iinkai (Ed.), *"Nani ga dekite, nani ga deki nai ka": Souritsu 30 shuunen kinen "jiko kensa hyou"* (pp. 177–188). Osaka, Japan: Osaka Jogakuin Junior College.

O'Malley, J. M., & Pierce, L. V. (1996). *Authentic assessment for English language: Practical approaches for teachers.* Reading, MA: Addison-Wesley.

Paiva, V. L. M. de O. (1997). A identidade do professor de Inglês [The English teacher identity]. *Ensino & Pesquisa 1,* 9–17.

Parry, K. (1996). *Transformational leadership: Developing an enterprising management culture.* South Melbourne, Australia: Pitman.

Peregoy, S., & Boyle, O. (2005). *Reading, writing and learning in ESL: A resource book for k–12 teachers* (4th ed.). Boston: Pearson.

Popper, K. R. (1962). *The open society and its enemies* (Vol. 1). London: Routledge and Kegan Paul.

Prabhu, N. S. (1987). *Second language pedagogy.* Oxford: Oxford University Press.

Richards, J. (2001). *Curriculum development in language teaching.* Cambridge: Cambridge University Press.

Robinson, P., Strong, G., Whittle, J., & Nobe, S. (2001). Development of EAP discussion ability. In J. Flowerdew & M. Peacock (Eds.), *Research perspectives on EAP* (pp. 347–359). Cambridge: Cambridge University Press.

Russ, C. (1994). *The German language today: A linguistic introduction.* London: Routledge.

Schoppa, L. J. (1993). *Education reform in Japan: A case of immobilist politics.* New York: Routledge.

Silva, K. A. (2005). *Crenças e aglomerados de crenças de alunos ingressantes em letras (inglês)* [Beliefs and collection of beliefs of students entering languages courses (English)]. Unpublished master's thesis, Universidade de Campinas, Campinas, Brazil.

Skehan, P. (1996). A framework for the implementation of task-based instruction. *Applied Linguistics, 17,* 38–72.

Sockett, H. (1976). *Designing the curriculum.* London: Open Books.

Souritsu 30 Shuunen Kinen Iinkai. (1998). Osaka Jogakuin Tankidaigaku karikyuramu: 1998 nen hensei ni tsuite [Osaka Jogakuin Junior College curriculum: About the 1998 changes]. In Souritsu 30 Shuunen Kinen Iinkai (Ed.), *"Nani ga dekite, nani ga deki nai ka": Souritsu 30 shuunen kinen "jiko kensa hyou"* (pp. 147–153). Osaka, Japan: Osaka Jogakuin Junior College.

Strong, G. (1999). A report on the IE program and its evaluation by Alister Cumming. *Thought Currents in English Literature, 72,* 181–195.

Strong, G. (2004). Developing an EAP lecture course and assessing it with action research. In D. Smith, S. Nobe, P. Robinson, G. Strong, M. Tani, & H. Yoshiba, *Language and comprehension: Perspectives from linguistics and language education* (pp. 121–140). Tokyo: Kuroshio.

Sugimoto, Y. (1997). *An introduction to Japanese society.* Cambridge: Cambridge University Press.

Sunal, C. S., Smith, C., Sunal, D., & Britt, J. (1998). Using the Internet to create meaningful instruction. *The Social Studies, 90,* 13–27.

Swales, J. M. (1990). *Genre analysis: English in academic and research settings.* New York: Cambridge University Press.

Swales, J. M., & Feak, C. B. (1994). *Academic writing for graduate students: A course for nonnative speakers of English.* Ann Arbor: University of Michigan Press.

Swales, J. M., & Feak, C. B. (2001). *English in today's research world: A writing guide.* Ann Arbor: University of Michigan Press.

Takanashi, Y. (2004). TEFL and communication styles in Japanese culture. *Language, Culture and Communication, 17,* 1–14.

Tedick, D. (1990). ESL writing assessment: Subject-matter knowledge and its impact on performance. *English for Specific Purposes, 9,* 123–143.

TESOL. (1996–2007). *TESOL's mission, values, and vision.* Retrieved April 12, 2007, from http://www.tesol.org/s_tesol/sec_document .asp?CID=218&DID=220

TESOL. (2003a, June). *TESOL position statement on independent TESL/ TEFL certificate programs.* Retrieved April 12, 2007, from http://www .tesol.org/s_tesol/bin.asp?CID=32&DID=373&DOC=FILE.PDF

TESOL. (2003b). *TESOL/NCATE standards for the accreditation of initial programs in P–12 ESL teacher education.* Retrieved April 12, 2007, from http://www.tesol.org/s_tesol/bin.asp?CID=219&DID=2135&DOC= FILE.PDF

TESOL. (2006). *PreK–12 English language proficiency standards in the core content areas.* Alexandria, VA: Author.

TESOL Commission on Accreditation. (1998). *TCA standards for intensive English programs.* Alexandria, VA: TESOL.

Tripp, D. (1987). *Theorising practice: The teacher's professional journal.* Geelong, Australia: Deakin University Press.

Tyner, K. R. (Ed.). (1998). *Literacy in a digital world: Teaching and learning in the age of information.* Mahwah, NJ: Lawrence Erlbaum.

Undergraduate certificate in teaching English as a foreign language. (2006). Kent State University. Retrieved April 12, 2007, from http://www.kent .edu/english/UndergraduateStudies/EnglishMinor/CertificateTEFL.cfm

Vieira Abrahão, M. H. (1992). A prática de ensino e o estágio supervisionado como foco da pesquisa na formação do professor de língua estrangeira [Teaching practicum and supervised teaching as a focus of research in foreign language teacher education]. *Contexturas, 1,* 49–59.

Vieira Abrahão, M. H. (Ed.). (2004). *Prática de ensino de língua estrangeira: Experiências/reflexões* [Foreign language teaching practicum: Experiences/ reflections]. Campinas, Brazil: Pontes Editores.

Vieira Abrahão, M. H., & Barcelos, A. M. F. (Eds.). (2006). *Crenças e ensino de línguas: Foco na professor, no aluno e na formação de professores* [Beliefs and the teaching of languages: Focus on the teacher, the student, and teacher education]. Campinas, Brazil: Pontes Editores.

Wallace, M. J. (1991). *Training foreign language teachers: A reflective approach*. Cambridge: Cambridge University Press.

Waring, R. (2006). *The word frequency lists*. Retrieved April 7, 2007, from http://www1.harenet.ne.jp/~waring/vocab/wordlists/vocfreq.html

Warshawsky, D., & Byrd, D. R. H. (1996). *Spectrum: A communicative course in English*. Englewood Cliffs, NJ: Prentice Hall Regents.

Widdowson, H. G. (1978). *Teaching language as communication*. Oxford: Oxford University Press.

Willis, J. (1996). *A framework for task-based learning*. Essex, England: Addison-Wesley Longman.

About the Editors and Contributors

Denise M. de Abreu-e-Lima is an associate professor of English language in the Department of Languages and Literatures at Federal University of São Carlos, in Brazil. Her research focuses on the use of multiple intelligences theory in teacher education and materials development.

Eliane H. Augusto-Navarro has been a professor of English at Federal University of São Carlos, in Brazil, for 5 years. She holds a PhD in linguistics and a master's degree in applied linguistics. Her research interests involve the teaching and learning of EFL grammar, TESOL teacher education, EFL writing, and English for specific purposes.

Anne Bollati has 20 years of experience in teaching ESL in higher education in New York, Minnesota, Ohio, Illinois, and Ecuador. In 1991 she founded the academic ESL Program at Black Hawk College, in the United States. In 1996 this program won an award for comprehensive programming from the American Council on International Intercultural Education.

Michael Carroll is an associate professor at Momoyama Gakuin University, in Japan. In the 1990s he led a curriculum renewal project in the Centre for Applied Linguistics at the University of South Australia. He has edited and is a reviewer for several journals. He coedited, with Jill Burton, *Journal Writing* in the Case Studies in TESOL Practice series.

Steve Cornwell is a professor at Osaka Jogakuin College, in Japan, where he has worked since 1995. He is currently editor of the *JALT Journal* and is on the Editorial Advisory Board for *The Language Teacher*, and he previously served on the TESOL Publications Committee. He has published on a wide range of topics, including teacher development, writing anxiety, and women's education in Japan.

Luciana C. de Oliveira is assistant professor of literacy and language education in the Department of Curriculum and Instruction at Purdue University, in the United States. Her research focuses on the development of academic literacy in the content areas, second language writing, and nonnative-English-speaking professionals in TESOL.

Klaus Gommlich is an associate professor at Kent State University, in the United States, where he teaches courses in TESL and applied linguistics. His research focuses on cognitive aspects of second language acquisition and translation studies. He has taught ESL/EFL and English for specific purposes courses in Germany and in the United States.

Kathleen Graves is a professor of second language teacher education at the School for International Training, in the United States. She is the editor of *Teachers as Course Developers* (Cambridge University Press) and author of *Designing Language Courses: A Guide for Teachers* (Heinle & Heinle). In addition to curriculum development, her professional interests include helping teachers create learning communities in their classrooms and collaborative professional communities with fellow teachers.

Juanita Heigham is an assistant professor at Sugiyama Jogakuen University, in Japan. She has been teaching English for 10 years and has taught in the United States, Europe, and Asia. Her interests include curriculum design, independent learning, and teacher training.

Audrey Kucia has researched technology use and curriculum planning at Kansai Gaidai University, in Japan.

Jon Phillips is an educator who has provided technical assistance to projects in the United States, Southeast Asia, Africa, and the Middle East. During his 20 years of experience, he has been responsible for teacher training, curriculum design, evaluation, project coordination, and teaching. From 1997 to 2003, he was a member of an AMIDEAST management team and was responsible for the curriculum/testing component of the Military Language Institute's language program.

Sarah Rilling is an associate professor at Kent State University, in the United States. She teaches courses in applied linguistics, and her research interests are English for specific purposes, World Englishes, and online writing and the nonnative speaker. Her teaching, research, and language learning has taken place predominantly in the United States, Japan, and Germany.

John Shannon is currently a dean at the largest foreign language institute in the world and previously worked as the director of the Intensive English Program at the American University of Sharjah, in the United Arab Emirates. He received his PhD in second language education from Ohio State University and is currently working on a book on language program administration.

Gregory Strong is a professor in the English Department at Aoyama Gakuin University, in Japan, and coordinates its Integrated English Program for freshmen and sophomores. He has worked in China on a Canadian foreign aid project as well as in Canada as a teacher, teacher educator, and curriculum writer, and he has published widely on education, travel, and literature, including short stories and a nonfiction book, *Flying Colours: The Toni Onley Story* (Harbour Press, 2002).

Tamara Swenson is a professor at Osaka Jogakuin College, in Japan, where she has worked since 1991. She has edited *JALT Journal* (1994–1998); served on the Editorial Advisory Board for *The Language Teacher* (1998–2004); and published research on writing, materials development, and language attrition. She is currently pursuing research in communication.

Jean Turner is a professor in the Graduate School of Languages and Educational Linguistics at the Monterey Institute of International Studies, in the United States. She teaches courses in applied linguistics, including language assessment and research design/statistics. Her professional interests include the definition and measurement of advanced language skills and issues related to the integration of teaching and assessment.

Karl Uhrig is an assistant professor at Kent State University, in the United States. He teaches courses in applied linguistics and researches the relationships among sociocultural factors, academic literacy, and cognitive contributions to both. His teaching experience includes teacher education, intensive English, and serving in the Peace Corps in Estonia.

Index

Page numbers followed by an *f* or *t* indicate figures or tables.

Developing a New Curriculum for Adult Learners

F

Family Problems and Modern Society, Osaka Jogakuin College program and, 117*f*

Federal University. *See* Languages and Literatures Program

Feedback, curriculum change and, 4*t*

FEP. *See* Communicative English Program

Financial considerations. *See* Funding

Form, evaluation of, 61

Freshman English Program. *See* Communicative English Program

Functional proficiency, Military Language Institute program and, 55, 56

Funding

    Black Hawk College program and, 16–17

    Osaka Jogakuin College program and, 117*f*

Future "Senior Life," Osaka Jogakuin College program and, 117*f*

G

GED. *See* General Educational Development

Gender considerations, 107, 117*f*

General Educational Development, Black Hawk College program and, 14

Gesturing, discussion behaviours and, 164*t*

Goal-setting, Integrated English Program and, 157–158

Graduation ceremonies, Black Hawk College program and, 26

Grammar

    Black Hawk College program and, 21–22

    Communicative English Program and, 138–139, 138*t*, 144

    Military Language Institute program and, 55, 56

    skill building and, 20*t*

G-TELP, 136

Guess Who's Coming to Dinner?, 173

H

Harry Potter series, 193–194

High school, 212. *See also* Adolescents

Higher Learning Commission, Black Hawk College and, 14

History of the English Language course, Kent State University program and, 210–211

Homework, Black Hawk College program and, 21–22

Human rights, Osaka Jogakuin College program and, 110, 110*f,* 111*t,* 117*f,* 122–123

I

IEP. *See* Integrated English Program

IEPs. *See* Intensive Engish programs

Implementation

    curriculum change and, 4*t*

    Kent State University program and, 212–215

    TESOL/NCATE standards and, 208–209

Independent work, computer-assisted language learning and, 90

Initiatives, curriculum change and, 4*t*

Innovation, tradition and, 8–9

Instruction

    integration with assessment and, 59–61

    TESOL/NCATE standards and, 208–209

Instructors. *See* Teachers

Integrated English Program

    administration/teacher support and, 174–176

    conclusions, 176

    courses and themes, 158*f*

    curriculum design and, 155–168

    evaluation of, 168–173

    institutional context of, 154–155

    introduction to, 153–154

    listening class solutions and, 172*t*

    skill integration and, 160*t*

    thematic units and, 160*f*

    themes and tasks of level 1, 167*f*

Integrated instruction/assessment, Military Language Institute program and, 59–61

Intensive English programs. *See* American University of Sharjah

Intensive reading, 9

Interaction, teacher education and, 200

Intercultural Communication course, Kent State University program and, 205, 208, 211

Interdisciplinary teaching, Languages and Literatures Program and, 187–189, 188*t*

Internal assessment, 60

International Student Association, 29

Internationalization, Osaka Jogakuin College program and, 110, 111*t*

Internet use

    computer-assisted language learning and, 94–98, 95*f*, 102

    Osaka Jogakuin College program and, 124–125

Interpersonal skills, Kent State University program and, 216–217

J

Japan

    characteristics of English instruction in, 7–8

    Communicative English Program and. *See* Communicative English Program

    Integrated English Program and. *See* Integrated English Program

    Osaka Jogakuin College and. *See* Osaka Jogakuin College

Journaling, Integrated English Program and, 165

K

Kent State University

    conclusions, 215

    course and program connections and, 211*f*

    curricular context and, 201–203

    evaluation of, 212–215, 217–219

    introduction to, 199–200

    program cohesion and, 210–212

    program design process and, 203–210

    program implementation and, 212–215

    program motivation and, 200–201

    reflective guide for, 216–217

Keyboard use, 93

L

M

P

Professionalism

    teacher education and, 199

    TESOL/NCATE standards and, 210

Proficiency. *See* Ability

Progressive education, 185

Projects From the University Classroom, 145

Psychology, Osaka Jogakuin College program and, 117*f*

Purpose, importance of, 10

Q

Quad Cities, Black Hawk College and. *See* Black Hawk College

R

Reading

    Black Hawk College program and, 21–22

    Communicative English Program and, 138–140, 138*t*, 144, 145, 146

    extensive/intensive, 9

    Integrated English Program and, 160*t*, 167*f*

    Military Language Institute program and, 56

    Osaka Jogakuin College program and, 110*f*, 117*f*, 124–126

    sample curriculum from American University of Sharjah program and, 46–48

    skill building and, 20*t*

    test specifications and, 76–77

Research, teacher education and, 200

Research-development-diffusion model of curriculum change, 4–5, 4*t*

Resident students, Black Hawk College program and, 21–22

Resource education, computer literacy for teachers and, 103

Rhetorical patterns, Osaka Jogakuin College program and. *See* Osaka Jogakuin College

Rights, teacher education and, 199

S